"Jake's story is my son's story. Burwell's pain, fears, anger, and misery are mine. I read *Saving Jake* at a time when I really needed strength, and I found it. Burwell is a great writer and a greater humanitarian for sharing her life, giving us the gift of hope and commitment."

— CARLOS B., father of an addict

"Reading D'Anne Burwell's brave and powerful memoir, I knew: this could be my child, and this mother's harrowing story could all too easily be my own. It could be yours, too. Love alone won't save us from the epidemic of addiction ravaging our kids, but love and better information, together, will help our families and our children survive and heal. Rooting for Jake on every page, we come to share in his struggle and in his family's hope for recovery. We also see just how tough a road that is, and how essential it is for stories like this one to be told. *Saving Jake* should be read by every parent."

— KATRINA KENISON, author of *The Gift of an Ordinary Day*

"A remarkable, gripping story...honest, vulnerable and thoughtful."

— SHARON HOFSTEDT, Psychiatric and Substance Abuse RN

"It is a brave act to tell your truth. Burwell has opened a fragile window into her life, allowing us to have a look in. She has written a beautiful account of her harrowing, heartbreaking journey, helping us understand what she has endured, learned, lost, and gained. It is her honesty and vulnerability that will keep you reading."

— JONATHAN BARLOW, MSW

"Beautifully written, exquisitely detailed, this book chronicles the long and often tortuous journey to recovery for both addicted individuals and all those who love and care for them. If your child is 'struggling,' you will find comfort in the pages of this book, knowing you are not alone. And you will discover solace and much wisdom in the author's loving quest to find the points of light on the pathway to healing and wholeness."

— KATHERINE KETCHAM, coauthor of *Broken* and *Teens Under the Influence*

"Poetic in its precisely chosen words...a page turner."

— DOROTHY M., mother of three, former wife of an alcoholic

"Too much shame and silence surround addiction. Burwell's terrific memoir will move dialogue forward on one of the top health problems of our time."

— GREG WILLIAMS, director of *The Anonymous People*

"I shed many tears, reading this book. Burwell's willingness to bare her soul—to communicate not just the pain and terror she lived through but the wisdom and determination of her entire family—is courageous and selfless. *Saving Jake* will not only touch people deeply, it will teach them about the disease of addiction and provide a beacon through the darkness."

— AMY TEMPLE, MS, school psychologist

"Addiction is not just about craving. It is also about chaos, love, fear, anger, shame, and sadness and how they wear you out over time. They can also make you into a better person, transform families, and—sometimes, with luck and a mother's determination—alter the course of disease."

— THOMAS HOFSTEDT, PhD, board member, HealthRight 360

"*Saving Jake* will help many families survive difficult and confusing times."

> — DR. KEVIN MCCAULEY, The Institute for Addiction Study

"With stunning honesty, Burwell depicts the quicksand that is life when dealing with a loved one's addiction."

> — LENNA BUISSINK, parent in long-term recovery

"*Saving Jake* is a story that will touch the heart of every parent; indeed, Jake's story is a cautionary tale for any family that has ever thought 'it could never happen to us.' Through it all, Burwell remains unswerving in her love for her son, dedicated to doing whatever it takes to support Jake's recovery—even when letting go is the most painful choice imaginable."

> — CHARLENE MARGOT, MA, The Parent Education Series,
> Sequoia Union High School District

"Burwell concisely and vividly unravels the heart-clenching, intimate details of a family's journey through addiction upheaval. Devoid of direct instructions, *Saving Jake* reads like a gripping, moment-to-moment guide for parents. Admirably, there is no self-justification, but rather raw authenticity and frontline truth. Rich with characters who climb into your heart, this beautifully told story is a powerful contribution to the literature."

> — BARRE STOLL, PsyD, licensed clinical psychologist

SAVING JAKE

This is a true story. Some of the names and details have been changed.
The chronology of events—an important element of the story—is accurate.

Library of Congress Control Number:
2015945053

Burwell, D'Anne
Saving Jake: when addiction hits home / by D'Anne Burwell.

ISBN 978-0-9962543-0-4

FocusUp Books
Los Altos, California

SAVING JAKE

WHEN ADDICTION HITS HOME

D'ANNE BURWELL

FocusUp Books

To my husband, my daughter, and my son,
as simple as that

There is a vitality, a life force, an energy,
a quickening that is translated through you into action,
and because there is only one of you in all of time,
this expression is unique. And if you block it,
it will never exist through any other medium
and it will be lost.

— MARTHA GRAHAM

PROLOGUE

I STOOD GRIPPING THE KITCHEN COUNTERTOP, taking short panting breaths, feeling as if I'd been squeezed inside the darkest tunnel. *Just get him to the airport,* I told myself. *Get him to the airport.*

I could hear Jake walking down the hall from his room, pausing to cough, a deep, racking sound. He stepped into the kitchen, wearing his usual shorts, T-shirt, white Vans, and Giants baseball cap, carrying his duffle bag, which he dropped on the floor. My nineteen-year-old son was so thin I wanted to cry, his skin so pale it seemed translucent, tinged slightly green.

"Do you want breakfast?" I asked, barely trusting my voice. He shook his head. His pupils were huge. He averted his eyes from mine.

For months, like cloud cover, my son's minimizing and omissions, his lies and excuses, had obscured that his life was falling apart. Over the past few days, I'd suddenly strung it all together—the soot on his forehead, the hollowed-out Bic pens in his rented room, the ruined finances. Jake was addicted to OxyContin.

I was about to send my son to a rehab facility I'd scrambled to find. *Was it the right one?* My husband was away on business, and seemed more resentful than supportive. My seventeen-year-old daughter was deep in her own crisis, her boyfriend threatening suicide. I felt completely alone, torn in too many directions, exhausted, forging ahead because someone must.

That moment in the kitchen felt at the time like the lowest point of my life. I didn't yet understand that addiction was a disease. I hadn't yet learned how to step back and let my child fight for his own soul. If I had known I was only at the starting gate, I might not have had the strength to pick up the keys, put my hand at my son's back, and steer him toward the car.

In the wrenching months that followed, my family witnessed firsthand the ways that society sidelines addicts and alcoholics, believing it is their choice to use drugs or alcohol to destruction. Years into our crisis, a thought surfaced in my consciousness: a book could help uncover this untruth. A book could tell the story of my family's battle, the lessons learned, the patterns repeated, the growth and change, the love. A book could help shine a light on the family disease of addiction, and let other families know that they're not alone. One book at a time, one story at a time, we might help halt some of this devastation.

Addicts are burdened with shame because society holds them to blame. I hope this story will help Jake and others to absolve themselves from that shame and blame. In describing this fierce fight, I hope to illuminate the challenges posed to a person with this lifelong disease, and help make sense of the chaos. I want readers to know how an entire family can be consumed, that addiction can make us prisoners, that it will grow stronger if we don't continually attend to it. Drug overdoses now claim a life every fourteen minutes. Overdoses are the leading cause of accidental death in the United States. While most major causes of preventable death are declining, death from drugs is not.

If we have conversations about drug and alcohol addiction, and add our faces and voices to the grassroots recovery movement that is emerging nationally, we can talk about solutions, and unite to bring about change to America's enduring drug problem.

I will tell the story of my own family, honestly and truthfully. Addiction has changed our lives completely. We have glimpsed silver linings along the way. We will keep looking back to find a way forward. We will keep reminding ourselves to live one day at a time.

Part One

PUZZLE PIECES

1

SWEET START

Making the decision to have a child—it is momentous. It is to decide forever to have your heart go walking around outside your body.
— Elizabeth Stone

IN 1992, I WAS A thirty-two-year-old new mother, living in Portland, Oregon, with my husband, Bruce, in a brand-new house that bordered a green space. One night, I held my beautiful baby, fresh from his bath in his blue-footed jammies, and sang him a lullaby in his darkened room, watching for signs of sleepiness as he gazed into my eyes. My own eyelids were drooping, so I switched to humming. Immediately, my son kicked me. Startled, I switched back to singing (*"Stay awake, don't rest your head. Don't lie down upon your bed..."*) then succumbed to weariness and hummed once more. He kicked me again. Was this nine-month-old child of mine communicating his displeasure that I wasn't using words? I experimented a few more times; each time I changed to a hum, he kicked. I felt sheer amazement that this tiny being was absorbing my words, and expressing his need.

So many memories crowd into my mind as I look back on the trajectory of Jake's life. Those early days in Portland, I would push his stroller through the park, our yellow Labrador at my heel. "Cheep, cheep," my son would say as I pointed to birds. "Sky," he would say, and "Moon." As we set out one rainy day, just before his seventeenth month, he shouted out his first sentence, "Need brella cuz wet!"

At two and a half, Jake was mostly inseparable from his little sheepskin baby rug, his "lambie." He was ever so tender with our dog; he would spread his lambie over her belly when she was sleeping and use her as a pillow. One day, he walked over to my nine-month-pregnant abdomen, shaped his small hands into a megaphone, and spoke directly into my belly button. "When you come out," he announced to his unborn sibling, "you kin have a lambie an' a binky."

Jake showed great concern whenever his brand-new sister cried. He whacked her on the head one morning as she was nursing—either accidentally or to see cause-and-effect—and turned white with shock at her screaming. I could see in his eyes how sorry he was.

When Jake was three and Alea two months old, Bruce's job as an economic consultant took us to Palo Alto, California, where I was born and raised. My parents still lived in the rambling house where I grew up, and most of my siblings lived nearby.

My parents were thrilled to have us so close. Not much backyard came with our rental house, so I often packed baby, dog, and three-year-old Jake over to my parents' place while Bruce was away at work. Jake would hop on his low-slung Hot Wheels tricycle and speed off on the path around the house, cornering like a madman, calling out, "Pops, watch me!" My dad—father of six, grandfather of eight—was incredulous at Jake's athleticism.

One of my younger brothers, Tom, a division-one soccer player throughout college, ran a soccer camp every summer on my parents' sport court. Jake bounced with excitement on the sidelines, watching the six- and seven-year-olds during trap and dribble drills. Finally, Tom rolled a soccer ball his way, and Jake trapped it and sent it back, using the side of his foot just as he'd seen Tom do. After a few shy moments, he responded to his uncle's beckoning and went off to join the big kids.

Alea began to crawl, walk, and climb onto the dining-room table before we finally found a house we could almost afford to buy, a three-bedroom ranch-style on a quiet street in Palo Alto. On moving day, Jake checked out every nook and cranny inside and out, peppering me with questions as Alea followed behind dragging her own lambie. "Momma, how will that piano fit there?" "Momma, why don't bees have blood?" "Why does the sun move, Momma?" After a day spent moving furniture, answering Jake's questions, and chasing Alea, who had discovered she could climb just about anything, Bruce and I fell into bed, exhausted.

We talked about waiting a year before sending Jake to kindergarten—his birthday was early October, so he wasn't yet five—but he seemed so confident and eager to start school, and we waffled. In August, Jake decided to create a special family holiday—Presents Day.

"What do you want for Presents Day, Momma?"

"One whole day of cooperation."

"Well, maybe Alea could get you that—what else?"

I realized I *needed* my son to go off to kindergarten.

He settled right in, loved his teacher, and made friends. His teacher had a special rule just for him: at recess, when Jake was "up" at kickball, he had to stand *way* back from home base, so as not to flatten another kindergartener.

Throughout the elementary-school years, our doggie stood at the window and watched for Jake and Alea to return home. Fortunately for us, Palo Alto schools were some of the highest ranked in the state, and the grade school was a few blocks away.

Jake's teachers consistently told me what a pleasure he was to have in class, that he was precocious and intellectually stimulated, that he was the first to quietly put his arm around a thoughtlessly ostracized kid on the playground, that he followed rules and was respectful, and that he earned his high marks.

In the late afternoons, out kitchen windows, parents kept an eye on the neighborhood boys as they bounded down the street like huskies in the snow. Each year, when the autumn leaves fell from giant elms, the kids raked up massive piles to jump on, then used the heaps as obstacles to rollerblade around.

Alea looked up to her older brother, and he looked out for her. He liked nothing better than to get into rough-and-tumble games with the boys, but he also played long hours with Alea, on her terms, setting up houses made from sticks and rocks for bugs they caught. They liked to dress up outlandishly and dance together.

"Put on that rock-'n'-roll song, Momma," Jake called out one memorable afternoon.

"Momma, look at *meee*," purred Alea, wearing a black cat costume complete with long tail and little ears, pouncing and pawing completely in character. They must have gotten into the Halloween box. Jake, in oversized glasses, a long-haired wig, a rainbow vest, and funky pants, gyrated his shoulders as Alea wiggled and spun.

The music blared, my children danced, and I laughed watching them.

Jake's joy in his athleticism funneled him right into sports. All through grade school, his baseball coach checked with me to be sure Jake would be in town before he finalized any game schedule. The soccer coach signaled Jake to take corner kicks with his reliable and strong left foot. He was tall and steadfast, so the basketball was naturally passed to him. "So many sports, so little time" was his motto.

When Jake was in fifth grade, he switched to a more competitive soccer league. I organized and managed his team, made up mostly of Jake's competitive friends, and persuaded Uncle Tom to coach it. The boys loved Tom, and stayed long after practice to bask in his compliments, competing to launch the ball the hardest into the back of the net. When my parents came to Jake's games, Pops—who had coached his own three sons in soccer for years—proudly cheered both his grandson, playing left wing, and his tall son Tom, tripping over players on the sidelines as they vied to stand next to their coach.

At the end of sixth grade, on Father's Day, Bruce and I and my parents crammed in with the other spectators at Jake's important end-of-the-season baseball game. Alea, always barefoot, climbed around under the stands looking for caterpillars to capture. Jake stood on the mound, firing his left-handed fastballs, frequently adjusting his cap due to the warmness of the day. The crowd chanted, "Go Rocket!"—the nickname he earned because of his lightning speed and the strength with which he could launch a ball from his wiry frame. In a flash, he caught a line drive and sent it on to his teammate on first base. Double play. The next inning, at bat, he was down two strikes. A pitch floated in and he smacked that baseball out to the trees and jubilantly circled the bases. On his way back to the dugout, he winked at Bruce and mouthed the words, "Happy Father's Day." What a kid.

In midautumn, after Jake had begun seventh grade and Alea fourth, on a rare Saturday morning when we weren't driving Alea to gymnastics or carpooling Jake to a soccer game, Bruce and I sat sipping coffee on our sunny patio.

"Would you ever want to go live in Europe for a year?" Bruce asked, setting down his coffee mug.

"*What?* Are you serious?"

"All I do is work. That'd be one way to cut back."

We had often discussed how Silicon Valley could feel like the Gold Rush days, when miners, looking for the mother lode, never rested. The dot-com boom had added crazy wealth to the area, and despite the crash in 2000, and economic decline elsewhere, the region remained resilient. Bruce's growing responsibilities kept him tied to the Valley's frenetic pace, and my sense of responsibility as a mother kept me constantly battling the prevailing culture of full engagement calendars, and expectations that young children needed professional coaches, tutors, and supplemental classes to lead them through their afternoons. Bruce tried hard to maintain some balance between work and family life. I tried hard to carve out slow time for bike rides, hunting for tadpoles, picnics at a nearby redwood grove, and cutting dough into heart shapes and sprinkling them with pink sugar on Valentine's Day.

"Remember how wonderful Italy was?" Bruce said.

"Yeah, I do."

Fifteen years back, we'd spent two weeks in a rented villa outside of Rome. The livable rhythm of life there seemed to work for everyone—kids, grown-ups, old folks. We'd loved everything about Italy: pizza and pasta, espressos and cappuccinos, midafternoon naps, history and ruins. Italy was where we'd gotten engaged.

"We could share it with Jake and Alea," Bruce went on. "I've been thinking I could work as an independent contractor, finish up some projects, then just take some time off. We could rent the house while we're gone. We could make it work."

I didn't know what to say. I didn't want strangers living in my house. And what would we do with our dog?

Bruce knew how I needed to mull things over, so he let it rest. But a few weeks later, he tried again after Jake and Alea were in bed.

"Could you imagine a completely unscheduled weekend? I bet the kids would love Rome," he said.

I wasn't so sure. On school mornings, Jake eagerly rode off on his bike to the newly remodeled junior high. He'd made every sports team so far. He liked band even if he didn't practice his clarinet much. Alea had a nice group of girls in her fourth-grade class, not many boys.

Still, I was starting to feel a little bit excited. Maybe just the right renters would be okay. Maybe my mother would take care of our dog—my father had passed away the year before, and the sweet presence of a Labrador might be a comfort to her. Then my perspective shifted even further. I'd completed fifth grade in New Zealand—exactly the grade Alea would be in if we took the leap—when my dad's work had taken us there. I knew travel to be transformative.

"Okay," I said both nervous and enthusiastic, "let's talk with them."

When we told the kids we wanted to live in Rome, Alea's reaction was to slam her bedroom door and sit in her closet, refusing to speak to us. Jake was less dramatic, but lay quietly on his bed for a long time. Eventually I slipped a note under Alea's closet door, "Will you come out and talk about it?"

She wrote back furiously, "You are *ruining* my life. I will NOT leave all my friends for a *WHOLE* year. They'll forget me!" She wouldn't come out.

After what must have been lonely hours in the closet, I slid in another note. "I've made a yummy dinner and it's ready. Please, won't you come out?"

A few minutes later she joined Jake, Bruce, and me at the kitchen table. "You guys won't believe how great the pizza is in Rome," Bruce said. "All the pasta, too. And they have the best gelato in the world."

"We'd get to travel to some neat places," I added.

"Can we go to London?" asked Jake, starting to get behind the idea. "I've read about prisoners in the Tower of London."

"Maybe," said Bruce. "How about seeing where gladiators fought lions in the Coliseum?"

"I'd rather see tulips in Holland," Alea said, flipping like a switch.

"Your friends will think it's cool, all the places you'd get to see," said Bruce. "They won't forget you."

We arrived in August, a few weeks before the beginning of the school year at the American Overseas School of Rome. The city was blistering hot. We didn't know a soul. Our Italian consisted of "buon giorno," "grazie," and counting to ten. Braving the heat, we ventured out for basics at the bustling open-air market at Campo dei Fiori, a piazza named the "field of flowers" in the Middle Ages and later used for public executions. It took the four of us, dripping with sweat, to lug bags of beautiful produce, cheeses, pasta, juice, and olive bread down several cobbled lanes, up ancient stairs, and into our apartment. Our refrigerator back home seemed the size of Montana compared to the tiny one here. We quickly adapted to frequent small purchases in the cool of the early morning.

One day, we poked our heads into the Pantheon, but it was difficult to appreciate the grandeur of the enormous circular building.

"Ugh," I said, "I don't want to share this place with hordes of tourists. Let's come back another day."

"We're tourists, too," said Jake.

Alea bristled at that. "*I'm* not a tourist. I *live* here now!"

We'd been working hard, figuring out how to do the simplest things. We decided to act like Romans and head for the coast. A few days later on a sparkling Mediterranean beach, we swam in the calm warm sea then spread out on rocks to dry. Jake stayed at the water's edge, skipping stones. A cute girl in a green bikini separated from the group of teenagers lounging behind us, curious about the American kid with the rocket arm. When Jake launched a rock way out, one of the teenaged boys stood up and swaggered over. The competition was on.

The two boys alternated shots, aiming for a small buoy well out in the water. Not a word was spoken between them, though the gang provided plenty of encouragement, or maybe they were rooting for Jake, we couldn't tell. The guy cast furtive and frustrated glances at his unlikely rival as the girl in the green bikini looked on. At last, the Italian hit the target, quit the game, and went back to lounging, taking his girl along by the waist. Jake looked over his shoulder, smiled at us, then hit the buoy four times in a row.

———

Over the year, which eventually included adventures in London and in Holland, we drew together as a family. Bruce never regretted quitting his job; he soaked in the luxury of spending time with the kids and me, though he worried about employment when we returned.

Arriving back to the swiftly paced Silicon Valley was a shock. Alea was jubilant that her friends hadn't forgotten her; her brother was more quiet. A week before Jake was to begin high school and Alea sixth grade, I took them to the mall. Both kids had sprouted up, were badly in need of new clothes, and were suddenly concerned with the latest labels their friends were wearing. The outing ended in a battle. Clearly they had outgrown their mother weighing in on what they should wear.

I sought advice from my older sister, who suggested a book about teaching teens financial responsibility. After some discussion, Bruce and I landed on a plan. Each child would receive a monthly clothing budget plus a modest spending allowance.

During dinner one night, I explained the new program to Jake and Alea.

"Okay guys, here's how it works. The next time we go to the mall, my job will be chauffeur. I'll *only* give my opinion if you ask me for it...kinda like a consultant. You decide what you want to buy with your own money, and when there's no more, there's no more."

Jake puffed up a little, receiving this news as emancipation.

Alea lit up. "Let's go shopping!"

The very next Saturday we gave it a try. In the car driving home, my son and daughter meticulously added up their receipts to see who spent less and who got more. They both stuck to their budgets. It wasn't long before Jake got a few neighborhood mowing jobs to supplement his income.

Plenty of students in Jake's high school came from educated families driving their children toward the Ivies. Jake took the requisite AP classes, but during his junior year he began to coast, doing just enough work to stay competitive with the bright kids. His interest and success in sports dropped away. He didn't run with a wild crowd; we didn't suspect drunkenness or drugs. He spent most of his time with three close athletic friends, competing with them at hoops, video games, and even a girl.

One spring day, though, during his junior year, I opened his bedroom door and smelled marijuana. I took two steps in, my mouth hanging open.

"Jake, what's going on in here? I smell dope."

He was sitting on his bed, alone, with both windows wide open.

"Momma, it's *weed*, not dope," said Jake, pretty relaxed.

I stood completely dumbstruck.

"I got a bad grade on my trigonometry test, and a friend told me I'd feel better if I smoked weed, and he gave me some. It's no big deal."

"There're better ways to cope than *smoking marijuana*. It's illegal! How did it get here? In *our* car?"

"Momma, weed is harmless," he said. "Everybody does it."

I could see from his red eyes that it wasn't the best time to argue. "We'll talk about this when your dad gets home."

Bruce arrived just before dinner. I filled him in, including Jake's "harmless" argument.

"Harmless? If he thinks it's harmless, maybe he should research what happens if you get pulled over with dope in your car."

"It's *weed*," I corrected him.

"Fine, what happens if you get pulled over with *weed*." He shook his head, processing things. "I guess it's no surprise that he tried it. Most kids do, at some point."

"Right here in our house?"

"Maybe that's better than smoking in an alley with his buddies."

"What are we going to do, though? What's the consequence?"

"I meant what I said about research. I think he should research how much it would cost him if he got caught. He should learn what marijuana does to your response time, your memory, your motivation."

We assigned Jake a paper answering all those questions. In addition to writing the paper, he lost his driving privileges for a long while.

The summer before his senior year, Jake completely surprised us by asking if he could see a psychologist. We didn't want to pry, but did want to support him if he felt the need to talk to some-one outside the family. I tracked down a sought-after counselor connected to Stanford with a jammed practice. He fit Jake in every other week. Jake appeared to like going, and commented that Dr. Nolan was insightful.

Jake's grades slipped a bit over the winter, but there were no further incidences involving marijuana or alcohol. Throughout his senior year, I struggled with the challenges all parents face as their children move into their own lives. I wanted to be there for my kids, yet give them freedom to make their own mistakes; I wanted to pay attention to what was going on in their lives, yet "butt out"; I wanted to teach values and keep them safe, yet allow them room to explore.

We always assumed our kids would go to college. "We'll fund your educations," I told them, "as long as you don't do drugs—or get a tattoo." Still, I discussed with Jake the possibility of a gap year between high school and college. I felt he could benefit greatly by taking some time to work or do service, but he insisted he wanted to stay in school. We made several trips to visit colleges. When application deadlines loomed, I found myself prodding, cajoling, and finally demanding that he write his essays and submit his applications. And he did. Acceptances and a few scholarships began to roll in. I felt huge relief when the onerous process yielded results.

Jake debated between the University of California at Santa Barbara and Colorado University at Boulder. In the end, he chose Boulder and was proud his partial scholarship would contribute. All he had to do was keep his grades above a 2.75 GPA. *That's easy enough for him, I thought.*

Jake and Ella, his girlfriend of four months, were a striking couple at his senior prom. He was tall and handsome, dressed in a rented tuxedo. She sparkled in a short aquamarine dress and high heels, showing off tanned runner's legs, her dark curly hair framing her sweet face. Jake was clearly smitten. He worked all summer to save up spending money for college and spent most of his free time with Ella. They'd soon be far apart; she was heading to college in Tacoma, Washington.

Ella and Jake's three best friends showed up unannounced for breakfast the morning Jake left for college. I put four extra plates on the table, hustling around cooking more eggs while Bruce and Jake loaded up the car. His friends all stood in our driveway waving when we pulled away for the airport.

2
DAWNING

The truth of the matter is all people who begin using alcohol
or other drugs do so believing they are in control of their chemical
use. This belief, however, does not change the fact that one out of
eight people who choose to use mood-altering substances
becomes addicted and never foresees it happening.
— Jeff and Debra Jay, *Love First*

OUR TABLE SUDDENLY SEEMED EMPTY. Alea was beginning
her sophomore year, and her long hours at gymnastics—
right through dinner—helped keep her from missing Jake too
desperately. Every once in a while, we got a brief call from Jake.
The third week of school, his voice sounded apologetic when
he explained that he and his roommate, Scott, got cited by the
Boulder police. "I *now* know it's a *law* that you have to ride skate-
boards on the road not the sidewalk," said Jake.

"What happened?" asked Bruce.

"We were skateboarding home from a party and got stopped
by two cops. They asked if I'd been drinking."

"What'd you tell them?" I asked, barely stopping myself from
launching into a lecture about wild off-campus parties.

"Two beers."

"Hmm," said Bruce. He was better than I was at not reacting. We'd figured Jake would do some drinking at college, and we'd talked about how we'd need to take a giant step back as Jake figured things out for himself. But I didn't imagine he'd get caught breaking the law his third week away from home.

"They handed me a ticket for underage drinking," Jake said, "so not only do I have to pay *that* but I have to take a stupid class on alcohol, *and* go in front of a judge in three weeks."

"Well, it sounds like you're taking care of it," Bruce said, making it clear he viewed this as Jake's responsibility.

"Yeah, I guess. One good thing is I'm supposed to appear with a parent, but they'll let me show up without either of you since I'm a registered college student."

"Well, that's lucky," I said. "Saves *you* the cost of a plane ticket for one of us."

Jake grunted in reply.

Jake turned eighteen six weeks into college. He told us he'd taken the alcohol class and paid the $100 fine, and the judge had cleared his record. He didn't give specifics about how he celebrated his birthday. When he flew home for Thanksgiving break, he'd lost weight and had a rough cough. On Thanksgiving Day, he was holed up in his room. I knocked, then stuck my head in.

"Jake, I'm making extra mashed potatoes and gravy. You look like you're not eating much at school."

"The cafeteria food's horrible, Momma."

"You seem kinda down. What's up?"

He was silent for a long moment, his whole body sagging. "You know I saw Ella yesterday, since she's back?"

"Yeah."

"Well, we're breaking up. She just told me that the whole ten months we've been together she's been sleeping with one of my friends. She *says* she's so sorry. Can you believe that?"

"Oh, Jake."

"On top of *that* she says my best friends all *knew* and didn't tell me. Friends don't do that. Why would they do that? I don't know what to think."

I was stunned. Jake's heart was broken and he felt betrayed all at once. I hugged him, and then the doorbell rang. Extended family began to arrive, so I couldn't ask him anything more about Ella. Usually Jake would be elated to see his cousin, Tara, but he was quiet and hurting. He must have confided in his sister because Alea put her arm around him toward the end of the evening. She'd felt left behind with him gone these past few months.

———

At Christmas break, Jake seemed tired, quiet, and still sad. His grades were okay but not great. I knew the first semester could be tough on freshmen. By his second week home, after lots of sleep and good food, he seemed in better form. I came home one afternoon to find him scanning rental properties on his laptop. He told me he needed to nail down housing for the following year.

"What about staying on campus?"

"No way. Everyone moves off after freshman year. And I hate the dorm food."

He showed me pictures of a few rentals. I raised an eyebrow at the large houses but said nothing more.

Then one day in February, Jake called to say he and Scott had found a rental they wanted to lease in the fall with four additional friends.

"Wow, Jake, that's six guys living together. That's a lot."

"Momma, it's a big house and really cool. You'd love it. It's on the Hill, close to everything, exactly where we want to be."

Bruce and I had reservations about him living with so many guys—would they do more partying than studying? We'd recently learned that Scott had been busted for weed in their room and given a citation from the housing office. Jake, by association, had been cited as well, but assured us there were no consequences unless you were cited three times. We didn't know anything about the other four kids Jake wanted to live with. A big house full of guys would be packed with distractions, yet Jake was forward thinking in securing his own housing. When he excitedly pressed us, we cosigned the lease.

As the spring semester progressed, we felt less connected to our son; he hardly ever called. When finals were over, he missed his flight home. He called to say he'd fallen asleep while waiting at the gate in the Denver airport and didn't hear his name being paged. *Must have been exhausted from those tough exams.*

A couple of days into summer break, on our sunny patio, Jake sat Bruce and me down. "I got an A and two B's but I didn't do very well in two of my classes."

"What happened?" Bruce asked.

"Well..."

I tensed. *He's stalling.*

"I did fine on my midterm in Business Calculus. I was confident, especially since I already took AP Calc, so I skipped some sessions. By the end, I didn't know what my professor was talking about. I couldn't catch up. I got an F."

Bruce's eyes went wide.

"And I got a D-minus in statistics."

I sat speechless.

"This is serious," said Bruce. "How are you planning on handling it?"

"I checked, and there's this grade-replacement program, I can redo the class. I already signed up with my professor...I can do it over the summer, take the tests by proxy. I already registered for it and paid half the tuition. I can earn the rest this summer. I want to go back in the fall. I can do this."

"What about your scholarship?"

He looked away. "My grades don't make the cut-off. I've lost it."

"Give your mom and me some time to think about this."

Later in our bedroom with the door closed, Bruce said to me, "I'm *not* paying out-of-state tuition for those kinds of grades."

I nodded, my head in my hands. "I never thought he'd fail. What do we do?"

"He seems to have a plan. I'm just not sure I'd agree to it."

"Well, he could come home and take classes at the JC, but he's pleading. He really wants a second chance."

"He could get a job and put school off for a year," Bruce said. I felt myself resisting the notion of Jake detouring from college. We both wanted him to be there, flourishing.

"What about his lease?" I asked. "We're on the hook for that rent. What if Jake works at your office this summer and makes enough money to pay for his lost scholarship?"

"Maybe," Bruce said. "And replaces the F."

"We could decide semester by semester if we would continue to pay, depending on his grades. I think he should *at least* make a 2.75."

"I'd agree with that," said Bruce.

———

Jake worked all summer but he didn't finish the calculus class. When I nagged him about it he said he had six months to complete it, and not to worry. He severed ties to his cheating friend but a contrite Ella worked her way back into his tattered heart. I didn't understand that relationship.

When school started up again, there was tension in the house. Alea, a junior, joined the water-polo team in addition to her year-round gymnastics. She worked out sometimes four hours a day and complained that she never saw her friends. She was unhappy with Jake back at school because there was no one to share her parents' scrutiny. She mentioned a boy; we kept telling her we'd like to meet him but she felt sure we'd pepper him with embarrassing questions so she refused to bring him around. She did her best to keep out of our way. The more she closed up, the more

I fretted. Again, I was trying to step back, to let her make her own choices, but it didn't feel that way to her. She argued that I was overbearing and didn't trust her.

At Thanksgiving break, Jake arrived home thin, colorless, and completely lacking any luster. I was dismayed to hear his cough was back. *Is he staying up late? Sleeping the morning away? Holing up playing video games? He used to be better at budgeting—now he never has enough for groceries. What's going on?* To Bruce I said, "From the looks of him, he isn't spending much on food. And he's certainly *not* conversational."

"Let's see what his grades are," he said. "There's less than a month till the end of the semester."

On the last afternoon of the Thanksgiving break, after Jake had already flown back to school, Jake's best childhood friend, Christopher, called and asked if I would come over. He and his mom met me at their front door and we all sat down in the living room. They looked so serious, my chest tightened.

"I'm worried about Jake's risky behavior," Christopher blurted out. His words did not match the image I had of my son. *Does he mean drugs?* The door to my foreboding intuition cracked open.

"But you're not at the same college," I managed to stutter.

He wouldn't meet my eyes. "I saw him last summer. And this weekend. And I see what he posts on Facebook." Christopher's face contorted as he grappled with how much to tell me. I could see that he didn't want to betray his friend, yet needed to voice his fear. He didn't elaborate on exactly what that "risky behavior" was and I had no words at all. Christopher's mom looked as if she might cry. *They must be softening all that they know.* Christopher had sounded the alarm and I wanted to bolt home to absorb the shock. I mumbled my thanks for his courage and hurried out.

Back home, alone, I thought hard about what I'd just heard. Could Jake be partying out of control and experimenting with hard drugs? That could certainly explain the dysfunction and disconnectedness. Something indeed was wrong.

When Bruce came home that evening I shared what I'd learned.

"All kids party in college," said Bruce.

"Did you hear what I just said?" Growing panic ignited my anger. "This is more serious than that. Go hear it from Christopher yourself."

We quarreled about it for a few more days until Bruce made the call.

When Bruce set down the phone, he rubbed his forehead for several minutes before he said to me, "Jake seems to be throwing an all-expenses-paid opportunity in our faces, *and* he's taking some immense risks with his future."

"We should stop paying for college immediately," I said.

Bruce was more adept than me at stepping back to consider a situation. "There's only about ten days left, then finals," he said. "It'd be better to talk with him face to face and see those grades."

I agreed to wait, though I knew I'd be stewing in panic, anger, and fear for nearly a fortnight.

When Jake arrived home at Christmas break, we confronted him.

"So I did a little partying. What's the problem? I can handle it." He didn't deny anything. Then, when his grades came in, his GPA fell short. At first, he was livid about a C in a music class where he'd expected a B. Then he seemed sad and resigned. Bruce and I felt sad and disappointed as our son's path forward veered sharply. We told Jake he'd have to get a job since he would not be going back to school.

Alea couldn't believe that we wouldn't pay for Jake to continue school, though she only heard it was because of some partying. But she was happy to have her cool brother home again. Bruce and I felt unsettled; a nagging thought kept surfacing that maybe we needed help in navigating our way forward.

Jake started seeing Dr. Nolan again, who suggested a battery of diagnostic tests. According to a specialist, Jake had a very high IQ; he scored extremely high in some executive functions and extremely low in a few others. He was diagnosed with ADHD. Jake wanted to know if he could get some medication for it. I couldn't exactly name why, but I reacted by putting him off. This didn't feel like the reason Jake was not being successful. We badgered him to get a job.

After a month, Bruce and I joined in a session with Dr. Nolan and Jake.

Dr. Nolan said, "Some of my clients have benefited tremendously from wilderness therapy with a company called Soltrails. This time of year, they offer one-on-one programs in New Mexico, since it's snowy everywhere else."

Then he described the positive effects that this kind of outdoor therapeutic intervention could have. Participants were paired with a highly skilled wilderness counselor and spent time with a licensed therapist. They received support and guidance to examine personal issues and roadblocks toward their success, while having some fun in a natural environment. Graduates walked away with a better sense of who they were and who they wanted to become.

"How long is the program?" Bruce asked.

"Six weeks, I think."

Jake stiffened at that.

Observing his reaction, Dr. Nolan said, "Jake, why don't you call Soltrails and ask all your questions?"

At home, Jake made several lengthy calls to the director and spent some days considering the wilderness trek. Bruce and I encouraged him, hoping he would go. What if he didn't? I felt anxious. Parents walk a fine line between holding back and making decisions for their teens. Isn't that challenge at the crux of parenthood? How do we know when to step in to keep our children safe and when to allow them the dignity to choose for themselves? From where I stood, Jake had just derailed himself from college, couldn't seem to get a job, and appeared lost. I didn't understand why. Intuition told me that soul-searching in the wilderness would refocus him, empower him, get him back on track. When Jake finally agreed to go for four weeks, not the full six weeks, Bruce and I felt relief and didn't push it. He said he'd decide out on the trail if he'd stay the extra two weeks.

3
UPSIDE DOWN

The best way to influence teens to become irresponsible and fail at life is to become highly involved in making sure that they *do* make it. This is because the implied message in that involvement is, "I don't think you're going to succeed, so I'd better get in here."
And the teen lives up to that.
— Foster Cline and Jim Fay, *Parenting Teens with Love and Logic*

A WEEK BEFORE JAKE LEFT for his wilderness trek, Bruce was away on business, and I was tossing in bed late at night. Mighty gusts tore through the branches of our giant magnolia. The rain gurgled down our noisy spouts.

Alea had been home since her eleven-thirty curfew and was safe in bed. I wanted to sleep, too, but my son was still out somewhere. Where could he be? I struggled not to imagine the worst in the dark of the night. Midnight came and went. More wind. Pelting rain. Just before one a.m., I heard his key turn in the lock. With a big sigh of relief, I nestled down, expecting his footsteps to patter down the hall and his door to click shut. Instead, Jake strode purposefully into my bedroom and switched on the light.

I sat bolt upright.

"Momma, I need to tell you something." His voice was a little too loud, too amped up. "I was in a car accident!"

My heart squeezed. Questions whizzed through my mind. *Where? Is everyone all right? Why didn't you call?* He clearly still had adrenalin pumping through his system. For a split second, I wondered if it was more than adrenalin, then pushed that thought aside.

"Me and Wade and Logan were on 101 going to get ice-cream..."

On the freeway going for ice-cream late on a Sunday night? In a storm?

"...and this other guy changes lanes in the rain at like sixty-five miles an hour and clips the front of Wade's SUV, and both of us went spinning."

"Oh my god," I said, my own head spinning. Then I thought, *Wait, wasn't Wade the guy who gave Jake that weed back in high school?*

Jake kept talking, half amped, half matter-of-fact. He told me how they spun across four lanes of traffic, how he braced himself to get hit again by other cars, how they landed upside down, him and his buddies hanging suspended from their seatbelts.

"It was surreal, Momma, like time had stopped. All that screeching and spinning and then everything went quiet. And I couldn't get my seatbelt undone and when I did I fell on my head. I had to kick the door open to crawl out."

"And you're all *okay*?" I asked, stunned and incredulous.

"Yeah, the cop said he's never seen two cars upside down on the freeway with no one going to the hospital. I took a picture on my phone. Look."

He held out his phone for me to see. How did he have the where-withal to snap a photo? Tears sprang to my eyes as I took it all in. The roof of Wade's car was flattened—smashed into the mud. They all could have been headless, but *they were alive*. My heart was pounding as I climbed out of bed and gave Jake a huge hug.

With tears in my eyes, I said, "My god, honey, I'm so glad you're all right."

"Me, too. I'm gonna go to bed." He flipped off my light as he headed for his room.

I stood there frozen as he closed my door, then crawled under the covers and hugged my knees. Why didn't Jake seem shaken? Why didn't he call me from the scene of the accident? Why did they only call Wade's dad? Why did they spend the last two hours at his house? Exhaustion and suspicion wrestled with each other. *What is there to hide?* I wished Bruce were here to hold me close.

But he's alive, I told myself. *He's alive.* I just wanted him to get going on his trek. I just wanted him to find his way.

In the coming week, Jake seemed more nervous about the wilderness than upset by his brush with death on the freeway. He departed early on the first of March and called me from his stopover in Albuquerque.

"Momma, I have two big problems."

Without realizing it, I took a big breath and held it.

"They canceled my flight to Silver City *and* I can't find my driver's license anywhere."

Big exhale. "What happened?"

"With the plane? Some kind of mechanical problem."

I envisioned someone from the wilderness program standing at a tiny airport holding a sign for "Jake," but no Jake.

"What about your license?"

"I had it in San Jose when I went through security, but I've been through every pocket, and my backpack, too, and I don't have it now."

"I'll check with the airport's lost and found. You'll have to plead with the airline to let you keep going without it."

"They're bussing everybody to a hotel and I have to be back at the airport at 5:30 tomorrow morning."

"Ugh—that's early. Don't forget to set your alarm. I'll call Soltrails and let them know what happened."

I tracked down his license. He must've left it at the security checkpoint. I spent my evening alternating with worry—a familiar place I lived these days—that he wouldn't wake up in time or they wouldn't let him on the plane. Wondering what was to come kept me from falling asleep. Miraculously, as slivers of daylight streaked the sky, the guy from Soltrails called to say Jake had arrived.

———

Lorri Hanna orchestrated things at Soltrails. As the psychotherapist who spent time with clients in the wilderness, helping them process their dominant life issues, she requested that families write impact letters to loved ones, which her team packed out to the campsite along with food and supplies. She encouraged us to convey all our truths in words—messages of support, pages full of our joys, worries, frustrations, love, sadness.

After a few days, we received Jake's first letter, which Soltrails scanned into an attachment.

> *... Our first campsite is only about 100 yards in from the van, so I guess we're starting out slow. I'm pretty anxious right about now. I'm wondering how I'm going to fill my days. It is seriously peaceful and quiet. It's a little eerie because it's just me and my thoughts...*

Bruce and I spent practically whole days working on our writing assignments. On the phone, Lorri patiently spoke to me in a kind and even tone, offering me tons of discerning edits, guiding me to transform my frustration and judgment into words my son could "hear." She planned to sit with Jake as he read and processed our messages. From what Christopher had told me at Thanksgiving, I understood that my son had hidden some dangerous and frightening drug use. *But all that was just experi-mentation, right?* After Lorri helped Bruce to tone down his own frustration—he felt that Jake, through his partying, had thrown away the privilege to attend college—we combined our letters into one.

Dear Jake,

We can only begin to understand how challenging backpacking and camping for a month might be and how tough it must feel to slow down and examine your thoughts and feelings. We know that it takes great courage on your part to do this and we are proud of you. Your willingness to do this trek says a lot about your acknowledging some issues that need dealing with and shows a commitment on your part to resolve them.

You used to relish being active, could hardly wait to get outside on the street to run, ride, throw, bat, kick, skate, and compete. It doesn't look to us that you have that joy in your life now. Is that accurate? As parents, we can see the clear connection between partying with drugs and disconnecting with most everything else. We recognize the damages that drugs can cause and fear that you are risking your very life. What were you using, how much and how often?

When we were at your Boulder house packing up, I (Momma) observed Scott waking up in the early evening to start his day, and you told me that the other housemates are pairing off to live together next year but Scott will be living on his own. Are you worried about Scott? We are troubled about what we see as you embracing a social scene that has a downward spiral; choosing to live in a party house, choosing friends who do drugs.

Your low GPA is a direct result of these choices. Do you agree that there is a connection? What do you think about that? While kids go away to college and make lifestyle choices, they make errors and learn from them, mature and move on, yet it appears you believe that you can "handle it" by continuing these behaviors. We observed that you lost weight, stopped exercising, ran out of money at the end of each month, procrastinated nine months to finish the calculus replacement program, and have pulled away from us. While your grades were not a disaster, you lost your scholarship. There are plenty of kids who graduate, don't get much in the way of a job or career path, and bumble along because that is what they did during college. We don't want that for you and we don't think you want that either. Is that true? We do realize this is part of a young person's journey in self-discovery; however, we also can't help but feel there is more going on here than that.

I (Papa) would like for us to explore why we don't often talk. It feels like you pull out your phone to text with someone as a way to block interactions. I would like for us to talk more about real life stuff, not just the casual, everyday surface stuff. What are your thoughts about this?

Though we don't mean to, we wonder if you think that we tend to focus on faults, as opposed to successes. We suspect that you might feel that all we ever do is point out how you could improve, and don't acknowledge often enough your accomplishments and successes. Is that true for you?

We welcome your feedback as to how you have experienced us supporting you in healthy ways as well as your comments on how we are enabling negative behaviors. We recognize we need to listen to you more effectively and that we need to take care in how we respond to you so that our words do not come across as judgmental, negative, or controlling. It is our hope that this trek will help bring some clarity to all of us and that you get on a path of health and direction toward adulthood. We believe that what you discover about yourself will help to determine what the next right step is for you.

Love,

Momma and Papa

Jake, meanwhile, had the birds to listen to in the morning, and the owls at night. He wrote that his tent had been dusted with snow several times in the night but he slept wearing two fleece pullovers, thick wool pants and socks, and a woolen cap to keep warm in his sleeping bag. There was no place to bathe except a tiny trickle of a creek where he could awkwardly scrub himself. Jake had been paired with an outdoor wilderness instructor who taught him the necessary skills to camp in the high desert. They went on hikes, moved camp, and in between Jake had long conversations with Lorri and worked on his letters responding to ours. He completed a twenty-page letter answering our questions of what had gone on in college.

I was home alone when I opened the email.

... You may not like what you hear but I hope you can listen to what I have to say. You're right, I used to love being physically active. I forgot that about myself somewhere in the last couple of years. I'm rediscovering that out here in New Mexico.

... Something never clicked after Rome. I came back missing the key to social success. My old social group hardly remembered my name. I figured the key to social success was simply building a repertoire of good times with everyone, precisely what I lacked after being gone, so I did my best to

create one in high school. That's the reason I was always dying
to get out of the house, because of my social insecurity, I was
trying to maximize time with friends. But I was not successful.
Then it felt like you both had blazed a path of success for me
to follow. I felt you were disappointed in me. It became easier
not to try ... then I won't have failed, plus I'll have a blast on
the way down. I gave up and pretended like I agreed with you.
I was quiet but my mind was raging that I was never going to
be as morally bulletproof as you. It felt like David and Goliath,
only there were two Goliaths and David had no idea what he
was fighting for. You both clearly knew what you stood for;
I didn't. I only knew it wasn't what you stood for, and that's a
short platform in an argument about what's right or wrong ...

My eyes opened wide as his words jumped off the screen.
I had no idea he'd felt socially insecure in high school. I felt hurt
that he experienced me as an insensitive merciless parent. What
would Bruce think when he read this?

... I never felt the permission to make my own decisions. I had
to know why not before I could know why. I understand you
still have questions, questions you may not be sure you want
the answers to. I'll take you as far down the rabbit hole as you
want to go ...

And here he described his drug use in college: beginning with
mushrooms and LSD, then moving on to lots of cocaine, alcohol,
and ecstasy at raves. *What? Could all this be true?* I pushed my
chair back and felt blood draining from my face. I'd known since
Thanksgiving that Jake used more than just alcohol and weed,
but somehow I'd denied the extent of it. *I don't really know my son.*
   But there was more.

*... I would be the first to admit I went overboard. I know I need
to make changes. Drugs fixed my problems for a couple of
hours. Drugs enabled my social aspirations. I want to learn
how to do those things for myself so that I don't feel I need
drugs to be who I want to be ...*

Oh, here's hope, I told myself.

Surely on this trek he would step back and recognize the error
of his ways—make the decision to stop embracing this terrifying behavior. Did he really feel he needed drugs to be a popular
guy? There was so much to try to understand, and the weeks with
Soltrails were racing past. Jake adamantly insisted that thirty
days was enough, though Lorri advised him to stay the full six
weeks. Bruce and I were constantly wondering, discussing, and
arguing over where to go from here.

In another letter exchange we heard growing entitlement
from Jake—he wanted to make his own independent decisions
with no hint of responsibility, no plan going forward. He main-
tained that using drugs was no big deal—he was not ready to
promise that he'd never use again. We were not willing to put
up with that. Paying expensive tuition bills for poor perfor-
mance and prodding him to get a job wasn't right. The drug use
he described seemed way beyond normal experimentation. Lorri
recommended he continue on to a supportive young-adult therapeutic program—a structured, substance-free place with therapy,
counseling, and life-skills education with real life responsibilities—an opportunity for Jake to learn, and figure out what he
wanted to do. But Jake wanted to come home.

Bruce and I found ourselves right back on what felt like a
tightrope. We couldn't *make* our nineteen-year-old son do anything. And we believed at his age he *should* be making his own
decisions, yet we were afraid. We wobbled, suspended over what

felt like an unknown void, not sure which way to lean. With input from Lorri, we came to a decision—our boundary—and sent an email, difficult to write, telling Jake that he could no longer live at home; he'd have to support himself.

> ... We recognize that you will probably need to spend some time living at home while you search for employment and make living arrangements. We would expect you to move out of the house within two months. If during that time you have not found employment sufficient to support yourself, we would pay for you to participate in a young-adult therapeutic program. We are willing to pay for such a program because we believe you will continue to benefit from being in a structured, substance-free and healthy environment. Earning an income and moving out on your own is part of the journey to self-discovery.
>
> We agree with you that you will not learn from our words, but instead will learn from trying to be independent, from failure, from hurts, and from hard work. We believe we would be depriving you of valuable lessons and experiences if we were to allow you to continue living at home. If working and supporting yourself does not work out, then it makes sense to us that you participate in a program. After either working or participating in a program for at least six months, our paying for college would be back on the table if you were drug free. We want you to know that we are here to listen and help problem solve as you figure this all out.
>
> Love,
>
> Momma and Papa

There was no time to receive his reaction, because we had to leave for Silver City, New Mexico, to be there when he came out of the woods for his "graduation." I hoped the new, respectful way of communicating we'd all been practicing would bind us together on this yellow brick road.

Before our meeting, Jake showered at a campground and arrived at our hotel with Lorri. We could hardly believe his transformation after thirty days on the land. He was fifteen pounds stronger, spoke with new confidence, and had eyes burning with life. He'd grown a beard. Lorri was athletic, well tanned, and had a deliberate calmness about her, which I instantly liked and admired. In a small conference room, she pulled chairs into a circle and we all sat down. With her encouragement, Jake started at the beginning of his days on the trail and described some of what he had learned about himself. He spoke with assurance as he looked into our eyes, and I could feel Bruce, like me, swelling with pride. I found myself assuming that Jake would reach the end of his story and say he'd thought about our final letter, and was ready to commit to giving up drugs.

Instead, he told us he was not angry that he was facing moving out in two months—he'd had some time with a professional to process the idea. He did admit to anxiousness about it. I fought back my disappointment that he wasn't choosing to go into a therapeutic program—a structured place would feel much safer to me. Maybe truth and respect were as much as we could ask for, for now.

Lorri was beaming at Jake's respectfulness and truthfulness. She said, "Jake, I think your mom has a surprise for you."

"Yeah, I do. Jake, I'm not going back with you and Papa. I'm going on a seven-day trek with Lorri's women's group. We head out tomorrow morning."

"Wow, Momma," said Jake, a glint of admiration in his eyes. "I'm totally shocked."

Five days earlier, Lorri had suggested that I join her next group out. At first, I balked. But at the last minute, I got a tetanus booster and tossed my hiking boots into my suitcase. I was by no means a backpacker. *A week without a shower?* Yet, I couldn't pass up the opportunity to spend time with the psychotherapist who'd just spent a month with my son. Plus, I'd begun to question myself. Was my parenting the cause of Jake's troubles? What was I doing wrong?

"I'm a little nervous."

"I was too, Momma."

I looked at Jake's strong suntanned arms and smiling face, his whiskered cheeks and confident stance. While Bruce helped Lorri put the chairs back in place, Jake gathered up his journals and loose papers. We sealed the session with hugs all around. As we walked out the door together, my son appeared ready and willing to take on his life.

————

On April 1, I followed Jake's footsteps into the Gila National Forest, setting down my heavy pack in camp with three women.

"That's Jake's tent you're unpacking," Lorri said, "and you picked the same place he did to pitch it."

I stood, unfurling Jake's bedroom in my hands, in what had been his home for the past month, where he'd done a lot of heavy reflection. I saw a large anthill about ten yards away. I guessed we both had the same thought to avoid that. *Will inhabiting this same space help me come to understand him more?*

Jake wasn't kidding; the tiny trickle in the creek was barely enough to slowly fill up water bottles, let alone accomplish any bathing. At the dry altitude of 6,500 feet we had to drink constantly, at least a gallon of water each day, to keep the dehydration headaches away. It became my job to fill all the water bottles regularly and add eight drops of bleach into each, then set them aside for thirty minutes before we could drink. It tasted like pool water but it was purified. On that first day, I seriously questioned my decision to be there.

The days became simple. Lorri's assignments kept me reflect-ing on important relationships in my life. I sat in a meadow of dry scratchy grass and occasionally looked up from writing in my journal to ponder the surrounding hills and stare at a deep blue sky. A wall of rocks in the distance looked like a climber's dream. I positioned my little cushion so that the slanting sun shone on my back. Lorri joined me and we talked for hours, sit-ting, sometimes hiking. She responded to my need for validation as a mother. And what about that blame I heard spilling from my son's letters—that my words conveyed mistrust, judgment, and negativity? Could lack of honest communication be at the core of our family's troubles? I wanted to engage with my chil-dren so they could safely share their thoughts and feelings, their joy and sorrow. I wanted to feel trust and love instead of con-flict and struggles. Alea had become argumentative, increasingly disrespectful, and was bucking against me. Under this strain, Bruce and I were at odds. Our family desperately needed wide-open communication right now. Lorri kept me focused on the power of language in communicating and how that impacted others. She helped me wade through the blame—blame from my son, and blame from myself that I should have the answers, that I should be less judgmental, more empathetic, a better mother.

Seven days sailed past. I couldn't wait to shampoo my hair.

Back home, I used one of my new phrases over and over: "Wait, that's not what I intended to say, let me try again..." My new awareness—the power of my words *and* that solving my family members' problems was not what they wanted—strengthened me as a parent. Somehow I felt buoyed by rediscovering truths; I *was* a patient, capable, good mother and I needed to trust my intuition. I felt renewed and willing to take on the hard work ahead.

4
SOOT

Addiction takes the healthiest parts of love and smashes
them into worry, helplessness, and hopelessness.
— PATRICK MACAFEE, PhD, Afterword, *Stay Close*

EASTER SUNDAY DAWNED DAMP with rainbows. Jake was
spending long hours in his bedroom with the door closed.
I assumed he was hunting for a job and searching for housing
on his computer. Suddenly, he burst out and announced he was
going to a job interview at an upscale coffee house.

"Where is it?" I asked.

"Over on University Avenue. It's perfect because I know a little
Italian and it's full-time work."

"Well, you're tall, dark, and handsome and could certainly pass
for an Italian. Good luck!"

He returned home two hours later grinning. Bruce was doing
paperwork at the kitchen table and I was at the counter chopping
vegetables for dinner. "Got the job," Jake said. "Tomorrow I start
an intensive two-week training."

I felt deeply relieved. Nearly a month into our two-month deadline, Jake was following through on his commitment to get a job.

"I'm gonna learn to make these elaborate foam designs, and I have to memorize the menu. Then I get to work the cash register."

"What's the place like?" Bruce asked.

"It's really upscale. Seems like a bunch of venture capitalists drinking coffee and making deals. Different languages at all the tables. I think professors and students from Stanford come in."

Jake did well in his training and began to earn a paycheck. Bruce and I felt hopeful that this job would be a good fit, for now. Knowing where Jake would be and what he'd be doing settled some of my anxiety. Our son had a plan.

At first, Jake borrowed my car to get back and forth to work. Every once in a while he came home especially late. Most of his friends were away at college, but a few were around. We didn't see evidence of drinking or drugs and trusted he was focused on moving forward. After another month, he found a room to rent in a house about a mile from his job. Rent was steep every-where in the Bay Area and would consume a big portion of his paycheck, but again he was following through on a commitment, this time to find housing.

Bruce wrote a check for the first- and last-month's rent; we agreed that Jake would cover all rent going forward. A few days before his move, Jake said the landlord needed an additional month's rent as security deposit, because Jake didn't have any credit history. I wasn't home; the way Bruce later remembered things, neither he nor Jake knew for sure how to spell the landlord's name. Jake said, "Why don't you just leave that part blank? I'll fill it in later." Bruce made out the check as suggested and handed it to Jake.

On June 1, Jake moved out precisely on our two-month dead-line. We loaned him our air mattress. A week later he bought a real mattress from a student graduating from Stanford, and we strapped it on top of our car to transport it to his new place. We donated a lamp, a desk, and a chair. Bruce loaned Jake his bicy-cle. He now lived fifteen minutes away; we agreed that one of us would pick him up once a week so we could all have dinner together. It felt like we were settling into a fresh start.

On our third family-dinner night, our plates were green with basil pesto linguine and salad.

"Are you getting enough sleep, honey?" I asked Jake. "You look tired."

He shrugged. "Not really. I finish my shift at midnight, and then I bike home, and then I have trouble getting to sleep, even though I'm *not* drinking the coffee."

I fought back my worry. He also seemed to be losing weight. "Do you make dinner at that hour?"

"Sometimes I just skip it because I'm so tired." He stared at his plate. "Ella's back in town so I see her sometimes. And some of my high-school friends are beginning to get back. It's a pain not having a car. I'm isolated."

Alea said, "I want to come in and have you make me a fancy latte."

Bruce smiled at her. I didn't know what to say, so I got up to clear the dishes.

————

Bruce and I had been seeing Dr. Nolan without Jake. One day, we sat on the familiar couch as Bruce let out his sadness. He'd gotten a call from a childhood friend who had recently lost his twenty-one-year-old son to an overdose of heroin. "His mother found him dead in bed one morning. Neither of them had any idea their son was using drugs. I can't imagine how awful this is for them."

A chill ran down my spine every time I thought of the immeasurable pain of those parents.

"I told Jake about it yesterday," Bruce said.

Dr. Nolan asked, "What was his reaction?"

"Not much. But I told him, 'Don't ever do that to your Momma and me.'"

It was too awful to contemplate, so I switched the subject to Jake's finances. "Jake says he doesn't have enough money to do anything. He feels isolated and miserable."

"I'm frustrated that he can't get by with what he's making," Bruce added. "It could work if he's careful."

Dr. Nolan looked thoughtful. "If it isn't working now, and he's miserable, you might consider supplementing his income."

"I guess we'll have to think about that," Bruce said, just as I blurted, "Something about that doesn't feel right."

We looked at each other. I thought, *We are just navigating in the dark here.*

The next time Jake came over for dinner, after the dishes were cleared, Bruce pulled his chair next to Jake with a spreadsheet and began offering some helpful tips for budgeting. After all, Bruce was a certified public accountant. From the kitchen sink, I looked over to see him bent over the worksheet talking away about credits and debits, while Jake leaned back in his chair, nodding off. Every week it seemed that he'd been diminishing, thin and pale, his eyes deadened, his answers evasive. There was a streak of what looked like soot on his forehead. *What IS that? What's wrong with him?* Bruce might as well have been speaking Russian.

I asked Jake if he would join me walking Bella, our five-year-old yellow Lab. I used my best communication skills from Soltrails to get him talking. "Jake, tell me more about what's going on for you." Then I was quiet.

"I feel anxious at work. Everyone there is older than me and more experienced. It's always busy and it's hard for me to know what I should be doing every minute. Then when I get home I can't sleep."

"Hmm."

"People at work go out to bars afterward since they're all over twenty-one but I can't do that. Anyway, I don't have money for going out." He continued to enumerate his woes. "I feel isolated being away from college and all my friends. And things aren't going well with Ella."

"Is she the right girl for you?"

"Nobody else'd be attracted to me since I'm all skinny again. Anyway, she's trying to make up for hurting me."

"Your life sounds tough, Jake."

"It is."

I didn't feel I was getting the whole truth, so I just went straight to the point. "Are you using drugs?"

There was a pause.

"I've had some beers with a guy from work. And, well, I fell off my bike last week when I was riding home in the dark and hurt my wrist. It was really hurting so I used Oxy."

I thought, *Where did he get that?* "Why didn't you just take some ibuprofen?"

He looked at me strangely.

The next day, a program came on TV showing an addicted young man smoking OxyContin, a narcotic pain reliever used to treat moderate to severe pain. On a piece of foil, he melted the white pill using a lighter from underneath. As the Oxy slid down the foil, he inhaled through the outer casing of a hollowed out Bic pen. The soot.

My son must be smoking OxyContin.

My hands were sweating as I rubbed my pulsing temples.

I paced the house, then picked up the phone and got through to Dr. Nolan. After pouring out my fears, I punched in Jake's number and breathed in long and hard to calm myself. I needed to make this call quick before I lost my nerve.

"Jake, can you meet me tomorrow at Dr. Nolan's office? At noon?"

He hesitated. "Sure. My shift got cancelled so I'll bike over."

"Okay. I'll see you there."

When Jake showed up the next day, relief swept through me. Bruce had left again on a business trip, and I hadn't been able to reach him by phone, so it was just me and Jake with the counselor. I sat on the edge of my seat and voiced intense worry.

"Jake, I've tried everything I can think of to help you and nothing seems to be working."

Dr. Nolan added, "Jake, you look awful."

He shrugged. "There're some problems at work with my shifts. They're not giving me enough hours."

My tears threatened to spill. "I think all your money is going toward drugs. I think you have a problem. This can't go on."

Jake's eyes, deep dark spheres, shifted up from the floor to meet mine. In that instant, I saw that he was shaking and scared. My own fear was vibrating inside me.

He said, "A coworker asked me if I was anorexic. That shocked me. I'm only eating a slice of bread every couple days. Drugs instead of food." He looked down. Then more softly, "Thought I could control it. I'm isolated from my friends. I hate my life."

Dr. Nolan seemed surprised at Jake's admission and glanced at me. I imagined he was acknowledging the power of a mother's intuition. My heart was cracking into little pieces. I looked at my helpless hands. I wanted to hold Jake the way I'd held him when he hurt himself as a little boy, to make everything all right. But I knew I couldn't.

"Your mom and I spoke yesterday," Dr. Nolan said. "She thinks you need to go to rehab. From what you've just said, I agree. I can give you the names of several. What do you think?"

Jake murmured, "I'll go."

I felt dizzy with relief and utterly overwhelmed as we loaded his bike into my car. We'd agreed that he'd come home with me. I didn't want him alone or using drugs. Enduring the past few hours without Bruce had been desperately hard. *What do I do now?*

Jake retreated to his room when we got home and I turned on my computer to research rehabs. I wasn't sure how much Dr. Nolan knew about the places he'd recommended. One was so far away, in Minnesota. I felt assaulted by marketing on the various websites. I didn't know the right questions to ask. I was shocked at the tens of thousands of dollars some places cost. I kept listening for Jake to come out of his room as I slogged through flashing advertisements and rosy pictures. He needed to go *now,* but I didn't know where. An urgency burned inside me, big as a bonfire, pushing me to make calls, to try to understand what each place offered. Some programs were longer than others, and some said adolescents needed to be separate from adults. The only consistent advice I kept hearing was the longer the program the better for a nineteen-year-old.

The next day, I drove Jake to his rented room to speak to his landlord. We got there first and started packing up. Lighters, dismantled pens, and crumpled pieces of singed foil were strewn around the floor of his rented room, mixed with dirty clothing. As we filled boxes, I could barely breathe; I felt like a corset was being tightened around my middle. We were loading the last of the boxes into the back of my car when the landlord finally pulled up. Jake walked over first to explain that he was moving out, and I followed.

The landlord said, "I'll prorate out the month, but I'm keeping the last month's rent since you didn't give any notice."

I said, "But we should get the security deposit back, right? If there isn't any damage?"

The landlord looked irritated. "There isn't any security deposit. It's first and last."

I felt too exhausted and overwhelmed to argue it. Jake and I climbed into the car, then drove in silence to the coffee house so he could give notice. This time I let him go in on his own, waiting in the car with my eyes closed and my chest aching.

"She wasn't very happy," Jake said when he climbed back in the car. "It's lousy timing. She asked me to do one more shift, tomorrow from two to ten. I said okay."

That night, between calls to find a bed in hopefully the right rehab, I got through to Bruce. In a hurry, I relayed all that had happened.

"Is it too much to ask for him to do a simple job?" Bruce demanded. It sounded as if my husband resented the timing of this crisis, as if I had anything to do with it. "Jake is young and smart. This doesn't add up. What the hell's going on here?"

I needed him to say something like, "It must be awful for you and I'm sorry I'm not there. What can I do to help? Should I come home now?"

Instead, he seemed preoccupied, presuming I would handle everything. Perhaps, deep down, he was immobilized by anger and fear. I was speechless with hurt.

Alea came through the front door just as I put down the receiver. My eyes flicked to the clock—she was home before her curfew—before they came to rest on my seventeen-year-old daughter's beautiful tear-stained face.

"Honey, what's wrong?"

"Ben's depressed. He's threatening to commit suicide. He's with his parents right now."

"Oh my god, Alea, that's awful. What can I do?"

"I don't want to talk about it." She turned and walked quietly to her bedroom.

I'd been trying to douse one fire, and here was another. I couldn't get to Alea; she had erected a stone wall. Jake, too, had walled himself in; each was disappearing behind an impenetrable barricade. I wanted to scream, to pound on their walls, *LET ME IN! Let me help!* I sank on the couch in my own hell, feeling torn in two. I couldn't stop crying. I'd never felt so alone.

Sleep never came for me that night, so I started back up on the computer before dawn. Midmorning, Alea dragged herself to her summer job. Jake needed my car to go finish his last shift. I told him I expected him back as soon as work was over.

After he left, like a battered explorer, I scoured his bedroom and found one lone white OxyContin pill in his desk drawer. *Should I throw it down the toilet?* I picked it up—I didn't allow drugs in my house. *Should I leave it?* He was out of money, and his body was demanding he get loaded. Maybe that's why he was so pale, pathetic, and irritable. I'd heard how awful it was to detox and I didn't know how to handle that. If he couldn't find the pill, would he go out and get more? I put it back in the drawer.

Between frantic calls to admission directors of treatment centers, I looked at our bank statements, hoping to discover what had gone wrong with the security deposit. I identified the check number, found the image of the cancelled check online, and froze. The name on the "Pay to the order of" line wasn't the landlord's. The check was made out, in Jake's handwriting, to his high-school friend Wade, the driver in the car crash. *He must be Jake's drug source.*

Our son had lied to us, taken our money, and handed it to a drug dealer. Fury and betrayal kept me searching for rehabs. I was still going strong at ten-thirty when Jake got home. We didn't even speak. At last, my calls resulted in securing an open bed at a place several people had recommended. Cirque Lodge in Utah offered a ninety-day program. I told myself Jake would get the best help there and I bought him a plane ticket for the following day. Falling on my knees that night, exhausted, I cried into the darkness. *Help.*

The next morning, after a breakfast he didn't eat, I drove my son to the airport. At security, I gave him a long hug and told him I loved him. Then I watched, hoping he would continue walking toward his gate.

Part Two

BEGINNER'S EYES

5
DISEASE

By calling addiction a disease, we don't remove choice and
we don't absolve the addict's need to take personal responsibility.
— Dr. Kevin McCauley

BEGINNING WITH THE MORNING I first sent my son off to
rehab—the morning he stood in our kitchen hushed and
cowed and I realized, with beginner's eyes, that I was staring
at the face of addiction—our family's journey snaps into sharp
relief. As I write, I am living those days and months once again.

Back home from the airport, I crash. I don't know how I've
carried off these last few days. I want to crawl under my covers,
pull the sheet over my head, and not get out of bed.

When I hear that Jake has arrived safely at Cirque, I'm washed
by enormous relief. It's the first of August. Surely he'll be fixed by
Christmas. If he listens and does what they say, he can get back
on track. I know he's terrified, but he's a compliant guy. If he
does the time, he'll be fine.

I have no understanding of the nature of this beast.

Bruce returns from his trip and we stumble through the first few days with Jake gone. I've learned that Cirque holds a "family week" every three weeks, a program they call "our most effective instrument in the recovery process." The next one will begin on day sixteen of Jake's rehab, and I want all of us to attend. Alea—soon to start her senior year—is torn. She wants to see her brother, but she doesn't want to miss the last week of summer with her friends, and she's still wrapped up in her relationship with Ben.

Bruce has been moving around the house in a tense, spooky silence. When I check with him about flight times it's almost a relief when he bursts out in anger and frustration. "Why couldn't Jake just keep his job, take care of himself?" he says, then shakes his head. "Is family week really a *whole week*?"

"It's four full days plus travel time, so pretty much." I'm upset too, but I'm walking around more numb than angry.

Bruce is staring across the room. When he finally speaks, I hear resentment. "Jake's problems are all we ever talk about," he says quietly.

It's true. I can think of nothing else. I hurt with continual self-blame—*I didn't teach him well, I couldn't get him to eat better, to organize his stuff, to calendar his life.* For months, when I haven't understood why his finances are in shambles, why he hasn't latched on to any passion, why he keeps losing weight, why he seems to routinely sabotage himself, I've blamed myself because I'm his mom. My brain has not been turning off at night and I unconsciously grind my teeth, cracking a filling.

I say, "I'll go make the reservations," and walk out of the room.

Bruce, Alea, and I withdraw into ourselves, each on our own island. A comment here and there gives me a glimpse into their jungle of thoughts. Finally, I drag my burden of guilt and blame onto the plane when the three of us travel to Utah to learn about addiction.

Cirque Lodge is situated opposite stunning mountains that rise right up from the parking lot. It would be a spectacular day for a hike, but that's not why we're here. Rehab residents and their family members all file into a big room for the first morning's lecture. I've learned that the residents—men and women both, age eighteen and up—attend lectures together and share meals, but spend most of their time in group sessions separated by gender.

The speaker, Dr. Kevin McCauley, is in long-term recovery himself, and has devoted more than the last decade to answering the question, "Is addiction a disease?" Patiently and passionately, Dr. McCauley demonstrates how addiction fits the disease model that doctors adopted more than a hundred years ago. Dr. McCauley uses hard facts from neurobiology and earnestly demonstrates how drugs hijack the brain. *A disease?* A puzzle piece falls into place, or tries to. This isn't Jake being lazy, making poor choices, and just wanting everything handed to him. This is his brain working against him. I sit up straight. My mind is screaming to make sense of all this chaos—to get our lives back. Dr. McCauley explains that in the famous Olds Rodent Experiments, where American psychologist James Olds injected drugs into the prefrontal cortex of mice, the part of the brain where choices are made, addiction did not occur. Cocaine was administered into all parts of a mouse's brain and not until it was injected directly into the midbrain did mice become addicted. The midbrain's function is to keep us alive by handling the next thirty seconds; a processing station that deals with life-or-death decisions. Olds' experiments show that drugs work in the midbrain, not in the part of the brain controlling choice. In other words, an addict's brain is telling him to get and use drugs for his very survival—drugs have become life itself.

Those addicted mice just keep hitting the lever for more drugs, overriding all necessities of survival (eat, kill, defend, procreate) as their midbrain convinces them they need the drug at all costs. Dr. McCauley says it plainly; it is not about mouse parenting skills (is he right?), or their personalities (lacking moral fiber), or any potential outside influence from mice gangs (environment). Drugs affect the midbrain and when threatened the prefrontal cortex shuts down. When addicts, observed in a scanning machine, are induced into a state of craving by watching videos of drug use, the midbrain lights up and the prefrontal cortex goes dark. The midbrain is in control, convincing the addict that the drug is the answer to everything. The thought flares in my mind—when Jake fell off his bike, his brain must have been telling him, "Your drug of choice is the answer," so he went home and smoked Oxy.

For a moment, I don't hear what Dr. McCauley is saying. I've suddenly realized that Jake was probably placating me when he told me about falling off his bicycle. He made it sound like he simply took a pain reliever for his wrist when he was likely abusing Oxy all along. Or was he telling me as much as he dared, hoping I'd make the connection he was in trouble? Tormenting myself with blame is futile.

Interrupting my thoughts, Dr. McCauley states a startling fact: 10 percent of the population has this disease. How do you get it? Dr. McCauley says there is a remarkable lag between science and the general public's understanding of "genetic vulnerability." In other words, this is both a psychological disease and a biological one. He says, "Genes don't get you there alone, just faster." Of course, there's the choice to drink or use drugs. It's a poor choice—but a common one—for a freshman to party away, drowning his sorrows, or reveling in the freedom and drug-using camaraderie of the environment of dorm life. Some brains can drink and drug their way through college and eventually get on with life; others activate addiction and there's no going back. Stress is a big factor acting on those genes. My thoughts race back to Thanksgiving break of Jake's college freshman year, when Ella admitted cheating on him and his friends all knew about it. Okay, that heartbreak and deception could count as stress slamming on a vulnerable adolescent brain in a poorly managed college environment.

Jake leans in to hear Dr. McCauley differentiate between an addict and a nonaddict. "After getting a DUI, a nonaddict would react by bringing that experience to bear in deciding to stop. An addict's thinking would be, 'I'll get high and deal with it tomorrow.' That brain has crossed the line to where the drug is life itself."

Dr. McCauley points out that the moral-choice argument—professing that an addict should just stop because that's the right thing to do—does not address craving. "Addicts don't have the choice not to crave. True craving..."

His voice trails off. Almost as if the audience is collectively holding its breath, the room becomes quiet as a coffin. Dr. McCauley breathes more deeply, then starts again. "Craving for the addict is not, *Gee, I want it a lot*. Craving is...up at night, can't sleep, sweat on your brow, pulse at a hundred and fifty, staring at the ceiling thinking *Just one more time*, every cell in your body screaming *Just one more time...* Make no mistake, that is genuine suffering." Tears sting my eyes. Jake and I both sit back. My compassion surges. I wonder what he's thinking. New information is swirling around my brain—survival instincts taking over, midbrains lighting up, addicted mice, cravings that crush—and some of my guilt drops away.

At lunch, I sit with a bowl of soup next to Bruce. He and Alea chat with Jake but I've heard so much in this morning's lecture I just spoon up the hot broth quietly. Looking around the cafeteria I begin to see I am not alone. I can spot who the visitors are. Like me, they're the ones sagging.

After lunch, the four of us head into a smaller room for an afternoon of group processing. We join three other families who are also here to support their addicts and alcoholics. The evident pain in the room penetrates my body—I feel raw, as if I have no skin, and my tears keep seeping out spontaneously.

We sit in a circle. One guy has a light in his eyes and I notice how solicitous he is of his mother, as if in every gentlemanly action he is bent on apologizing to her. He's a handsome hippie in his thirties and the only resident Jake introduces us to. He sparks a connection with our whole family, and during breaks we talk with him and his mother. Another thirty-something—a high-school English teacher—has been derailed by smoking weed. *A pothead? Wait, can you trigger addiction by smoking marijuana?* His mother, sister, and ex-wife are here, even his elderly father, who's battling cancer.

Each resident takes a turn sitting in the "Ring of Fire," listening while family members pour out their hearts. It can be searingly emotional to tell our addicts how we've been impacted by their addiction, so we all circle up to support each other. The counselor tells us this process helps break down an addict's strong denial that his drug use affects others.

The English teacher goes first. Each family member speaks to him, even his ex-wife. I find myself trembling as his mother describes her long road of agony. Next, a blond guy in jeans and a sweatshirt moves into the Ring of Fire. His mother speaks as his older sister sits silent and angry. At twenty-three, he already has a protruding beer belly and drinks to forget his father's sudden death. His mother is afraid his drinking will escalate to rages where he'll beat her. Her story is interrupted when a jittery young man enters the room. We learn that he's just arrived from detox. He's deathly pale, sick and disjointed, with veiled eyes. He bounces his leg continuously, almost violently. He looks a few years older than Jake. I remind myself to keep breathing.

Jake is next in the Ring, and Alea takes the seat facing him. The counselor prods him to ask, "Alea, how has my addiction affected you?"

Blackened tears of mascara stream down my daughter's face, and a floodgate opens. She blurts, "I'm so scared. I *need* you in our family." Aching with pent-up pain, shock, anger, and sadness she vents at my quiet pale son, telling him how alone she feels with him unavailable and how terrified she is that his drug use will kill him, leaving her brotherless. "Jake, what's happening to you? *Please* do what they tell you so you can come home." I look away, but my eyes fall on the ex-wife of the pot addict, who is weeping silently as she follows every word; there is no escaping inner turmoil anywhere in this room. The widowed mom is tense and clenching her hands, pain splashed across her face. The counselor starts the tissue box around the circle. Each of us has lived the hurt Alea is expressing.

Bruce goes next. He lets out his frustration that Jake has landed in rehab. "You're a smart kid, and you had a great opportunity to be at a good college. I don't understand how you got here." His thoughts get tangled. "Drug use impacts your ability to function. Don't you *want* to get out of bed and get a job done?" He shakes his head and looks down at his shoes. "I'm really worried for you, Jake," he says softly.

When it's my turn, I look into Jake's face. He seems passive. I can't imagine what it's like for him to sit across from me, waiting for me to bluntly describe my pain. I try to gather myself, placing my hands in my lap and taking a slow breath, but warm tears keep pouring down my cheeks.

"Jake, nothing has made any sense for so long. And I've been so worried about you. I'm glad to be here now, to see you in a place where you can get help. They say you need time here. You can't do it alone."

Pausing, I fight against the motherly protection that suddenly rears up from my depths. I resist adding my pain to his—resist telling him fully how badly I ache. But the counselors have told me I can best help Jake by being honest, so I forge ahead.

"Now that I know you were using right after your wilderness trek—while I was out there sleeping in a tent, drinking bleached water, and working hard to learn how to communicate with you better—I feel completely betrayed. In fact, I feel like *all* my attempts to help you have been thrown back in my face. Every day I wrestle with guilt that I should have figured out a way to keep you safe. I couldn't. I didn't. And I can't."

I don't say everything I could, but what I've shared has eased my fear and frustration. My nose is chapped. More tissues get passed around. Jake doesn't cry.

When we take a break, I pass an emaciated, hair-bleached-frosty ghost of a boy creeping down the hall, gliding his finger tip along the wall, eyes straight ahead. He doesn't talk or make eye-contact. Jake explains that he's been here a long time—he's schizophrenic—and that his family never comes to visit. A lump rises in my throat.

Exhausted and overwhelmed at the end of the day, Bruce, Alea, and I retire quietly to our hotel. Bruce and I go straight to bed. Alea, stunned by what she's learned of her brother's addiction and wanting to pour some of it back out, stays up to tap out her college-application essay on her iPhone as she lies on her rollaway cot. She is enormously impacted by the residents and impressed with the counselors, too. As I'm about to drift off, she whispers, "Momma, what do you have to major in to be a counselor here?"

"Not sure," I mumble. "Psychology, maybe. Got a title yet?"

"Yeah. 'What Do You Wear to Your Brother's Funeral?'"

I suck in some air. I thought I'd run dry, but more tears slide onto my pillow.

The next day, Jake seems set on minimizing the wreckage his drug use has left behind as he voices his budding plan in a meeting in his counselor's office. "One month here followed by three months in sober living should get me back to CU Boulder to begin the January semester."

But we've just heard from these professionals the full impact of this disease—the time needed for healing.

"Jake," Bruce says, "Dr. McCauley explained that the science shows how easy it is to relapse at ninety days, then again at one hundred and twenty days."

"Thirty days will do it for me," he says, digging in. "Ninety days here is *way too long*."

This sounds familiar. I remember when he insisted that thirty days in the wilderness program was enough, that six weeks was too long. Avoidance sits on one of his shoulders and denial on the other. Getting back to his friends in Boulder is foremost in his mind, and his counselor does not challenge this thinking.

Alea sits silently taking in her brother's resistance.

He asks his counselor, "What're the statistics of addicts who can successfully control their use when they've only been addicted for a little while?"

She answers with an AA expression. "Once you're a pickle, you can't go back to being a cuke."

Clearly, Jake is unable to accept what it means to be an addict. It has just been hammered into us in lecture after lecture, group after group, that an addict often fights this every step of the way. Our beginning education about a necessary sober life for him at nineteen is overwhelming. From all that I've just learned, the behavior and dysfunction we've been experiencing these past months now makes sense. *There is no quick fix*—we can't just all go on with our lives. This is so hard for all of us to accept.

There's one more thing I need to say to my son. We've been living with deceit for months, and I'm tired of deception.

"Jake, so far we haven't told anyone that you're here. It's going to be difficult to explain why you aren't at home."

"No one else has to know." He is adamant.

I'm trying my best to be forthright, yet respectful. "That means I'll be forced to lie whenever someone asks me where you are. It will make me uncomfortable not to be truthful."

"I *don't* want anyone to know."

I realize he's entirely focused on himself, he doesn't care what I'm feeling. Most likely he thinks he'll be judged, even by loved ones. I leave it for now, though I'm still in turmoil.

Later on, the counseling director, Sue, explains in a kind and straightforward manner to the assembled group of visitors that we each need to work on our own recovery. "This is a disease that spills into family relationships. You are already helping your loved one by coming here to learn about addiction. You are raising your awareness of behaviors that might need changing. The addict is not the only one who needs to recover. You can continue helping yourselves by going to Al-Anon meetings. Meetings are everywhere. Many people find tremendous support there and gain a newfound sense of well-being over time."

Her words sound full of wisdom. Still, a part of me resists. If Jake will just stop using drugs, we can all go back to a good life. But her remarks introduce the concept that family members need to work on recovery, too.

During the break, I prod Alea to go ask Sue her questions about majors and counseling jobs. She hesitates, but gets her chance when Sue stops and chats with us briefly. Sue invites Alea to meet privately in her office once she finishes up.

Afterward, Alea tells me, "Sue was super helpful explaining about an MSW."

"What's an MSW?"

"A Master of Social Work. She told me some colleges have a five-year program to get it."

Alea looks animated. She was gone so long I suspect she spent time questioning Sue about her boyfriend Ben and his ongoing depression.

After four full days at Cirque, I'm brimming with information and emotion, as if I'm loaded down with sacks of groceries in a tiny new kitchen. I need to set everything down then pull out each item and figure out where to put it. Jake's brain is telling him to use Oxy no matter what. What do I do with that? The disease is progressive. Is that why it took just two months on his own for his life to fall to pieces? Denial seems a primary obstacle, and as soon as I pull *that* out, I want to fling it aside, but I fight the impulse. I hold on for a moment and feel puzzle pieces fitting together. I think back to when Jake failed those two college courses and we sent him back for another semester. I recall Lorri recommending that Jake continue on to a transitional program after he bared much of his soul on his wilderness trek. Should we have insisted he go? Understanding addiction as a disease is what we've been missing. Right now, I trust Jake is where he needs to be. I need to repack my sacks and take them home.

It's time to say goodbye. Though strangers only a few days ago, shared anguish has drawn us together with the families of other residents, and we reach out easily to warmly hug one another goodbye. The immediate and total empathy is written on each departing face. I no longer feel so alone.

But I can't read Jake's expression as we squeeze him tight. Is he feeling abandoned? Frightened? Angry? Ashamed? I have no idea. As we depart, I take one last look back at all the addicts and alcoholics waving goodbye. Better understanding and compassion have changed my notion of what it's like to hang out with a bunch of drug addicts.

6
DIGGING IN

Drug addiction isn't as simple as a person making bad choices.
Rather, it reflects a disease of the very system
that makes good choices possible.
— Dr. Nora Volkow

"I PUT IN A REQUEST to change rooms," Jake tells me on a phone call. "I'm friends with Max, and he sleeps in this huge bedroom with a giant window looking straight out to the mountains. One of his roommates was just discharged so I think they're going to let me switch."

I held my breath when we passed the thirty-day mark—the period Jake insisted was all he needed at rehab—and I'm relieved to hear him talking about a new room.

"Hope that works out," I say.

"Me too. I'm not happy about my current roommates."

He tells me that Rick's a night owl. He sits up in bed in the night speaking gibberish for several minutes at a time—waking Jake up—then as Jake is just falling back asleep Rick wakes up again, more lucid, and tells Jake over and over how he's only there to appease his parents, he plans to never quit using. He loves drugs and they're a big part of his life.

"And Stephan isn't doing so well," Jake continues. "He took so many psychedelic drugs at a rave his brain never came back. He's created five different personalities. Stephan's right-handed, but he signs in every day as Sergio, using his left. Sergio's a twin who's the one who takes drugs, not him."

"Geez."

"Yeah. He's in and out of here and the hospital. He's not stabilizing."

"Sounds like being in a different room is a good idea."

"Yeah, I like Max. We like to work out together. We go to the gym every day."

Bruce travels to the family week in early September and I plan on the one after that. Bruce gets a second opportunity to participate, listen, observe, and interact with Jake as well as the other residents. When we talk his first night, he tells me several visitors commented to him how impressed they were in exchanges with Jake—that he's such a caring young man. As a distressed parent, Bruce feels comforted to have someone else notice what he's known all along in his son—that goodness. Jake's temporary dark disguise has left us both afraid the real Jake might at some point be lost to us.

Bruce tells me Jake looks good. He's smiling again. Working out at the gym is causing him to bust out of the little T-shirts he arrived in at 145 pounds—at six-foot-two. On day thirty-seven, Jake's put on twenty pounds. Bruce takes him out to buy a few new shirts on a specially earned pass. He treats him to his favorite at In-N-Out—a double double, fries and vanilla shake—and admires how Jake can wolf it down.

When we talk the second night, Bruce describes his day. "I went to the morning lectures and then had a spectacular afternoon outdoors with Jake. It's chilly—you can tell autumn is coming—but it warms up in the afternoons. We hiked to a water-fall and then took a chairlift up with bikes. Screaming down the mountain was great."

"That's not something *I'm* doing when I visit him."

"It was a real treat. He loved it. But he's still talking about leav-ing early, with aftercare in Boulder. I told him we didn't support either of those ideas. *That* really changed the mood."

My heart sinks. "He's talking about leaving?"

"I actually think he envisions getting on a plane to Colorado right after I head home. And his counselor seems to support his idea of aftercare in Boulder—though not as soon as Jake has in mind. I don't understand his counselor. Their aftercare person said returning to the same playground with the same playmates is definitely not a good idea."

Bruce becomes more and more frustrated with Jake's coun-selor the following day, particularly when she asks which after-care program we'll support and pay for, when Jake isn't even halfway through the program. Bruce and I agree that Jake needs to spend the full ninety days—we clearly heard in all the lectures and group sessions that the longer an addict stays in treatment the better. We also agree that Boulder would be the worst place for him, even after ninety days, and that college is out of the question until he spends some time in a transitional program. As for what we will pay for, we'll decide on that when the time comes. We thought we'd made all this clear.

We set up a conference call with Sue, the head counselor. Bruce sums things up. "Jake's angry because he feels like we're making him stay longer than he wants."

"You're not making him do anything," Sue points out. "You're giving him the opportunity to get treatment."

"Yeah," Bruce says. "And he's not happy about it."

Sue calmly continues, "I've explained to Jake that the longer he stays here—the more stabilized—the more mentally clear he'll become. There's no hurry. Many residents have that same urgency to leave."

"So what do we say when Jake gets so angry?" I ask.

The savvy head counselor quietly repeats herself. "It sounds to me that you support treatment. Tell him, 'Ninety days at Cirque, that's all we'll support right now. I hear you're not happy about it.'"

"You make it sound so simple," I say.

"It's not," she says kindly. "None of this is simple. By the way, are you guys getting to Al-Anon?"

On his last afternoon, Bruce learns that Cirque has graduated some 3,400 residents since opening its doors ten years ago. Every September they host a reunion for alumni, during which a gong is struck to commemorate each graduate who lost his or her battle with addiction. This year the total increased to one hundred dead. One hundred addicted souls who had a chance at treatment, gone.

When Bruce returns home on Friday he tells me Jake is looking forward to the three-day reunion event, which is helping to distract him from his thoughts of getting out. Just before he left, Bruce made a point of asking one of the long-time counselors— who greatly impressed him in several of the group sessions— what he thought about Jake going to Boulder and restarting college in January. "Too soon," he said.

———

I've learned there's an Al-Anon meeting every day of the week in various locations close to our home. I suggest to Bruce that we try the Sunday evening one, over at a church a five-minute drive away.

"I'm curious," he says. "But I'm not wild about listening to a bunch of people talk about their problems."

He's only been home two days and I imagine he'd rather read a book or watch 60 Minutes. Luckily, he's fresh from hearing Sue encourage us to go. I say, "We know we need help and this one has a newcomer welcome right before the meeting starts. That's us—newcomers."

"Let's give it a try," he says.

We gobble down dinner in order to get there by seven o'clock. I ask Alea if she wants to join us, and she declines.

I wonder, *What's this program all about?* as we walk into what turns out to be the wrong room. Twenty or so seated couples, obviously in the middle of some assigned task, all turn to stare at us. I want to spin around and run. This, it appears, is a couples-therapy class. As we back ourselves out, one nice man whispers that Al-Anon is next door.

In the correct room, people are setting up chairs in concentric circles. Someone digs up a large electric coffee pot and spreads out cookies on a tray. By the time the meeting starts, about fifty people have trickled in. It looks like it could just as well be a PTA meeting. No one is in charge—yet everyone is. With tremendous honesty, one shares his pain, another her failings; some struggle to hope. One woman pipes up to describe her unexpected joy— she spent the day with her recovering husband. Quiet respectful-ness saturates the room. People aren't jumping in to make their point; instead, they listen attentively and consider what's being said. There's something soothing and freeing about listening to their dreadful narratives—stories that parallel mine—and rivu-lets of tears start coursing down my face. I keep expecting a clear leader to spell out what we should do, but people are simply shar-ing their experience, offering it to those who will take it. Not an ounce of judgment anywhere. Some people notice me crying and glance understandingly, as if it happens here all the time. At the end of the meeting, before I can duck out to find something to wipe my face, a man, a total stranger, comes up to me. "I was a wreck when I came in here a few years ago," he says. "My wife's an alcoholic, and this program helped me turn my life around." And then, "Keep coming back."

In the car I dig up an extra packet of tissues. I finish sniffling and wiping my nose, which is continually raw these days. Bruce is used to seeing me cry and doesn't comment. "What did you think?" I ask him.

"Everyone was especially welcoming."

I nod in agreement.

"I didn't like holding hands at the end and saying 'Dear God.' That made it feel like a religious group. And I hate to hear 'grant me' in a prayer because I just don't believe in some god *granting* me one thing or other. But besides that, I think the meeting was helpful.

"Me, too."

The next day—Monday—I talk to Jake's counselor. "You got him here," she says. "Now he has to want it. You can't do the work for him."

"I can't just sit and brood," I tell her. That leaves too much time to question over and over why this happened. Latching on to a reason, any reason, feels better than having no answers. "What about the high incidence of those with ADHD, especially boys, and addiction? Could ADHD be a factor in Jake's self-medicating?" I refuse to let go of control.

The counselor says, "Jake admits he was using Oxy at the time he was tested for ADHD, which invalidates those findings. Maybe he has ADHD, and maybe he doesn't."

"Jake was *using* back in February?" He was living at home then. Revelations like this one hit me like falling rocks.

The counselor ushers Jake into her office to participate in the call. He's furious that Bruce and I won't support his return to Boulder.

"I was yanked out of college," he says, "And now you're trying to control me and keep me from the friends I made there."

I stiffen in my seat against the onslaught of blame, denial, and anger.

Entitlement comes next. "The bar was set higher for me than my friends and Boulder was where life was *fun*."

His words draw me in to a swirl of familiar emotions—fear, guilt, anger of my own. "Jake, that 2.75 GPA was the minimum set by the college to keep your scholarship and a baseline we all agreed upon for our continuing to pay."

He thrusts a spear laced with manipulation. "Well, the *real* using of drugs was when I came home, where I was isolated from my friends, and had to get a job."

I need armor. If only I knew to stop responding to his flinging blame and not react to this angry manipulation. If only I could contain my outrage at his expected privilege. We go round and round and get nowhere.

My fear of what's happening and what might happen is all-consuming. My grief over time wasted and what might have been is intense. Imagining a relapse sucks up all my energy. My spirit feels dead—but a mother can carry on half-dead.

Fix, fix, fix.

"Jake, why don't you explain your aftercare plan," the counselor says. "And of course we hope you'll stay the full ninety days."

"I want to make it on my own, in Boulder," Jake says, agitated. "It's eating me up, whether I can do it. I'll get a job, and use my clothing budget."

"Honey, there's no more clothing budget."

Silence.

"How much money do you have?" I ask.

"About seven hundred dollars plus my last paycheck, which should've come by now."

"Papa deposited it into our account to reimburse us for that security check you stole."

More silence.

"I'm still considering leaving."

He is water slipping through our fingers. Unwilling to do the work an addict needs to do, he's rejecting all professional advice—complete ninety days, then transition to a structured aftercare facility. He's unwilling to take the time to learn to protect his sobriety, even if his parents are willing to pay the bills.

"Scott's offered to buy me a plane ticket to Boulder. He's living with a couple of my old friends—Paul and another guy you don't know—and they'll let me stay on their couch."

"Scott uses drugs."

"Mom, he's had some trouble with the law but he's clean and sober now because he's being drug tested."

Jake's main concern is clearly to get back to his friends without regard that they use, or precisely because they use. You can't hold water cupped in your hands for long. His idea of getting back to the party renders me powerless.

I've felt an urgent need to fight for his very life by intensely trying to fix this problem, certain that I could convince him to do it my way. My mind is opening to the suggestion that there could be another way to fight for him. I've heard the experts tell us that many addicts and alcoholics fall into the trap of believing they can do it alone and if they experience the consequences of their decisions it can help with this subterfuge. Hard as it is for Jake to hear, I know it's right to refuse any assistance for him to get back to those college guys. I may have to stand, arms hanging loosely at my sides, and watch him choose to go it alone—betray himself, go back to the party, go back to his using friends. My part may be to let him go and to just be sad about it. Can I bear it if he returns to the very situation an addict cannot survive in? It's awful to contemplate the risk he'll take if he walks out. Somehow I'll have to let him if that's what he chooses. Pure motherly love has proven not to be enough.

Sue calls on Wednesday, and Bruce and I quickly pick up our two cordless phones. "I gave Jake a pass yesterday to go to a movie with two residents. He's on 'no-contact' with a particular girl, because last weekend at the reunion they were seen lying together on a picnic blanket. As I believe you know, we don't allow fraternization here at Cirque—clients need to be focused on themselves, focused on the work of recovery."

I remember reading that rule when I first researched Cirque and learned that they admit both men and women.

"The girl just moved to her brother's house and has been participating in our outpatient program. I asked Jake if he planned to meet her at the movie theater and he vehemently denied it, but one of our staff members just happened to be at the theater last night and caught them together."

"Oh." It's all I can say.

"So she's being kicked out of the outpatient program. I've given Jake the chance to stay, but on restriction, meaning no more passes."

"What's he saying?" asks Bruce.

"He says he'll probably leave, but he's thinking about it and will give me his answer this afternoon. I'll let you know."

When we hang up, I feel defeated. The disease is drawing him back in—just like the experts warned—controlling his thinking and decision making, derailing him. He has a little bit of money, a few friends willing to put him up, and zero impulse control. *Does he think he can manage his illness alone? Is his midbrain urging him to protect his drug use?* He turns twenty in a few weeks. The last thing he wants is his parents in control of him, yet he might choose to leave with no financial resources and a lifelong disease.

On what should have been Jake's forty-fifth day of rehab, we get a second call from Sue. "Jake's leaving. We've tried to get him to choose to stay. He's being respectful and even thanked his counselor for the work they did together. He asked her if he can return if things don't go well. He promised to call you when he gets to Boulder."

Fear stabs between my shoulder blades. From across the room I see Bruce close his eyes. Though I never imagined he would, Jake is walking out of rehab. I don't recognize this as a decision the Jake-I-used-to-know would make. Stunned and powerless, Bruce and I can only hope that someday soon Jake will look closely at his actions, his life, his blame—and accept his disease. But first he has to survive the consequences of this impulsive decision.

7
TEEN BRAINS

Addiction takes our hearts and twists them. It takes our thoughts
and contorts them. It takes our souls and fills them
with dread, shame, guilt, and burning fear.
— KATHERINE KETCHAM

THE NEXT MORNING, when I glance in the mirror, the lines
on my face have deepened. There's more gray hair. I thought
I'd get a break with Jake in rehab, that I could at last sleep
soundly knowing he was safe. Instead, the past forty-five days
have been an all-consuming struggle over him completing the
recommended ninety days, traveling, attending family weeks,
researching aftercare, fielding long phone calls with experts, collapsing in tears, making therapist appointments, and coordinat-
ing conference calls with the counselors. Bruce and I are bone
tired. We just lost the fight over what Jake is "willing" to do and
we both look like hell.

When I let Alea know her brother walked out, she indignantly
stomps off to her bedroom to call his friends.

"What'd you say?" I ask when she comes out.

"I told them Jake's leaving rehab early because *they* offered him a place to stay. They claimed they had no idea."

"Huh."

"*And* I told them he needs to get his butt back in treatment."

I hope Jake doesn't think we put Alea up to that, but secretly I'm glad they get an earful.

"I don't care if Jake is mad I called them. I hope he'd do the same for me if the situation were reversed."

She can think with a clear mind, that one.

Rehabs ask for full payment up front because clients often walk out. The price tag is the cost of the year of college Jake is missing. Can we get a refund? I harbor a tiny bit of hope that he'll realize his plan is foolish and decide to reenter Cirque so I hold off pursuing one. Bruce and I agree there's nothing more we can do. We've been pushed back on our heels, fallen on our rumps, thunderstruck at the size of Jake's entitlement. *Did we contribute to that?* Parents don't get "do-overs," just the choice to struggle on or stay knocked down.

For several days, we don't hear from Jake and are left with our own thoughts. How will he manage in the dysfunction that his friends live in? Is he using? Will he reconnect with dealers? Will he deal himself for a source of cash? Will he remember the increased risk of overdose after being clean? Will he be able to get a job? Can he really do it? *What is Jake thinking?* Four days go by before Jake returns a text saying simply he's in Boulder and everything's fine. Just before bed that night, Bruce looks at Jake's bank-account activity and announces that he has just purchased a $68 concert ticket. That's one tenth of his entire net worth. What nineteen-year-old goes to a concert completely sober? Now I can't sleep at all.

Incredulity that Jake is not working away in rehab causes me to constrict physically and emotionally. Guilt, grief, and fear seal me up. Hope isn't allowed in, nor do I permit these ugly three out. Inside me, they act like rabid dogs, attacking my stomach and tearing it apart. I'm exhausted by day and tossing all night. The meridians of my arms and legs fall prey to intense itching, and a twitch in my eye, like a forgotten car blinker, goes on for days. I'm silent. I'm wooden. I have nothing left to give my daughter, my husband, anybody. A friend trying to offer support can't break through.

Uneasiness gets thrown in; Alea's applied to Boulder and has already received an acceptance letter. Did the place itself trigger my son's problems? Should I try to convince my daughter to go somewhere else? I listen to other parents boast about their kids being wooed by the Ivies, and my ears modify their crowing into white noise. I seek out people who've dealt with an addict in their lives, who understand the deep hurt as well as the futility of this comparison game.

Bruce and I continue going to Al-Anon each Sunday, and I sprinkle in a few more weekday meetings just for me. This disease has brought me to my wit's end and I need help. Each time I walk into a meeting the room is packed. One day, someone mentions the three-C's slogan—*I didn't cause it, can't control it, and can't cure it*. For the rest of the hour, I can't hear anything else. *Yes,* I think. It's an hourly battle to dispel the guilt that wants to creep in or that a well-intentioned yet judgmental comment can evoke.

I didn't cause it. What if I had kept Jake back in kindergarten so he wasn't one of the youngest? What if we had not moved overseas for his eighth-grade year? What if the social scene in high school had felt more welcoming and inclusive to him upon his return? Would any of it have changed his course, warding off addiction?

I can't control it. Plenty of kids are not taking control of their lives, don't have good time management, make poor choices, party and experiment with drugs, have parents that are providing too much—still, they don't land in rehab. When I see a healthy, purposeful young man I feel waves of emotion, of longing and jealousy. I can hardly stand for people to have determined sons who are moving forward with their lives.

I can't cure it. I'm angry; then grief consumes me. When I get home from the meeting, I curl up in a ball on my bed.

But I'm driven to fix this horrid problem. I *want* to cure it. This is what spurs me to get up. I begin, bit by bit, to discern a blueprint for what to think and do, what not to do, and how to move forward. I get it that enabling drags this out. But my son's brain is not functioning properly so I feel I have to come up with what will be best for him. These past months, it's as if I've donned a Superwoman cape, honing my skills at swooping in to solve crises. Now I'm hearing I should hang up my cape, but fear keeps it firmly on my shoulders. A whisper gets my attention, then becomes a constant murmur, until I finally hear at full volume that solving an addict's problems is exactly what a parent should *not* do. *Do nothing?*

Jake doesn't want us to tell people about his addiction. Bruce has confided in his oldest sister but has been tight-lipped with anyone else. I've fended off queries from my own family but my sisters know something is up. The secrets feel awful locked up with the ravaging dogs. I shun questions, judgment, and advice. I don't feel strong enough to explain, yet I need support. I'm a mess. I'm so low, I tell one of my sisters the truth when she calls. She's caught off guard and asks all kinds of questions. With each answer I feel like I'm sinking in quicksand.

A few days later, a neighbor joins me while I'm out walking our dog. She innocently asks about Jake. This mother has watched Jake grow up and was always glad to see him coming up her walkway to fetch her three boys outside to play. She's fed him stacks of peanut-butter sandwiches and gallons of chocolate milk over the years. I'm struggling, convinced that the truth would floor her, stuck in the notion that telling would breach Jake's privacy. I'm avoiding shame, too. I tell her Jake moved back to Boulder to look for work since he's finding this area so expensive. It's been hard for him to balance his checkbook. He really misses his friends there. My words are not false, but I feel dishonest not telling the whole story.

Back home, I sink into a chair. "It's about time Jake answers for himself," I say out loud. The house is empty; I'm talking to the walls.

I glance at the *National Geographic* on the side table, containing the article "Beautiful Brains" by David Dobbs. I thumbed through the pages yesterday and felt overwhelmed. I pick up the magazine again and read more closely.

Dobbs writes compassionately and compellingly about the teenage brain. Technically, Jake will no longer be a teenager after his upcoming birthday, but my guess is that he's operating at the level of a fifteen-year-old. Drug use, I learn, stunts emotional brain development. The dilemma for adolescent addicts is that their fight with this brain disease comes at the most difficult time in their lives, because their brains are not fully developed. Not only is their prefrontal cortex incompletely formed, natural rebellion pushes them to break away from their parents, and new research shows that teen brains perceive that being with peers is of the utmost importance and may even see being isolated from friends as a threat to their existence.

Dobbs explains that teens gravitate toward peers to invest in the future rather than the past, and that they prefer the company of those their own age more than at any time earlier or later in their lives.

> This ... makes peer relations not a sideshow but the main show. Some brain-scan studies, in fact, suggest that our brains react to peer exclusion much as they respond to

threats to physical health or food supply. At a neural level, in other words, we perceive social rejection as a threat to existence.

Jake is working with a juvenile brain that is still years away from full judgment—if he were to stop using today to give himself a chance to catch up and recover. His brain is telling him to distance himself from his parents and desperately wants him to stay connected to friends. He's just learned at rehab why he also has an insistent voice inside his particular brain urging him to protect his drug use as if his very survival depended upon it. Is it any wonder he's bolted back to friends, back to drugs? It seems an impossible task for him to embrace recovery.

I recall Jake sounding like a victim when he sat in the rehab counselor's office and complained of being disconnected from his Boulder friends when he came back home and from hometown friends when we moved overseas. He wrote on his wilderness trek that entering high school after being away was a social disaster. Reading more about the teenage brain helps me appreciate how strong that friend connection is. Was his brain telling him his fate depended on those connections? Did he "perceive social rejection as a threat to his existence," which then caused him to begin self-medicating? What level of peer exclusion was happening to a previously well-liked, tall, smart, athletic, handsome boy? Did Jake "go wild" with the freedom of college to rebel against his parents?

My anger at his disease spills over, and I once again blurt out words in my empty living room. "When is he going to move on from playing the victim?" I grab the throw pillow at my side, make a fist, and punch it hard. A bit of anger siphons off, but fear creeps in to take its place. I fold over crying, wrapping my arms around the pillow. Eventually I straighten back up, and the thought comes: *Jake first has to acknowledge his addiction before there will be any change.*

Drained, I get up to start dinner.

The next morning, Alea shows us a picture from a new posting on Jake's Facebook. "Momma, look," she says with a mixture of anger and sadness. "He's obviously loaded."

The shot shows Jake partying at a rave two weeks after leaving Cirque. Next to him, "Sober Scott" looks completely wasted.

"I thought Scott is the one who's supposedly being drug-tested regularly," says Bruce, clearly upset about the photo.

"That's what Jake told me," I say.

"Why don't you guys cut off his phone?" asks Alea.

We haven't given Jake a dime ever since his substance abuse became clear to us, except for his phone. It's on our family plan and we've paid for the monthly service.

"I think we should keep it on since it's our only way of contact," says Bruce. He heads out the door to work leaving me wondering and worrying if that's the right thing to do. Alea walks down the hall carrying her laptop to her room.

It's easy to feel appalled at Jake's choices. It's hard to keep it sorted out that the disease has hold of his brain. What other disease causes you not to want to take the medicine? Did Jake simply hear that he faces a life of partylessness and can't imagine a life like that? I fear for what could happen and feel sad for the time he's wasting. Like a dark gray cloud, powerlessness envelops me. I sit down heavily at my empty kitchen table, my thoughts going in circles.

8
STANDING IN THE RAIN

Where is there dignity unless there is honesty?
— MARCUS TULLIUS CICERO

ON JAKE'S TWENTIETH BIRTHDAY, the Indian summer turns to a dreary rain. Jake was born by Cesarean section. I developed complications, and it was two weeks before I was able to step outside into a fresh fall day carefully holding my newborn. My arms seemed destined to cradle him, my fingers to stroke his porcelain cheeks.

Right away, baby Jake refused to breast feed. As I struggled to nurse him he seemed besieged yet wanting. I wondered then if there was a connection between the medications I was given— labor inducer, general anesthesia, antibiotics—and the way he rebuffed nursing. Today, watching out my window at the falling rain and hoping he'll return my call, I contemplate how we've come full circle; he's still besieged yet wanting, and we're both struggling.

At Jake's fifth birthday party, I handed out hand-sewn bat-man capes to ten little boys. Jake's black cape lies tattered now in our old dress-up box after years of make-believe. When he turned thirteen, we were living in Rome, just figuring out where things were. We nearly lit our apartment on fire when I tried lighting what I thought was a candle and it turned out to be some kind of firework. On his seventeenth birthday, Jake beat his longtime Ping-Pong rival, Uncle Tom, at a family party. Drug use never entered my mind on any of those birthdays.

Where is he now on his twentieth?

Bruce is in Portland where his father—Bopa—has been hospitalized for a hemorrhagic brain aneurism. The prognosis is dire. I feel debilitated from sadness all around. I remember Bruce saying last year that he sometimes felt guilty at how well his life turned out. Well, look at us now standing in the rain.

It's been nineteen days since Jake walked out of rehab. I feel desperate, looking at the road stretching ahead. Bruce and I are going to need support and some wise council, so I track down Kevin McCauley. He remembers Jake and me from Cirque. I ask if he can recommend a good addiction therapist, telling him Jake's silence is torturing me and I know he's oblivious to the pain it causes. Dr. McCauley hears my voice tremble and swiftly apologizes on Jake's behalf; he himself tormented his own mother during his active addiction. He tells me how he withdrew deeper into his disease even as a flight surgeon in the U.S. Navy and later when he flew helicopters and Hornets for the Marine Corps. His mother called his Colonel and begged him to stop his paycheck so he would not have a source of money to buy drugs. I know how frantic she must have felt. I scribble down the names he gives me.

Instead of a birthday card for Jake, an empathetic note from my sister arrives in my mailbox later that day. She's tossing and turning at night too, wondering about Jake. The pain of loving an addict spreads out like a pool of blood.

I gradually begin to tell more friends and family, then wish I hadn't. Everyone has a theory. The military will straighten him out. Anti-depressants are the answer. His high-school curfew was too early. He needs to live at home. He needs to prove himself at college. The party environment in Boulder did it and we'd be out of our minds to allow our daughter to go there. He can't be an addict; he has wonderful parents. If he'd just keep his drug use under control. There's a monster in his soul that keeps him self-medicating. He'll fall into dire circumstances living on his own. Our speedy intervention will certainly resolve the problem quickly. Just find the right rehab.

Nodding with a fake smile, I'm unable to close discussions down. My stomach turns to stone. Mostly, their well-meaning concern and advice is fraught with misconceptions—at odds with the science of the brain, addiction experts and literature, even my firsthand experience. The fact is, one out of eight people who choose to use mood-altering substances becomes addicted. I'm exhausted explaining, then defending myself to those who remain safe in their well-ordered thoughts about the world. Instead of feeling supported, I increasingly isolate from those who haven't endured the family disease of addiction.

Sitting at my computer, I get an email from a friend who is freshly fretting. He writes that he heard a discussion on the radio comparing two different substance abuse philosophies. "You already know the 'disease' philosophy. The other emphasizes taking responsibility for substance abuse, so maybe you should look into that, too."

Philosophy? Addiction has been defined by the American Medical Association as a disease for years now, yet the public has not caught up. *Taking responsibility*? There's that misperception again—that addicts are just irresponsible. I never thought about any of this before Jake's disease thrust me into it, so I can't expect others to understand, yet I want to pound my fist on the desk when I see myths perpetuated. I shout at my computer, "I didn't cause this disease, and Jake isn't lacking moral character!"

One day at Al-Anon, I listen to a grief-stricken mother who lost her thirty-three-year-old addicted son to an overdose six weeks ago. She's been reduced to just holding up her hand, palm forward, to signal that she can't talk about it. Sounds like an effective technique to stop the onslaught. She drags herself to support meetings where she can grieve without filtering, evading, or explaining that addiction is a disease. Moral fiber is not at issue here.

Outside of a meeting, it's rare to find someone without an agenda, someone without the words "Why don't you just..." on the tip of his or her tongue. I long for more empathy from my friends, then recognize my own no-nonsense habit of skipping straight to fixing a problem, efficiently and without exuding empathy. Bruce would agree; I know he doesn't always feel heard and understood.

And one dear friend—I remember when I traveled to Phoenix to help out when she was on bed rest during her second pregnancy. I decided she needed to set up her toddler's bedroom so that he could safely spend time in his room by himself, and promptly told her so. She broke down in tears, feeling helpless and criticized. I realized too late that my advice was totally logical and totally unsympathetic to a woman stuck on the couch hugely pregnant with an energetic toddler running around. I'm embarrassed now that I could open my mouth and dish out advice like that.

Being able to give comfort is a special skill. When disaster strikes, most of us want to make things better; we don't want to accept that sometimes we *can't* make things better. Sometimes it isn't within our power. Resisting the impulse to jump in is often the greatest comfort we can give.

One day when I'm out with Bella, I pass a neighbor looking for her ancient gray tabby.

"I'm worried because she didn't come in last night and I think she might've gone off to die."

Stopping, I consider her words while my dog sniffs around our feet. She has just named my exact worry ever since Jake walked out of rehab.

"Maybe she found shelter somewhere out of the rain and will be back soon," I offer.

My neighbor smiles ruefully and sadly. "Pretty sure this is the end."

My heart constricts at her words, and tears, for me, are never far away. I'm about to walk on when I realize I haven't offered much empathy, and I do know how much it hurts to have someone you love out there—somewhere. If I had stroked my own purring kitten on my lap and shared my home with her for eighteen years, I too would be out madly searching.

Should I be out searching for Jake under bushes? Like my neighbor, I struggle to harbor hope—hope he'll come back in on his own. I touch her arm lightly and tell her it must be hard to wait and wonder, and I tell her I'll keep my eyes peeled for her gray cat in even the most unlikely places.

9
SEEKING ANSWERS

When the student is ready, the teacher will appear.
— Buddhist proverb

IT'S BEEN ALMOST A MONTH since Jake left Cirque. Late at night, the telephone rings. Bruce is still at his office and I'm lying in bed, *CoDependent No More* by Melody Beattie propped on my middle. I take a quick intake of breath—*Jake's on the phone*—then slowly exhale.

He sounds flat, tired, depressed, somewhat in a haze, even cowed. I resist the overwhelming temptation to offer advice, especially when he keeps repeating, "I don't know what to do."

In our relationship, it's hard to tell if Jake sometimes sets me up to swoop in to do something for him, or if I offer help and advice before being asked. Melody Beattie coined this behavior as "codependency." There's a certain amount of self-sacrifice in parenting, and as you become crazy with worry, jumping in to help appears to be the loving thing to do. You can find yourself adapting to addiction's insanity and end up doing for the addict what the addict should do for himself. I can now look back honestly and see I've crossed that line frequently. Surely it must bewilder Jake when I respond, "I know you'll figure it out, honey."

Dejection spills into my ear. "All these months I've been away, I was sure I was missing out. Now that I'm here, I don't feel connected. Everyone seems plugged into classes and parties and friends."

"It sounds frustrating. Have you done any job hunting? Gone to any AA meetings?" When he was leaving rehab, he argued he would pursue both.

"There's lots of distractions, Momma."

I suddenly remember Lorri's words from our long conversations about parenting. She encouraged me to ask my kids open-ended questions. It's as if her voice is whispering in my ear, guiding me now. "How is it living with Scott and Paul?"

"Pretty tight." He doesn't admit he needs help.

"What'd you do on your birthday?"

"Nothing. I spent it all alone."

"Oh." His words and tone cause me incredible sadness. I squeeze my eyes shut to erase the image of him all alone on his twentieth birthday. Then I climb out of bed and begin to pace.

There's silence as I grapple with what to say. I'm certain he would like me to ask him to come home. But then where would we be? "Jake, I love you so much and I'm thinking of you all the time."

"I gotta go," he replies, skittish as a cat.

When I set the phone down, grief reduces me to a heap on the floor and huge sobs leave me shuddering. How can Jake be this dysfunctional so quickly? Every fiber in my being wants to rescue him, but my brain's telling me it won't help in the long run. I know it is right to hold a boundary, but as a mother it's tearing my heart out.

In the brighter light of morning, I deal with my need to stay connected. Because I still think he listens to my advice, and hoping he can check email, I send him encouragement.

> *Jake,*
>
>   *I wanted to let you know that I am thinking of you every day and that you are not forgotten here. I hold you in my heart and think of your handsome face and your kind heart. I know it must be a difficult time for you. Fighting addiction is an enormous challenge. I trust that you will make the right decisions for yourself. I believe in you, that you will succeed in whatever you wish for. I believe that you want to do what is right and good for yourself and I wish you strength for that.*
>
>   *I love you very much,*
>
>   *Momma*

All of us in an Al-Anon meeting unhappily drag ourselves in because of colossal turmoil, yet I marvel at the generosity of some who've been in the program a long time. The suffering in their lives has created room for transformation. They have been humbled by addiction—the draining feeling, the powerlessness, the pain is not hard for them to recall—still, they offer great compassion. They tell me, "You can call me anytime," or "You sound like a wonderful mother, doing all you can." They are changing my notion of "doing all you can." In my search for straightforward guidance through madness, little nuggets of their wisdom get through. I struggle to let go of controlling others, replace worry with gratitude, listen, and for God's sake stop forcing solutions. Doing nothing, just accepting what is, might help Jake best. I've stopped to ask myself: What if my help is not helpful? They tell me if a person changes his attitude, his situation will greatly improve. I've been sure Jake is the one who needs to change his attitude. Yet I keep hearing that my own attitude is the only one

I can control. Can this be the ray of light to follow out of these deep dark woods? What will happen if I do things differently?

That very day I get my chance to try parenting another way. Alea walks into the living room where Bruce and I are sitting and plops down on the couch.

"Guess what? I just got an invitation to go to Puerto Vallarta with nine girlfriends over spring break. We can all stay at Joanna's vacation house—it's right on the beach *and* there're places to go *dancing*."

My eyes lock with Bruce's. At the image of pretty seventeen-year-old high-school girls enjoying an all-expense-paid opportunity to dance (and drink) until dawn in a foreign culture, my thoughts scream, "Not gonna happen." Before I can open my mouth, Bruce says, "We'll have to think about that." His words save me from voicing my knee-jerk reaction. I admire how he is able to put things aside to think about or talk about later.

When Alea's not around, Bruce says calmly that he thinks we should tell Alea she can go, as long as she pays for it. I struggle the rest of the day—first capturing, like big brown moths, dozens of visions of disastrous scenarios, then releasing them—until I finally come to agree with Bruce.

Before she goes to bed, we pause in her doorway. Bruce says simply, "You'll be eighteen soon, and it's time you start making decisions about how you want to spend your money. You can decide whether to go or not, but you'll need to pay for the trip yourself."

On the spot, without anger, she decides not to go. Perhaps she wasn't all that comfortable with the whole idea, anyway; maybe her parents' unwillingness to pay is just the excuse she needs to go back to her peers and blame it all on us. It does seem to make sense to her that if you want something, you need to make it happen and pay for it. The absence of a fight amazes me.

By opening my hands and letting go of the reins, I transfer her choices to her. Our relationship makes a small shift for the better.

Calmness comes in bits and pieces, even with Jake rebelling, couch surfing, and using. A big weight is shifting, by no means gone, and knowledge is beginning to settle in that I don't have to fix it—I can't fix it.

But 114 Americans die every day from drug overdoses.

I limp along with my hazard lights blinking. Fear crowds my lungs, making it difficult to breath. When I hear that just as many people die in Al-Anon as in AA because of stress-related illness, I stop putting it off and make an appointment to get a scope down my throat. At the pre-endoscope appointment, the little elderly doctor asks me questions about stress and I break down right there in his office. He is so sympathetic yet professional, and like a true gentleman, he actually hands me his handkerchief. Shaking, I can attest that at this moment my stomach is twisting tight. He writes down the procedure appointment time, hands it to me, and pats my shoulder.

Usually by midafternoon the load of worry has me exhausted. Time is passing by; my head is not in the present. Can it be days since I washed my hair? Where did those days go? Driving, I suddenly wonder where I am. In conversation, I can't hold a detail in my head. *How can autumn leaves already be dropping off the trees? What will Jake do for the approaching holidays? What will he do without warm clothes?* My husband tries to draw me back into family life. We plan a weekend getaway. I drive my daughter to visit several colleges. I host a birthday dinner for my mother and sister-in-law. Throughout life's motions, I drag my heavy heart.

The result of the scope shows that my stomach lining is irritated, nothing more, so I try some medication. It doesn't help. My way of coping is to learn all I can about this disease, to know the experience of others. I read about addiction until I'm dizzy—*Love First, No More Letting Go, Teens Under the Influence,* and *Broken* are stacked on my nightstand.

I keep coming across common repeated symptoms—addicts and alcoholics feeling empty, separate, disrespected, and without purpose. Jake recently described that he felt that way in high school. I never saw it back then. How could a mom not know that about her son? Can I convince him he's a talented and lovable human being when addiction is telling him otherwise?

I'm so steeped in everything about addiction that I'm seeing it everywhere—or do I have a growing stock of knowledge that allows me to recognize it? A friend speaks with a sense of chaos about her thirty-two-year-old son. She's angry because he rages at her, then she rationalizes away his behavior. She wants to know if his years of pot smoking make him an addict. Her notion of a drug addict, like many, is someone lying in the gutter completely high, tripping out of his mind. She wonders how a person could hold down a job and function in the workaday world and still be an addict. *Is this what denial looks like?*

I've heard stories about the craving going away completely once the addict or alcoholic embraces a higher power. *How is that possible?* I ponder my concept of a higher power one day while I'm walking Bella. Mother Nature certainly has delicate power in turning autumn leaves scarlet and gold—several flutter down, a visual marker for the passage of time—and her cataclysmic power is undeniable when she brings it to bear. Do I believe in a higher power?

What portion of this world is choice, luck, coincidence, instinct, intuition, or fate and what part accident? I can't get behind the idea of a god sitting up in the clouds with an individual plan for each of us. I'm like a tree losing all its leaves yet still intact, trunk and branches sturdy after a turbulent storm. Part of me resists branching into unknown patterns. I stay rooted in myself yet begin to trust those who have gone before me, to allow the advice from Al-Anon to guide me. Nobody is forcing me to swallow a dogma or belief system whole. Take what you like and leave the rest. For now it's enough to send my roots into the collective energy and wisdom of a support group as my kind of higher power, certainly a collective power greater than myself. When I feel that seep in—that fellowship of complete understanding and lack of judgment—it chokes me up. Perhaps I cry in meetings because, bathed in acceptance, I relax and drop my guard. With defenses down, leaf-size pieces of my sadness drop to the ground unbidden.

From bank transactions, we can see Jake's money disappear, but we hear nothing from him. Bruce sees a charge for another concert ticket. Jake withdraws $200 cash and has just $80 left. I'm angry all over again. What's he going to do when it all fizzles out? I want to shake my son and shout, "Why are you jeopardizing your very life? Why won't you embrace the road to recovery?"

The doctor says it's only a matter of time for Bruce's father. Bruce tells me he wishes he could spend some time in Portland supporting his mother and sister but he's scheduled for a crazy two-week stint of meetings and conferences. Am I looking at everything through lenses smudged with addiction? Has Bruce become a workaholic? Any crack in a marriage will widen in the face of addiction. Our family has been and is coming apart at the seams. Where is normal?

Parenting responsibilities continue at home with our daughter. While Bruce is out of town, Alea comes home in tears *again* because her boyfriend has just been admitted to the hospital for a seventy-two-hour involuntary psychiatric hold.

Can we get a break here?

"Momma, his parents are texting me constantly."

"Why? What do they want?"

"Ben won't talk to them—they want information from me. I don't really want to talk to them but I'm afraid for him."

"How about asking them to come over right now and you can talk to them here with me?"

"Great idea," she says, texting them as she speaks. Her phone pings. "They'll be over in ten minutes."

I hold her in a long hug.

When the doorbell rings I caution myself not to talk too much, to leave things to Alea. We sit down in the living room. Ben's dad just wants to emote and his mom wants to process what she hears my daughter saying—that Ben doesn't want to leave the house, that she's tried to get him interested in basketball again, tried to get him to take her to school dances, to do *anything*. I listen with dismay. Even though her boyfriend repeatedly breaks up with her, Alea's been trying to "save" him; she's learned from me well. His mom unwittingly dumps more of a load when she tells Alea, "You're Ben's only lifeline to the outside world." I glimpse the pressure and unhappiness my daughter has been under. She's kept her feelings buried. Ben's parents are looking to my seventeen-year-old to advise them. There's insanity every direction I look.

And then, later that day, when I open up my inbox I see an email from Jake. I blink; can this really be a response to my email from ten days ago? As eager as I am to read it, pent-up emotion pours out in a rush and the letters spelling his name swim before my eyes.

Hi Momma,

Thanks for your email. I haven't checked my email in a while so I just saw that. Unfortunately my phone broke completely and I can't afford a new one. I want to call you and papa soon in the next couple days to talk about how things are going. I've been all right here, I just once again feel like I'm not really going anywhere and everyone else here is. Sort of like I don't belong. Which is certainly a new feeling for me in Colorado. I love the guys here but it seems like I'm trying to live in the past and recreate something that won't ever be the same. Also, I didn't get the job at the restaurant and that sort of bummed me out and basically made me feel more like I didn't belong here. All in all, I'm realizing Boulder is not what I thought it would be.

I'll give you and Papa a call tomorrow or the next day.

Love,

Jake

When Bruce arrives home the next night, I read him the email, and he digs up our phone plan.

"His phone seems to be working just fine for certain friends. He's sending hundreds of texts."

"Maybe he feels the need to lie since he doesn't return our calls." I know he hasn't returned his cousin Tara's calls or my mother's or a few others who've tried.

Bruce says, "Maybe he's afraid we'll stop paying for it."

"Should we?"

"I think we should leave that line of communication open."

My need to act keeps me struggling. As I change into my pajamas, I wonder if Jake might get back to rehab faster if I called Paul's mother to tell her my son—a drug addict—is sleeping on her son's couch. I met her briefly last year when the guys all moved in together. She asked me what I thought about hiring a house cleaner, especially for Paul and Jake's bathroom. I told her I'd bought them a bucket, rubber gloves, and some Lysol and stuck it under the bathroom sink. I'm sure Paul never told her why Jake had to leave that rental house last January.

Bruce knows exactly what I'm thinking when I say, "I desperately want to contact Paul's mother."

"That's not a good idea," he says, climbing into bed. He's tired from his trip and worried about his dad. Bopa's getting worse.

I take one last stab at it. "I'm pretty sure she has no idea she's supporting Jake."

"Stay out of it," Bruce says.

On my nightstand, *Moments of Clarity* now sits on the top of the stack. Individual recovery stories make me feel closer to Jake and I want to pour their wisdom into his brain. In one chapter, Mike Early writes that it took ten years before he became willing to get sober.

Willingness...in a word, that's it. I became willing to look at alternative ways of dealing with my addiction and dealing with myself. I became willing to look at this program, willing to follow it. I had been in it but I hadn't been willing to participate. I hadn't been willing to be a part of it, to live it. The only thing I was willing to do was change it to my liking.

Jake must have said a hundred times back at rehab, "I'm not *willing* to work on sobriety for six months before going back to school... I'm not *willing*...not *willing*. Is it going to take years for Jake to accept the work he has to do to move forward with his life?

I switch off the light to brood over that in darkness.

10
NOT THE SAME MOTHER

Nobody sees what's happening because that person is deft
at conniving, scheming or outmaneuvering the world
on the way to another drink or drug.
— WILLIAM C. MOYERS

IN THE MIDST OF PASSING out Halloween candy to costumed
kids ringing the bell every few minutes, and our doggie sticking her head between my knees to lick small hands reaching
into the candy bowl, the phone rings. Bruce left this morning
yet again for out-of-town meetings. Alea has morosely gone off
to her emotionally-draining boyfriend's house instead of trick-
or-treating with her girlfriends. Juggling the door, the dog, the
candy, and now the phone, I'm completely surprised to hear Jake
on the line. It takes me several seconds before I register it's him.
His strong, clear-sounding voice confuses me—for weeks I've
imagined him incapacitated in a drug haze.

He tells me he just got a new phone (*for free?*) at the Apple
store. He's calling for our health insurance information because
he thinks he has bronchitis. It may be that he's purposely calling

at a time of lucidity, knowing I'll evaluate the quality of his voice. That voice is all I have. He coughs. My heart wants to believe that perhaps he's not as bad off as I suppose.

He wants something. Sorting out the lies from any truth seems impossible. As I read off the numbers of our insurance policy, I wonder if he intends to misuse it in some way. Drug addicts these days don't look and present to doctors like they used to. I hate this broken trust.

"And Momma, can you send me my new debit card? It must've come in the mail by now."

I pause to stop and consider: Is paying for a stamp enabling?

"I misplaced my wallet so I had to cancel the old one," he continues.

Months later I would learn his wallet had been stolen. I would discover he'd been able to get a doctor to prescribe Xanax—a central-nervous-system depressant regularly prescribed as a sedative, to induce sleep, to prevent seizures, and to relieve anxiety. The Center for Disease Control reports Xanax is a commonly abused medication. Privacy laws in health care written many years ago totally pave the way for a young addict's manipulation. Since Jake was over eighteen, the clinic wouldn't tell me what any appointment was about, but certainly expected that we'd pay the bill.

"Jake, Bopa isn't doing well at all. He's not long for this world."

"Oh geez."

"What do you think about going to Portland to say goodbye to him?"

"Yeah, I'd like to do that," he says, no doubt sure we'll pay.

"It'd mean a lot to Gigi and Bopa. Think about it."

When Bruce returns a few days later, he and I discuss a possible trip for Jake. We assume he's broke, yet somehow he's making it work for himself in Boulder.

"It's important for him to see Bopa," says Bruce.

My brain starts to formulate a manipulative plan even before I'm aware of it. I want him to go, I miss him, I want him to have the chance to say goodbye to Bopa, *and* I want him to get back to rehab. "What do you think about offering to pay for half a ticket and let Jake figure out his return?"

"Where will he go after that?" asks Bruce.

"Exactly," I reply, hoping he'll choose to go back to Cirque.

Jake should be the one to pursue going to Portland, but he doesn't follow up, which greatly annoys Bruce and saddens me. Who knows how many days Bopa has left? Our pattern has always been that we are the first to speak, but this time we don't. In a lull between business trips, Bruce flies up to see his dad without Jake.

I hold out another two days before my need to stay connected, to prod Jake, to hear his voice wins out. I'm usually in such emotional turmoil when we talk that my thoughts get jumbled, so I jot down what I want to say, planning to keep the note in my pocket until I'm able to get through. Refraining from rescuing him won't be as difficult if I'm prepared and clear, fortified with written words.

I'm surprised when he answers the first time I call, but manage to ask in a calm even voice, "Hey, how're you doing?"

Jake answers, "Not doing much. Everybody around here's pretty busy with school, though." He seems in a mood to talk. He admits to going to parties now and then, and drinking; "No hard drugs, Momma."

I want to believe—to trust. "What do you want for yourself?" I ask. "What do you think you need?"

"When I help someone with homework I feel smart. But then I get frustrated because I can't string my life together. Other kids carry on wildly here, you know."

"You have a disease, Jake. It's so common for smart people with this disease not to be able to connect the dots. You have to learn how to do it, with support, with recovering people." From my script I read, "Some people can quit for a while on their own, but no one can *recover* all alone."

Something seems to be triggered by those last words. Emotion flooding him, Jake begins to cry.

"Honey, you're a lovable human being, and I believe in you. You'll figure this out."

He sniffs. He whispers, "The highs are so high and the lows... so bad."

I swallow hard. "I can't imagine. But I believe you'll end up a stronger person."

"If I'd just done what my counselors said."

"Oh, Jake. It sounds like you're often your own worst enemy."

Silence, then a tiny, "Yeah."

"We all worry so much for you. We're learning how an addict's brain can be tricked into rationalizing away destructive behavior." I soldier on with ugly facts that he's certainly heard at rehab but is disregarding now. "The disease of addiction is the heart of your problems. It's a progressive disease and nothing in your life will get better until you deal with it. If you don't get treatment, the disease will continue to get worse. It will always be with you. Only you can put it into remission. Plenty of people die...it's fatal. You can die little by little in prison or homeless or you can die quick as a blink in an accident or overdose."

He's listening.

I keep on. "My own life is changing and—crazy as it sounds— I'm grateful to learn how to recognize when I'm trying to force situations and how to practice being less judgmental and more empathetic. My desire to help you is driving me down this path."

He exhales, then gets choked up.

"Your dad's in Portland right now."

"He is?" He sounds surprised and disappointed that Bruce went without him.

"I'm going in a week or so. Your dad and I will pay for half your ticket if you want to go see Bopa."

"Oh. I guess I'll look into flights." He doesn't object to paying his half.

"Bye, honey. Let me know."

"Thanks, Momma."

I hang up daring to believe he hasn't been in a drug stupor every day, that there will be an end soon to this bleak period of him trying to go it alone. He sounds to me like he's ready to make a change, to save himself. I'm yearning to leave anguish and despair behind and welcome in hope. Maybe these same highs and lows are what he's experiencing. Maybe he's "not that bad." Parents *want* to hope.

Here's where I should leave it alone; however, that afternoon I check for flights that would put us both in Portland at the same time. Am I *doing* something because I hate to sit and wait? I reason that I need to go see my father-in-law myself, Jake sounds like he may be ready to undertake a change, and Bruce has business trips lined up. Am I forcing a solution? There are some low-priced flights going fast so I buy them, but I get the return for Jake to Salt Lake City—near Cirque—not Boulder. Fear acts like a ferocious wind at my back. I'm trying to lead my son to water, like a horse, rationalizing he will have to drink as I salt the oats. From my wishful perspective it's a beautiful plan; Jake gets to see his grandfather one last time and visit his grandmother, and I get to spring into action to help. After learning about this disease these past months, I feel better equipped to talk face to face with him. Then obviously, he would choose to fly back to Utah to figure it all out with the experts, right? That's that. Neat and tidy.

When Bruce gets back, I relay the conversation and my plan to him. He agrees we have nothing to lose. He departs again the next day, this time to a three-day conference.

I've purchased tickets leaving next week; I simply can't wait until Jake calls back. I write down a straightforward message and punch in his number. After only the second attempt, he answers and I read, "Jake, in looking at my schedule, it works for me to go visit Bopa next Tuesday. Your dad's been there twice recently so it's my turn to go. I checked flights and as I waffled they were doubling in cost so I bought mine and bought one for you, too. It would mean the world to Gigi and Bopa to see you and it sounds like you want to go. I grabbed a return flight for you to Salt Lake leaving about the same time as my flight. I can easily get a refund if you have no interest. I thought you might consider returning to rehab. You can reimburse me for that ticket or buy one yourself to wherever you want to go."

Pause.

Then slowly, "I kinda expected something like that. Let me think about it."

I give him the flight times.

"Can you bring my laptop and charger with you?"

He's gonna go. "I'm not sure it'll fit with my stuff so I'm making no promises."

He pauses again. I imagine he takes his phone from his ear and looks at it thinking, "Who are you and what have you done with my mother?"

He has a week until that flight leaves.

As soon as we hang up I ask myself, *Am I manipulating him?* The answer is, *Of course!* The alternatives feel like death. Jake and I have always maneuvered each other in what we say and do—it's inherent in our relationship. Out of love, I'm trying everything I can think of to get him to choose recovery. I'm holding out a life preserver to him—drowning, stuck—sure he'll grab on, certain I'm the one to rescue him. It's been over three months since I've seen him, and I miss him terribly. I'm proud of myself for triggering the possibility that he might get back to rehab.

What are others in this situation doing? It's important to learn what neuroscientists have discovered—addiction alters normal brain functioning. When you're battling from the trenches, it's equally valuable to absorb the lessons from those who have lived it—addicts use fear, guilt, and pity most as they manipulate others. In *Addict in the Family,* Beverly Conyers writes, "Addiction has the power to wipe out reason, will power, and good intentions."

Evidently, Jake's power to reason has been wiped out. His good intentions to search for a job and go to meetings evaporated. He can't make sense of his life falling apart. He resists blaming his drug use because his addicted brain is reassuring him that he doesn't have a problem. As Jake continues to withdraw from us and either defends or lies about his drug use, we end up frustrated and hurt by what appears as a lack of responsibility. We struggle once again to understand these common symptoms of the disease. Will Jake ever admit complete defeat in the face of addiction and be so humbled by it that he will resolve to make the commitment to work on his recovery?

I'm always updating Bruce by phone—he's not *here*. When I relay my last conversation with Jake, Bruce is preoccupied with the conference he's attending. I'm stumbling, all alone. I'm hurt that I don't get much reaction nor any input. I'm expecting a "thanks" or "good job" for keeping at it. *Something.* While I'm obsessed with addiction, Bruce wants to avoid it, not read about it, put up a wall around it. He's angry at Jake for using up all our energy and emotion; he doesn't want addiction to take over our lives.

I actually get a call back from Jake, and my plan takes a direct hit. "Momma, there's no bed available at the rehab."

At least he checked.

"So after seeing Bopa I think I'll train up to Tacoma to visit Ella. It'll be just about her Thanksgiving break, so we could drive her car home for Thanksgiving."

I want to wring her enabling neck.

"I'm thinking of returning to Boulder after that."

A window slams shut. *Shit.* "Tacoma is a fifteen-hour drive. And you'll have to pay for a flight back to Boulder."

"I know."

"I guess I should work on getting a refund from Cirque for those last forty-five days."

Immediately, he says, "Don't do that," which is about the only hopeful thing out of his mouth.

There's no conversation about getting help, admitting defeat, moving on. A war is going on within his brain. Addiction is harping at him to protect his drug use at all cost. He is avoiding help, deflecting—his brain is the enemy of his soul. Yet somewhere in his core he hates his loneliness and dysfunction. I try to accept what I hear.

Twenty-four hours before we are to meet at the Portland airport, I call him. He still has not confirmed that he's in fact intending to make the trip. I'm utterly dismayed when his voice sounds like he's speaking through bubble gum. Panic flickers. I don't know what he's using—going there in my mind may shove me over the brink. He says he just woke up (it's afternoon), but I can hear his high—that disoriented lack of brain function comes from using hard drugs. My fingernails dig into my palms. I fear for his life.

————

On the plane, I reread Beverly Conyers' wise words. "Since addiction stunts emotional growth and keeps an addict's focus solely on self-gratification, addicts are prone to trampling all over other people's property, boundaries, and emotions." I've certainly felt crushed as I've tried to be emotionally supportive, held firm to boundaries, and consistently encouraged Jake to get back to treatment. There's no doubt in my mind that he's an addict.

Over the next few days—if he shows up—all I can do, as Conyers suggests, is to repeat the phrases that I know are true: "There are people who can help you." "You can't live with us right now because that wouldn't help you." "We can't give you what a recovering community can." "When you're ready to get help, we'll be here for you." "I know you'll get through this." "I believe in you."

At the designated meeting spot, Jake stands leaning against the rental car counter and I feel a rush of adrenaline as I stride toward him. I wrap my relief and hope around him. When I stand back and look at him, I see deep circles under his eyes. His cough would raise the hair on any mother's head. I have not set eyes on him since family week back in August. It's now mid-November. I didn't see him those weeks in rehab where he grew healthier and put on weight—now he looks even worse than when he first entered rehab.

Jake's cough is relentless as we drive toward downtown Portland. We cross over the Marquam Bridge, the dark Willamette flowing below—we can see five of the eight downtown bridges that connect the east side to the west. We drive on toward Lake Oswego where we'll sleep at Bruce's sister's house the next few nights.

In the morning as I'm brushing my teeth, I observe flecks of ash in the bathroom sink. He must have just used. I don't have to snoop, it's right there to see. I don't know exactly what, but if you smoke Oxy that would create ash. I bump into him in the hallway. Jake is surly.

"Jake, you look awful."

"I haven't slept well the last few days," he claims.

"I don't buy it that you're merely tired. You're using drugs, and it's causing you problems."

He doesn't like me calling him on his lie, and blazes an angry look my way.

Addicts don't respect people they can fool so I respond immediately. "The mother you left a few months ago isn't the same mother you're facing right now."

He stares, then moves slowly into the bedroom and climbs back into bed instead of getting dressed.

"We need to leave in fifteen. Gigi's expecting us."

I feel torn in too many directions. I am appalled at his lack of functionality. I want to take him by the shoulders, shake him hard, and yell in his face, *"What are you doing to yourself? Just stop this!"* At the same time I want to ignore this nightmare, deny it completely, and enjoy having him near after so long.

About a ten-minute drive away, Jake's grandparents live in a retirement community. After being in and out of the hospital this last month, Bopa is lying naked under a sheet, half paralyzed in the second bedroom of their apartment. He's in a hospital-type bed. A wheelchair and various care-taking equipment crowd the room. It's particularly warm and Jake peels off his sweatshirt, revealing his skinny chest and arms. Bopa's body is failing yet his mind has some clarity. His eyes are observant, and he's gently quiet. Jake spends some time with him while I talk with Gigi in the living room. In his last years, Bopa's been a prolific poet and Jake comes out after a while holding a copy of his book of poems that Bopa has just given him.

Bopa perks up having us there. "I'm not as sick as people think I am," he tells me.

"What's your level of frustration on a scale of ten?" I ask.

"Nine!" he blurts out, batting Gigi's hand away as she tries to pull up his sheet.

Lucky for him that he drifts in and out. After Bopa's little nap, Jake spends more time talking with him. He's gentle and kind with both his grandparents. Being with him is bittersweet.

My son took a baby step by getting here. Back at Bruce's sister's, he takes one more when he calls Cirque to check for openings. I try not to eavesdrop, but his side of the conversation doesn't sound good. "No beds for at least ten days," he tells me afterward. "I guess it's a busy time there, this close to the holidays."

We spend most of the next day with Bopa and Gigi. During a break, Jake researches flights and train schedules on his laptop—which I brought him. Maybe he finds me irritating and difficult to manipulate after just two days together, or maybe now he thinks it would be awkward to face all the relatives at Thanksgiving. In any case, he begins looking for flights from Tacoma back to Boulder.

"Now all the flights are too expensive—I can't afford it."

I stare at him and out of my mouth comes, "That sounds like manipulation. The deal is I fly you here and you figure out your return yourself." I amaze myself that I recognize the dance we do and catch it in time to name it.

Twenty minutes later, he hands me two crisp twenty dollar bills to pay for his train ticket north, immediate reimbursement for using my credit card to buy it online. This drives home a fact I already know—Jake has a source of money. Since he hasn't mentioned a job, I'd be crazy not to assume he's dealing drugs.

At the end of our second full day, the time comes to say goodbye to Bopa. I look into his clear blue eyes.

He says, "I hope you'll read my book of poems from time to time."

"I will...and I'll hold you in my heart. I love you." I tear up and squeeze his hand.

Early the next morning, I drive Jake to Portland's Union Station. When I hug him goodbye, I hear in his shuddering exhale the uncertainty before him. His somewhat deficient plan—train up to Tacoma, wait three hours until his girlfriend can pick him up, spend a few days with her—lacks a final destination. I watch him drag his overstuffed duffle bag in to find his train. The sight tears at my heart; I sit behind the wheel but can't drive away. I picture him looking all around for the right track, so lost. I want to run in after him, to hug him one last time. But I just sit. Then anger that he's searching for a train rather than heading for rehab pulls me up from this downward slide. I look over my shoulder and merge into traffic heading toward the airport.

On the plane home I drift in a sea of grief. The thought comes that I may very well have said a final goodbye to both my father-in-law and my son. The fragility of it all brings a huge lump to my throat and I feel pressed down in my seat by layers of sadness. Bopa has come to the end of his life; soon, he will no longer exist in this world. And Jake does not seem to be valuing the precious life he's been given.

11
HOLLOW THANKSGIVING

I thought of alcoholism as too many drinks, not as a disease.
I thought it was for other people's kin.
— BILL MOYERS, Foreword, *Now What?*

SOME TEARS FALL INTO THE STUFFING, not from chopping onions but from the emptiness of this hollow Thanksgiving. The day looms like an oppressive duty instead of the holiday I've always loved, the warmth of a large family gathering, the chance to spend the day with my brothers and sisters, our mother, and my nieces and nephews, big and small. Not everyone knows the truth about Jake's absence—most crucially, I haven't had the strength to tell my mother or my brother Tom—and I know it will take effort to keep the deception straight.

Before everyone arrives I chop sage and pecans, remembering past Thanksgivings, ping-pong competitions in progress, toddler nieces and nephews digging through Jake's old Legos and Alea's cast-off dolls, the dog's tail knocking over unattended wine glasses, and tantalizing smells of roasting turkey wafting through the house. In the final hectic minutes, many helping hands would always be ready to scoop out the stuffing, carve the bird, mash the potatoes, stir the gravy, and pull the two casseroles, corn and sweet potato, out of the oven.

Today, Bruce tries to alleviate the silence in the kitchen by turning on some music. When I ask Alea if she'd like to help me chop, she makes it clear she wants to be away from me—not under my control in the kitchen, and certainly not anywhere near a whiff of my suffering. In recent weeks, she's been reactive to everything I say, not wanting to have anything in common with her mother. I'm a good cook and value this skill, therefore she rejects it. When she was little, Alea would follow me to the garden, barefoot, in her pink sundress, and hold our big yellow colander as I pinched off fragrant basil leaves. She relished a steaming plate of al-dente linguine al pesto. And Jake as a toddler would sit in his highchair grabbing handfuls of "green noodles" off the tray, demanding "Mo', Momma!" Ultimately his face, his bib, his ears, even parts of his hair would be smeared emerald. These days Alea shuns learning how to cook and Jake hasn't eaten at my table in months. I feel rejected and alone.

I go through empty automatic motions cooking up this turkey feast. Everyone arrives bearing delicious contributions and bottles of wine. It's a smaller group than in years past, and with Jake gone, there's not enough interest to pull out the ping-pong table. One little nephew searches for the box of Legos. Cousin Tara steals away to suffer quietly in the dark of Jake's bedroom. As hostess I want to be calm and serene like a swan gliding on a lake, but my emotions are in turmoil, paddling like hell beneath the surface. I'm the last to sit down and just as I spread my napkin and lift my fork, someone asks, "So, how's Jake?" Tears, like icicles, suspend inside me. I force my face to remain expressionless. "He's fine," I say, then manage to change the subject.

My heart is not able to celebrate, my belly not able to feast.

My wine tastes like vinegar tonight.

The next day, as we are finishing washing and drying stemware, Jake calls. Apparently he's made it from Tacoma back to Boulder. I don't ask how. "Cirque will finally have a bed for me on December first," he announces.

Malevolent emotions drain away, and relief fills me.

He says, "The problem is I don't have any money to get there."

He might as well toss his debit card in the trash—there's nothing left. After we cleared out his rented room months ago we ended up storing his mattress in our garage. I got tired of it blocking my way, so I sold it and tucked the $150 in my sock drawer.

I tell him about the money. "Oh—that's great." He thinks for a moment. "Half of that will cover my plane ticket. Could you transfer the rest into my debit account? I want to give it to Paul toward the cost of me staying here."

"I'll send Paul a check."

Jake argues. "A check could get lost. C'mon, Mom, I'm going to rehab in a few days."

I hate it when he's irritated, needling me, and that tactic has worked for him in the past to get me to do what he wants. Just for a second, I get all wobbly, then I find some spine. I may never know if he wants the money for one last blow-out or if he truly intends to give it to his friend, but I'm not transferring it into his debit account. This dance has two partners; his tugging me into supporting his dependency and me complying or even offering help before being asked. I'm not partnering up now.

"I'll send Paul a check."

Jake gives up. He tells me the flight details and I purchase the ticket online.

Later that afternoon, we get another call—Gigi shares the sad news that Bopa has just passed away. It feels like powdery snow is floating all around me.

Part Three

TRYING AGAIN

12
RELIEF AND GRIEF

When you blame others, you give up your power to change.
— ROBERT ANTHONY

RELIEF AND HOPE, grief and sadness. Quietly Bruce processes his grief that his dad is no more. Each night he comes home from work, drained and tired. Alea is sadly silent about Bopa passing away, too, but her tears at dinner seem more about breaking up with Ben—again. Like the tree in *The Giving Tree*, Alea has bestowed all her love and care on this guy, yet he's stomped all over her. We've been hoping for a tidbit of her warmth but she hasn't channeled any our way.

Tonight, when she finishes eating, she heads for her room. Bruce and I both register the solid click of her door. I look sadly at her empty place at the table. Bruce looks over at me. How overwhelming it must be for her, with her brother running from his disease, her boyfriend unable to cope with life, her grandfather passing away, and her parents a mess. Her branches are being chopped off one by one. It isn't surprising she's walling herself in.

"It's hopeful Jake got himself back to Cirque," Bruce says, but his voice is flat.

"Let's hope he listens to them this time. And hears what they say."

Bruce looks like he just wants to go to bed early so I add, "I hope he gets a different counselor this time."

I think of how domineering I must have seemed when he first entered rehab four months ago, pronouncing to his counselor, out of tremendous fear, that we needed to guard against relapse *at all costs*. To my mind, if Jake accepted the best possible help and support, relapse would never happen. I was so intense, dictating what he *should* do. Now I get a second chance to step back and respond differently, though I still consider asking if Jake might be assigned to a different counselor, since we had such miscommunication with the previous one. Miraculously, I refrain, and Jake is assigned a new counselor without my trying to control things, a man with whom we all easily connected at family week back in August.

I now understand that a slip or a relapse will almost certainly happen, and did happen. An addict just has to pick himself up and get back to support. *Wanting* to get sober is what's necessary for lasting sobriety. Is Jake's mindset any different this time? Is it safe to hope?

During Jake's first week there, his new counselor calls when it's just me at home.

"How're you all doing?"

"Better now that he's there," I reply, eager for any news.

"Jake's taking fifteen milligrams of Theraquil, a low-dose anti-psychotic that aids in sleeping."

I take two quick shallow breaths—my lungs are most always in lockdown, and a deep breath is not possible. "That sounds frightening," I say.

"An addict's brain is prone to flipping into a psychotic state, so Theraquil helps. Jake's reactions are slow 'with affect,' which means his facial expressions don't always match the situation. I'm noticing there're no quick ready smiles. He's fragile."

"And his cough?"

"He's got a cold on top of that, and he's missing breakfasts because he has trouble getting up in the morning and making the regular nine-thirty group. Don't worry; we'll take care of him."

"What's his attitude? What's he saying?"

"He said to me, 'I'm here to figure out what the hell I'm gonna do with the rest of my life.'"

My chest tightens. *This is so hard for him, too.*

The counselor continues. "He admits that these past months he's been waking up in the late afternoons. Sleep disorders are common in early recovery—for you parents, too."

If you only knew.

"Drug abuse can severely deplete the level of dopamine in the brain's reward system, which can cause depression and anxiety as well. It may take months or even years to reestablish equilibrium."

What damage has he done to himself these past months? I hold back tears. "And what about antidepressants?"

"The treatment team and I will want to see him clear and strong first. So let's see how Jake appears and reacts in two weeks' time to decide further about any meds."

"Okay. Thank you."

Counselors always seem to be short on time. He's spoken kindly to me, and I wish I could talk to him longer to process my worry, but he's off to deal with another client. I take a moment to focus on breathing normally.

On a Monday morning two weeks later, Bruce and I get on a conference call with Jake and his new counselor.

"I'm feeling pretty good."

It's wonderful to hear Jake's voice. He sounds so clear and focused, so different from that bubble-gum voice. His rough cough seems to have faded.

He says, "I've been thinking... I've always wanted to live in L.A. I could go there for a follow-up program. I have some friends there."

God, I think, not that idea again of connecting with drug-using friends from college.

"I could go to meetings with Mel Gibson!" He sounds half serious. "And take some classes. I'm not really interested in getting a job right now."

Bruce glances at me with raised eyebrows. "How would that work?" he asks. We both hear Jake choosing the path of least resistance, maneuvering to see what we'll provide for him.

"I could share an apartment with a friend down there."

"What're your thoughts about dealing with your addiction?" I ask.

Jake's anger flares. "I can *handle* things, Mom."

His counselor interjects, "Jake, your parents would be crazy to trust everything you say at this point. They're looking to see what your actions say, not simply your words. Let's talk more about this with them next week."

When we hang up Bruce bursts out, "I hear denial again. We've already ridden that rollercoaster."

"Does he really believe he'd go to L.A. and work on staying clean and sober?"

"He still has a month to be *right there*. What is it with that place, that the minute he gets there he's already planning his next move?"

"It's Jake doing the manipulating, not the rehab," I say.

"I guess so. Look, I've got to get to work. I'm already late."

I watch as he goes out the door and pulls it shut behind him. His long hours leave me feeling sidelined. My daughter rebuffs me whenever I try to clear the mist between us. Once this week, I found her sitting on the cold garage floor, sobbing.

"Honey, what's wrong?" I asked, shocked to see her huddled there.

"I *don't want* to talk about it," she said, burying her head deeper into her knees.

I tried to gather her up in my arms but she wouldn't let me. I stood for a moment stroking her hair, then said, "At least come inside, honey, where it's warm."

Monstrous epaulets of worry and exhaustion crush me. I don't want to go anywhere, just stay home, read...the grocery store...walk the dog. Christmas shopping? Forget it.

That night, I manage to make dinner—I'm struggling to maintain the ties that bind us—but Alea doesn't come home at the agreed-upon time and Bruce stays late at the office. The food grows cold on the stove. I sit down heavily at my kitchen table. My family is splintering apart.

We need help. Searching through McCauley's recommendations, I choose an addiction therapist because she's a woman—I didn't always feel understood as a mother by Dr. Nolan—and of course because she has extensive experience with addiction issues. Bruce is willing to go but agitated at the time away from work. I pick him up at his office in the middle of the day and drive to the therapist's office. At this first session—in an old Palo Alto home that's been converted into offices—she gives us the homework assignment to remember the reasons we got married twenty-three years ago. Perhaps she is evaluating nonverbal cues—we're sitting wide apart on either end of the proverbial couch.

"I thought we were going to talk about Jake," I say.

"If you're not strong together, addiction will tear you apart, and you won't be much use to Jake," she responds.

I can tell Bruce likes her; he's been wanting to focus on our marriage.

I keep bringing her around to Jake's story. I need to know what she thinks about going forward.

"What do other parents do about aftercare?" I ask.

"They pick the place," she says.

I tell her and Bruce that I spoke with an admission's director who told me that even if I never talked to him again, he hoped I'd take his advice.

"What'd he say?" asks Bruce.

"He said, 'As parents, you should choose the place your addict goes for aftercare—otherwise, they'll pick it for the wrong reasons.'"

"You mean like, 'I'll get to go to meetings with Mel Gibson' and 'I've always liked the beach'?" Bruce says.

"Exactly," the therapist says.

"I've been thinking about the idea of offering a Christmas gift to Jake," I say. "More recovery—this time at Jaywalker Lodge."

Jaywalker is a rigorous ninety-day program for addicted young men, offering a variety of mountain-based activities built on honesty, accountability, and service to others.

"I like the idea, too," says Bruce, and turns to the therapist. "What do you think?"

"It's a good idea," she says. "And the important thing here is that you two are together on it."

At dinner, Bruce tells me he discussed it with his sister—a clinical psychologist—on the phone that afternoon. "She disagrees with parents selecting a specific facility. She thinks we won't get 'buy in' that way."

"What'd you say to that?" I ask.

"I remember at both family weeks hearing how drug use harms the brain—affects maturity among other things—so that a twenty-year-old may act a lot younger. So I asked her, 'Would you let an impaired fifteen-year-old choose?'"

I've been reading about the same subject. How alcohol and drug abuse impairs learning, attention, and memory, particularly in an adolescent brain, which isn't fully developed until age twenty-five. How early drug use can permanently affect a person's ability to mature. "What's scary is that it's not just about him acting younger than he is." I say. "If he keeps using, he could alter the course of his brain development. He could stunt his emotional growth for the rest of his life."

"That's terrifying," says Bruce.

We both get quiet. Like a frog in a deep pond climbing onto the tiniest lily pad, I'm struggling to get back to hope. I can't help but peer down at the mix of underwater predators from my tenuous perch. I want to turn toward the sun, believing Jake's willingness and attitude will be what takes him forward.

But Jake keeps at it, asking us to pay for going to L.A. I know there aren't any easy answers; however, seeking then digesting input helps me cope. Katherine Ketcham writes in *Teens Under the Influence*, "Decades of research and clinical experience confirm that adolescents who are coerced into treatment are just as likely to stay sober as adolescents who decide on their own to seek help." If we sit around waiting for Jake to "hit bottom," he could die. We have to expect his addicted brain will keep him fiercely fighting us as we try to help him. We have to try.

Bruce and I agree that offering continued treatment at Jaywalker is the best thing we can do. When I call Jake's Cirque counselor, he says he'll help Jake process the offer, though he underscores that it will take some time. Never mind that Jaywalker's filling up and might not have a bed available when he needs it. Santa's bringing the opportunity for longer treatment this year and we hope Jake will accept that gift.

———

One day, leaning wearily against my daughter's doorframe, I listen to her complain how she's being bombarded by questions from her seven cousins. Jake has been gone for nearly five months, and of course they all want to know what's up with him. They don't understand how draining addiction is, how neverending. Alea looks pale and tired stretched out on her bed. She dreads communicating with any of them because she's in pieces herself.

"Alea, it's the same for me when someone asks, 'Is he really powerless over drugs?' or 'You mean, he can never drink alcohol again?' I feel completely at a loss to convey all they need to know to understand addiction. But it's not my job to enlighten them."

"I'm sick of it. I can't remember who knows what—and I can't help them feel better."

"Our therapist suggests saying, 'We're getting support and we're circling the wagons on this one.' It helps me pull back and protect myself. Maybe we could think up words you can use to set a boundary."

"Circling the wagons *is* kinda old-fashioned, Momma." She rolls onto her side and props her head on her hand.

"Okay, yeah, whatever words work for you. If you realize you have a boundary, it helps give you confidence to hold it."

We both agree it changes relationships when we do that.

"I think I'll say, 'I don't want to talk about it,'" says Alea. "Or maybe something like, 'It's draining for me, so let's talk about something else.'"

"That'll work." Alea puts her head down, ready for a nap. I say no more and softly close her door.

This disease is too monstrous for any one person to handle. Withholding the truth from those I haven't yet told feels like an extra burden—yet I can't shore them up, and I can't help them process their grief.

Bruce is tied up at work during our next therapy session so I go alone. I mention how both Alea and I are struggling with secrets and boundaries.

"I don't want to lie about it anymore. That feels like a secret that can turn toxic."

"You're right," she says. "Having everything out in the open may even help some family members, because the secrets around this disease are so destructive." She waits a moment for her words to sink in, then adds, "Honesty will be supportive to Jake in the long run, because they can all begin to learn about addiction and understand him better."

"Honesty feels like relief," I say.

She says quietly, "You've been carrying this a long time."

Sadness and fear overwhelm me. I cry. There's nothing temporary about all this; there's no quick fix.

The therapist helps me focus on a plan for telling the truth. A few days later, my mother calls to ask for Jake's address so she can send him a Christmas gift. Instead of answering, I say, "Mom, can I come over tonight? Will you and Tom both be there?"

My brother sleeps in his old bedroom several nights a week because it helps with his impractical work commute. My mom confirms they'll be there. The minute I'm faced with telling, a sense of depletion spreads out from my middle. I'm acutely aware Jake doesn't want them to know, but it's too late for that.

Bruce is up against a work deadline so I go to a Twelve-Step meeting to bolster myself before driving to my mother's house. Even before I open the back door, a familiar whiff of fried chicken reaches me from her kitchen. Tom's eating a late dinner. I sit down at the table. My mother looks at my face, senses something's coming, and sits too.

"Jake hasn't been home because he's sick." My plan is to stick to the facts. "He has the disease of addiction."

My mother's face registers shock. Tom puts down his fork.

"We found out Jake was using drugs at CU. That's why he left school almost a year ago. We quit paying. And that's the reason he went to that wilderness program last spring, so he could figure things out. Then this past summer we told him he needed to support himself while working at that coffee place, because he wouldn't agree to quit using. I know some family members thought Bruce and I were acting harshly by not allowing him to live at home. *And that was hard.*" My voice shudders as I force out more words. "If we hadn't insisted he live on his own, his substance abuse might have dragged on even longer. The disease is progressive. He quickly lost a lot of weight and was having problems at work and with his finances. He clearly had a problem."

"Wait, what was he using?" asks my mother.

"Mostly OxyContin."

"Isn't that what I used for my back last year? That's a prescription drug."

"You're right. And it's a commonly abused drug among young people." I take a breath. "So he went to rehab in Utah last August. He was willing to go, so we thought things would get better, but he left midway through the program."

"Left and went where?" asks Tom, his dinner growing cold.

"Back to Boulder. That's why he wasn't home for Thanksgiving. And he won't be home for Christmas, because he's finally back in Utah. It's going to take a long time—kids his age don't want to accept that they're addicted. He's safe now—he's been back in rehab about three weeks and we're waiting to hear if he'll go on to a next step, a transitional place in Carbondale, Colorado."

My mom's shaking her head trying to understand what she's hearing. "Doesn't the campus have a policy for policing those dorms for drugs?"

And Tom asks, "Did those guys he was living with in that big house use drugs?"

"Yes."

"Did you and Bruce call the mothers of those guys?"

Blame is the first place we all land. "We didn't. We were pretty sure they already knew, and we just didn't feel it was our place." I pause, suddenly exhausted, then go on. "One of the things we've learned through this nightmare is that you can't control others. And that addiction is a really, really complex disease, affecting everyone in the family. The best thing you can do for Jake—and for me and Bruce and Alea, too—is to learn about it."

I can see they both have more questions, but I'm too drained to keep going over this. I've brought Dr. McCauley's DVD with me—*Pleasure Unwoven*—and I set it on the table. "This is a first-rate source of information," I tell them. "I think it'll help."

As I drive home, I tell myself they'll have to figure out a way to process their emotions without me. I can barely take care of myself.

With Christmas just a week away, more relatives ask for Jake's address, and I give it to them, hoping they'll deluge him with messages of love and support. Jake may hold this against me, and I can't control that. I can't control what they'll say to him, either. I feel relieved of my duties as gatekeeper.

———

I've learned about an Al-Anon meeting specifically for parents of addicts and alcoholics, and I go check it out. It's a thirty-minute drive through rush-hour traffic but I'll do anything to get more support. The room is packed. I listen as parents describe relapses as well as turning points in the progression of their son's or daughter's disease. One mother recounts how an intervention got her seventeen-year-old son into a year-long program, and she can finally sleep at night. A father relates how he himself is in recovery from alcoholism, sadly witnessing his daughter start down that same road. Some parents emphasize that they come to this meeting for themselves, to learn how to refocus on their own lives no matter what their child may do. Sensations of dismay and disbelief swirl inside me. Yet perspective sprouts like a living ladder reaching toward hope, and I jump on the bottom rung.

I convince Bruce to go with me the following week. On the drive home, he says, "There were over *eighty* people in there tonight."

"Pretty powerful, huh?"

"I think it's more useful to listen to parents in the same boat than people in that other meeting."

"Yeah. There's so many like us."

On the morning of Christmas Eve, I wake up so miserably sick that I can't pick up the rope in our usual tug-of-war with Jake. During a brief conference call with him and his counselor, we hear that Jake will give Jaywalker a try, though he'd much rather go to Southern California. His opposition and resentment simmer just under the surface.

I sprawl on the couch, looking at the twinkling lights on our tree, a raw throat squashing any intensity from me. Jake's counselors don't see a need for antidepressants, which should make me happy. Instead, Jake's absence empties me. Later, when Alea opens my mother's annual gift of homemade toffee, she says, "We have to send Jake some." Sadness hits us all as we picture him sitting in rehab on Christmas—no candy, no presents, no family. No hope? Will he have the will to fight back from this? After Bruce and Alea do the dinner dishes, my daughter quietly gets out old videos, and when I hear my children's sweet toddler voices floating in from the TV, I go in and sit beside her. No one can replace her brother tonight but at least she can feel my love.

In the morning, the three of us open a noticeably smaller heap of gifts than usual and then we load up the car with the piles of donated clothing we've been collecting from our neighbors. Our SUV is packed to the ceiling. We're not this altruistic every year but we desperately need to be of service today, to do something for others because we can't do anything for Jake. Last year, some friends gave away warm clothing and blankets to the homeless in San Francisco, and we decided to follow their lead. It lessens our grief just a drop—it could be Jake out on the street if addiction wins.

Only the homeless are out this early on Christmas morning; the rest of the population is tucked at home. We circle a grassy patch at the Civic Center where dozens of people are gathered, some sleeping in the sun, others clustered in twos and threes every ten yards or so. We place thick fleece, wool blankets, and fresh tangerines into appreciative outstretched hands. For a moment we touch each other's lives. A couple blocks over, it takes just ten minutes to finish handing out everything we have to the mobs of men standing on the steps of City Hall. One guy asks for the empty bag.

The most difficult holidays are over and we can just ignore New Year's Eve.

13
A PROGRESSIVE DISEASE

> When people do things because we told them to, we have
> deprived them of the satisfaction of solving a problem
> on their own and given them an opportunity to blame us
> for the outcome. Thus controlling perpetuates the very
> immaturity that we would like our loved ones to overcome.
> — BEVERLY CONYERS, *Addict in the Family*

WHEN ANOTHER OPPORTUNITY to attend Cirque's family
week rolls around, Alea says she doesn't want to spend
the end of her winter break listening to lectures, even though
she hasn't seen her brother since family week five months ago.
She drags herself from writing the last of her college essays to
sending in applications. She's nearly extracted herself from her
spiraling-down boyfriend but occasionally submits to his alternating rejection and desperate midnight calls. Like a drooping
flower, she needs water in her vase. She's trying to live on dew
in a drought; disregarded by both her brother and her boyfriend.
The day before I fly out, her deep affection for Jake and a rare
chance to see him wins out; she changes her mind and joins me.

I've been gearing up to see him. Like a whirlwind, I never stop
collecting information to help me deal with my own distress.

As soon as I finish reading a book about addiction, I don't hes-
itate to call the author and ask a question. I speak often with
directors of transitional programs, trying to understand exactly
what they offer. Professionals, fellow Al-Anon members, and
recovering addicts with years of experience working in the world
of treatment all give enormously of their time helping me understand. Mothers share coffee, their heartbreaks, and hard-won
wisdom. Counselors' words float through my head (don't pad
the landing; discuss agreements going forward). Some of their
ideas crash against my skull (a huge sense of entitlement is part
of this disease; there's a real art to an addict playing the victim)
and their words reverberate (it would be a good idea to practice
not giving Jake what he wants) until they sink in. The recovery
community helps me forge and refine a framework for upcoming
conversations and decisions.

My job is to learn to love Jake "skillfully." I'm struggling with
the line between loving him and staying out of his life, with
recognizing when I need to throw on the brakes. If I putt along
steering my own life, I'll convey to him that he's responsible for
his. I know that intelligence is not where the disease operates,
even though Jake attempts to outsmart it. I know that it's common for addicts to fight on their way into rehab and to fight on
their way out. I know that addicts like to live in the extremes
because of their brain chemistry and hate the fact that life happens in the boring. I know they are emotionally stunted because
their emotions are like a muscle that hasn't been used. I know
that denial comes back when they listen to other addicts and tell
themselves, "I'm not like those people."

There's a dusting of snow on the parking lot as Alea and I walk
inside Cirque Lodge to sign Jake out—he's earned a pass and
we're taking him out to eat. I'm apprehensive because I put pressure on myself to say the right supportive thing, to be on guard
for manipulation and lies, to watch out for and stop any blame

aimed at me, to practice detaching with love, to keep an eye on my tendency to control, to rescue or problem-solve. It suddenly seems a tremendously tall order just to go out to dinner with my son. The lobby is nice and warm. Jake comes around the corner and lights up when he sees that Alea has come, too.

My daughter comes alive being around her brother, pelting him with questions about his daily routine. She transforms before my eyes back into the-girl-I-used-to-know. Was it just a few days ago she was curled up in the fetal position in response to more mind games from her boyfriend? We drive to a Chinese restaurant. The conversation is light. We order family-style—my kids get just what they want and I quietly let go of what sounds good to me. Jake starts with potstickers, still craving carbs. I later learn that the menu at Cirque consists of fruits, veggies, and protein and leaves out most carbs, because carbs turn to sugar, and sugar is addictive. We didn't receive guidance about diet when we took Jake out on pass.

After dinner we stroll over to some shops. It isn't long before I'm unsure of what to say in the face of manipulation.

"Most of my clothes don't fit anymore, Momma. My style has changed—see, I really like this shirt."

"Hmm," I say as I wander away, madly wondering how I should handle this. Part of me wants to buy the shirt for him—isn't it normal for a mother to buy her son a gift? I can spot the manipulative pattern but can't depend on coming up with the right words. The moment to purchase the shirt passes. I follow Alea into the next store, still trying to form the right words in my head. Should I have given Jake direct feedback when he commented on the shirt? For all I know, he might be thinking I won't buy it because I think he's a loser, or that I'm disappointed or angry with him. But he didn't ask me to buy it. Should I have said, "So Jake, what are you saying—that you want me to buy you a few things?" That sounds so easy, but feels so hard to do. I'm living in confusion, wanting to cradle my son and rout the enemy at the same time. *God, this is so hard to sort out.*

In my zeal to deliver my son back by curfew, we end up with a few extra minutes parked outside Cirque. When I shut the engine off, the car's interior begins to get cold.

I decide to get a tough conversation over with. "Jake, I told your grandma and my brothers and sisters that you're in rehab. I was miserable trying to keep it a secret."

"I kinda figured, since I just got six cards. What'd they say?"

Trying to protect his feelings, I play it down. "They had lots of questions." Hmm, did he learn his communication traits from me? "They don't really know anything about this disease...but everybody loves you, Jake."

Alea adds, "It's much better not having to keep the secrets straight."

Jake says, "Uncle Steven wrote, 'Now you really need to find God.'"

"Well, take what you like and leave the rest—isn't that one of AA's slogans? Last time, I heard your counselors make suggestions of ways to think about a higher power."

"Yeah, they tell us anything you're in awe of equals G.O.D.— the Great OutDoors, a Greater Option than Death, Good Orderly Direction, the Gift Of Desperation."

Alea pipes up, "I like 'A Group Of Drunks.'"

Jake gives her a goofy look. "They tell us an addict needs help to get out of his own head, which can't always be trusted."

No kidding, I think. "So all the G.O.D.s can be of assistance," I say.

All three of us smile.

"Jake, the last time I was here they recommended to us parents that we read the Big Book. I bought a copy and there's a section in there that pretty much describes how I feel about a collective power. The author wrote that he didn't come to an acceptance of a god who intervened personally and directly in people's lives for many years, but he was able to accept the idea of a force that moved in the rooms, a power greater than himself, and *that* satisfied his spiritual needs for a long time."

"Hmm," says Jake. "I gotta go sign in. See you guys tomorrow."

Slowly over icy roads, I drive the few blocks back to our hotel. I'm drained and Alea seems ready for bed, too. She switches off the light.

———

Dr. McCauley lectures on the brain disease of addiction at each of the family programs so the next day we listen to him once more. Will I hear things differently? Jake really likes this talk, probably because McCauley has an incredible ability to draw on the latest neuroscientific research to explain the disease in a way that must help people in recovery to feel better understood. Jake has heard him four times now and is attentive, not bored. Like a sponge, I absorb the collective power in the room, listening, needing the strength, sensing that knowledge is powerful, seeing that recovery is possible.

During the long afternoon meeting with Jake's counselor, Bruce is patched in on a speaker phone from his office. Right away, the counselor includes Alea.

"You bring a unique perspective as the sister." She loves the guy for that. "Jake's time at this facility is just about up and our goal is to discuss agreements going forward."

Jake's erratic brain responses are on display. "I'd rather go to L.A. than Jaywalker," he says, renewing the debate all over again.

I'm on the verge of blurting out, "You can't exchange that Christmas present and you can't return it, either." Like a fish, as soon as I'm hooked I start thrashing. But the counselor smoothes the waters by saying what a gift it is that we're willing to pay for continued treatment—in a far calmer voice than I would have managed.

"Well, I guess Jaywalker's program is a better fit for me than the one in L.A."

Geez, Jake. Why did we just have to go through all that turbulence?

We hear Bruce's voice come out of the black box on the coffee table. "In the event of a relapse, Jake, a state-run rehab might be all that we're willing to pay for going forward."

Jake straightens up in his chair, looking shocked and aggrieved, but instead of arguing he says, "Let's change the subject."

Somehow Jake's sense of entitlement has grown to the height of the Wasatch Mountains outside the office window. It's hard not to wonder if he landed back at Cirque simply because he was cold, tired, and hungry. His words are often argumentative—what will we do for him? We've been stunned that he seems to bear no responsibility. As long as he's blaming us, there will be no change.

The counselor says, "Jake, I'm hearing that your parents are willing to pay for treatment, but that funds are not unlimited. There're all kinds of good places out there if you should need it."

Alea remains quiet but crosses her arms over her chest.

Jake has often convinced himself he has a problem with insomnia, or finances, or girlfriends, but not drugs. I remember back to summer, about a month before he first entered rehab, when we took a long walk together and he told me about his anxiety, mood changes, depression, isolation—certainly *not* his substance abuse. In essence, he was confiding in me and also lying to me. At the time, I didn't know the extent of his drug use, and he refused to link it to his life spiraling down the drain. Now I know addiction is a primary disease and that the behaviors often mimic mood disorders such as depression and bipolar.

It's common for parents, even counselors, to unwittingly deflect attention away from addiction by focusing on symptoms that are caused or exacerbated by drug use. If addiction is not treated it will obstruct solving mood disorders. If the ship you're on is sinking, you're not going to radio the coast guard to talk about the faulty electrical wiring; you've got to deal with the ship. Our son's whole life depends on him embracing sobriety, on that one thing. Bruce and I acutely feel his descent, even as Jake, like most addicts, resists connecting his problems to addiction.

Back at the hotel that night, Alea switches worlds, messaging with friends. I pick up my book. I'm rereading *Beautiful Boy* by David Sheff. I first read it back when Jake was a junior in high school, never imagining I would become the parent of an addict. I'm living the nightmare now.

When the alarm goes off the next morning, Alea and I, somewhat refreshed, respond to it like a battle cry. We suit up in armor, ready to combat Jake's denial as the disease marches on. It feels good that we're working as a team.

On this third day, the two of us are immersed in the resident's stories. A big guy in his mid-twenties—Cruz—survived thyroid cancer eight years ago. He turned to heroin when he learned his cancer had returned. His forearms are dotted with scars from cigarette burns and track marks. He tells us he entered rehab at Cirque then walked out one night and bought beer, which of course got him kicked out. For the next month he lived in a nearby sober house where, he jokes, "I took a little vacation from rehab." An avalanche of entitlement comes roaring down off the mountain when Jake proclaims that Cruz had it better than he did. "You got to live in a mansion and play cards. I had to fend for myself and couch surf." I marvel at this facile blame slinging.

Isaac sits with his mother and girlfriend, speaking so quietly I strain to hear him. Isaac's younger brother died of cancer when Isaac was just twelve. Cancer in one child and addiction in the other—too much for most parents to bear, and the marriage came apart. His father remarried and Isaac deeply resents his stepmother. His own mother has lost so much she grasps at her son to be her best friend. "I want you to choose *me*, not drugs," she pleads, leaning toward him. At twenty-two, Isaac has a long road to travel before he'll be capable of helping his girlfriend care for their baby.

Damian, a flight attendant, has beautiful brimming eyes as he listens. His parents disowned him when he came out of the closet, and he's wistful that there's no one here for him.

Where else is bare honesty and pain so openly discussed? Where can you feel connected so quickly? Where, after only a couple hours, do you know a person's deepest pain, cry together, witness budding hope, and warmly, naturally, and willingly give bear hugs to people who were strangers moments ago? When it's my turn, I sit facing Jake surrounded by this sweet group of druggies. This time I speak without a tear.

"Jake, I've spent these last months learning all I can about this disease. I get it that all of you sitting here want to go forward with your lives, yet you can't trust what your brain is telling you. I'm desperate for you to be able to move on, Jake, and I've been so worried for you... I'm trying to deal with that. You're the only one who can do the work to find your way to recovery. I can't help you, which is nearly impossible for a mother to accept. I love you and want to help, so I continue reading about this damn disease, and when I'm not doing that I'm going to support meetings, yoga classes... I'm journaling. I'm doing everything and anything to take care of myself. I'm struggling with getting out of your way so you can find your path to recovery."

Some of the guys are hanging on my words, wanting and needing me to be their own absent mothers. Some say they wish their moms had my awareness and understanding of addiction.

Alea remarks, "Mom, last time in the ring of fire you were just *freaking out* and now you're just calmly getting through this. I'm so proud of you."

Quietly, Jake adds, "You're an all-star, Mom. Whatever you choose to do, you go all out. You inspire me for my own recovery."

It feels good to have my children hear my words and acknowledge the change in me. I hope what Jake says is true.

Alea takes the hot seat. She doesn't miss a beat, hammering Jake and revealing her pain. She describes how difficult family gatherings have been, how she and I had to review beforehand which family member knew what and keep the storyline straight. She describes this past Thanksgiving, how Tara texted her from Jake's bedroom and Alea walked in to find her crying in the darkened room, missing him terribly. The counselor stops her there. "Wow, Jake, what a powerful image to visualize your cousin crying in the dark of your room."

Jake doesn't outwardly show any emotion.

Alea continues, "I can't deal with all their grief." She's angry and tired of cleaning up his messes.

Cruz interrupts, asking Alea how old she is.

With a toss of her long hair, she answers, "Almost eighteen."

I smile; that birthday is still three months away. Cruz just shakes his head, surprised at how wise she seems for her seventeen years.

Jake's counselor asks him if he has anything to say about his escalated drug use during his recent relapse. I sit up straighter. My eyes dart to the counselor's face. *Escalated*? Jake looks at me and admits he began using drugs intravenously these past few months out on his own. *Oh god.* Does he mean *heroin*? Is my son a heroin addict?

My carefully built beginner's foundation crumbles—*whoosh*—and there's nothing to hold me up. I fall back down the hole, with shock, anger, fear, sadness, and hopelessness tumbling in with me. I just finished telling Jake and these guys that I have newfound tools to help me cope, and in a flash, with the news of needles, I relapse into helpless desperation. The counselor asks if I have any last thoughts. "YES," I want to shriek at Jake. "*Shooting heroin*—ARE YOU FUCKING KIDDING ME?" Instead,

I flounder, overcome with emotion, trying to summon a whisper. Everyone in the room can see I'm real, no perfect mother at all. Dead silence. They may not understand why I'm falling apart; after all, there are other heroin addicts sitting here. But Jake knows. He speaks up, acting like it's no big deal and trying to smooth things over by saying that missing Thanksgiving and Christmas wasn't so bad.

This frees up my voice. "Jake, don't you *EVER* think you're not missed. There was a *HUGE* hole with you gone at Thanksgiving and Christmas. It was...*horrible*." And that ends our process group. Everyone trickles out to lunch—Jake, the fastest out the door.

14
WHACK THAT BLAME

That first hit off the crack pipe marked the exact moment when
I turned my back on marijuana, warm whiskey, cold beer, chilled
vodka tonics, and powdered cocaine. Crack was everything I had ever
wanted, and it gave me everything I had ever needed. Nothing else
mattered except reaching that peak of rapture over and over again.
— WILLIAM COPE MOYERS, *Broken*

L UNCH IS QUICK AND QUIET. Jake gobbles down his sandwich
before hopping up and away. Earl Hightower's lecture is next
on the day's agenda. Hightower, notoriously engaging, manages
to weave wit throughout the narrative of his tough, addicted yet
vindicated life. Alea and the rest of the audience sit spellbound
with occasional bursts of laughter. But I'm churning, shifting
around in my chair, and can't manage a smile. My mind is trying
to squeeze consolation from the counselor's last words to me, "A
drug is a drug is a drug."

Many parents have drugs solidly ranked in their minds, erro-
neous perceptions or not. Alcohol is legal, marijuana is not so
bad, prescription drugs are given to us by doctors, cocaine and
LSD are getting risky, crack is surely only in inner cities, and
you're pretty much a goner on meth. As for shooting heroin—we

picture the worst of the worst, bums out of their minds under a dark bridge, contracting AIDS from shared needles, homeless, lying in the gutter.

For months, like a needle stuck on an old vinyl record, I've been going round and round with the awful truth that my son is a drug addict. Each daily breath and every thought has revolved around only that: the recognition of it, the hiding of it, the uncovering of lies, the pushing past denial, the grieving, then unveiling the secret to others, finding support, weeding out the unhelpful advice, crying, more grieving, and then resignation with tentative hope. Now he's upped the ante. *My son is a heroin addict.* How will I move past this defining sentence? I want to run back in time, back to his sweet truths—Jake was such a good little reader (I'd find him under his bedcovers at night with his flashlight); he would put his arm protectively around his baby sister and play "kitchen" with her for hours; he was compliant and patient when his cousin Tara, her sister, and Alea all wanted to dress him up like Harry Potter (smearing on hair gel and make-up for the movie they were making together)—but this new reality overshadows them all. Will this ever get better?

When Bruce picks us up at the airport that night, I wrestle with how to tell him. I haven't come close to understanding how Jake could choose to use heroin—how can I explain it to my husband? Will it soften the blow if I speak gently? If I wait until morning?

Later, digging deeper into my reading, I will learn that straightforward economics plays a powerful role in the progression from prescription drugs like OxyContin to heroin. The latter—at only ten dollars a bag—is the much less expensive high. The rampant increase nowadays in young, middle-class heroin junkies is closely linked to the escalating prescription of Oxy, Vicodin, Percocet, and other pain killers. The amount of opioids sold per capita has more than *tripled* in the last decade. They're sitting right there in everyone's medicine cabinet, making it easy for high-school kids to get pills from home, or their friends' homes. High-school athletes are prescribed vast amounts of prescription painkillers for injuries and simply bring them to school or share them at parties. Twenty-four percent of high-school students—more than five million kids—have abused Vicodin and OxyContin. A 2012 study published by the *New England Journal of Medicine* found that when OxyContin was reformulated to make it more difficult to make soluble or crush, 66 percent of Oxy addicts moved on to heroin. Kids quickly find themselves following the Oxy-to-heroin path because heroin is cheaper and easily obtained. The most rapid growth in heroin addiction, according to the Substance Abuse and Mental Health Services Administration (SAMHSA), is occurring among young people under age twenty-one.

When we reach the house, Alea goes off to shower, unpack, and get set for her last semester of high school. Bruce can see that I'm depleted but he sits down in a comfortable chair in our living room and wants to hear more about family week.

There's no way I can wait, and I don't speak as gently as I hoped. "Bruce, I learned today that Jake started using intravenously after he left Cirque in September."

"*What?*" He actually jolts out of his chair at the force of my statement, as if he's been struck by a baseball bat.

"Heroin."

Words elude us for a few seconds. The nerve fibers in our brains these past months have been reorganized and bundled to connect straight to despair. Enormous fear roars front and center. Bruce's brow furrows and his lips press together tightly. Sinking back into his chair, he puts his head in his hands, his elbows on his knees. "We're going right down the road my friends traveled."

"Oh honey, this is different. We have to believe that. They had no idea, and then it was too late. At least we know." *Do I really believe this is different?* "You're right, though," I find myself whispering. "Jake's disease has moved quickly... He could die."

"People smoke, and put things in their mouths and swallow them, but *injecting*... There's something about that...that's so deliberate... My god, he's so sick."

I listen to Bruce wrestle with his emotions—exactly as I felt in the group earlier today. His voice rising, he says, "Is this disease really wiping out his reason, his good intentions, *and* his will power? Why can't he just be accountable for himself?"

It makes me ache to see him so upset—I've already had eight hours to process this news. "It might help if you talk with his counselor. He's a good guy, and he really helped me gain some perspective. He reminded me that *at this moment*, Jake's safe. That his shooting drugs was thirty-five days ago, even though I only heard about it today. He offered to talk with you if you want to give him a call."

An hour later when we climb into bed, Bruce is still silent. I snuggle closer and he wraps his arm around me. He and I have little choice but to move through the numbness. The counselor's right—Jake's safe at this moment.

One day slides into the next. Our addiction therapist continues to focus us on our suffering marriage. Each of us is dealing with this strife differently and we end up feeling misunderstood, angry, and lonely. I flatly state that Bruce's work has supplanted our family and me, and he counters that I don't understand his pressures and commitments and that I'm obsessed with addiction. Fighting over who's right isn't working. We try to follow her advice to work on listening and empathizing with each other. Still, it's hard to have energy left over for each other when you've misplaced joy.

My birthday rolls around. My daughter washes the dishes without being asked and willingly walks the dog. Her tiny gestures feel like gifts of sunlight. Besides tearing at my marriage, the disease has tightened its grip on my daughter and me. Alea generally has her claws out during our conversations; however, she caps off today with yet another gift.

> Dear Momma,
>
> I can see how much you have grown after learning about addiction and codependence. You have completely transformed. All the effort and persistence you have shown has really paid off and everyone can see how much you have changed. I think it's fantastic you are taking care of yourself and learning a healthy way to love Jake. Thank you for showing your unconditional love and support as I have been going through this rough time, it is comforting to know I have someone I can always count on...

Alea, herself, has come a long way. Witnessing my sorrow must make me more human in her eyes. Instead of fighting me, she's giving me the impression she sees addiction as the enemy. In any case, today it appears to be true that if you work on yourself, other relationships get better.

I do not expect (well, maybe just a smidge) nor receive a word from Jake. Even though I know some pipelines are broken in his brain—certainly the one stemming from his empathy spigot—his silence hurts. He's stuck squarely in the belief that he is a victim, asking *What will you do for me? What will you give me?* The dysfunction of his brain is causing him to look for a way out of recovery, not for a way in.

My head has its own dysfunction going on. Mothers can heap blame upon themselves in a flash. And it's exhausting to go back and forth with guilt. One moment I know I didn't cause Jake's struggles, the next I question how I contributed. I feel like I'm trapped in a ping-pong game, and the stakes keep changing. News of Jake's disease progressing to heroin scores one for hopelessness. When he lobs blame my way, my pattern is to concede the point. But I'm changing my grip and I don't have to stand in the same spot and swing. I'm learning that I can whack that blame back into his court where responsibility belongs, and I couldn't have made that shot on my last birthday.

Over on his side, Jake is blaming his counselor for "making" him tell me about his escalated abuse. And he's blaming me for making way too big a deal of his intravenous drug use. These last few days before transitioning to Jaywalker, Jake is consumed with anger at his counselor, stressed over the move, and ashamed that his parents know more secrets. I imagine his ailing brain might twist our strong reaction of fear into validation that he's a failure. I worry that he'll be tempted to ask a drug-using friend to pick him up at the Denver airport and throw all his hard-earned progress away instead of getting on that bus to Carbondale. *Jake, please get on that bus. I don't think you're going to make it if you don't. I don't think Papa and I are going to make it if you don't.* The ball is on his side of the net.

15
JAYWALKER

A grandfather says to his grandson, "I feel as if two wolves are fighting in my heart. One wolf is vengeful and angry; the other is loving and compassionate." When his grandson asks which wolf will win the fight, the old man replies, "The one I feed."
— Cherokee parable

MAYBE SOMEDAY JAKE will tell his children about the day a blizzard caused him long plane delays with no food or money, and how he continued on, hungry, in a little van traveling over slippery mountain passes and deep snow to get to the place which ultimately saved his life. I hope that's how the story turns out. For the past day and a half I've acted as if my worry vigil will keep his plane aloft, will avert any cravings or detours, will prevent any icy road accidents. But the only thing thirty-six hours of worrying has given me is a stomachache and two wasted days of my life. At last, my cell phone rings. Someone in admissions lets me know he has arrived, has checked out clean and sober, and is starting on their intake paperwork. *Breathe.*

Jaywalker's program has a therapeutic component that integrates the rugged mountains surrounding Carbondale. There's daily group therapy, Twelve-Step work, and a focus on developing a spiritual attitude to aid in long-term recovery. Not only do they channel all that male energy (ages eighteen through mid-twenties) into thrills and natural highs in the great outdoors, the small program is also set up to teach self-reliance. Residents build badly needed self-worth by mastering outdoor skills. Bonding as brothers, these young men build trust and learn to support each other in a small-town community. They have to wash the dishes, too.

Jake calls home after several days. At first, he's enthusiastic about the snow, then sounds like he's at a loss of what to do with "so much free time." He sounds a bit forlorn, telling me Jaywalker isn't as comfy as Cirque. He shares the top floor with five guys, has a twin bed and a small place to stash his clothes. Finally, a hint of defiance creeps into his voice. He wants us to increase his small allowance.

I hedge. "Why don't you email me your idea of how much it should be increased?"

"Am I wasting my time—have you already decided?"

I don't hear a shred of gratitude from Jake, no hint of self-reliance, and I feel my anger flare. What if he were one of those addicted kids whose parents couldn't afford a treatment program, never mind an allowance?

The very next day, the subject of parents' difficulty in saying "no" comes up in a support meeting. Someone jokes that Nancy Reagan's "Just Say No" slogan might be better aimed at parents whose inability to say "no" hinders recovery. I gain perspective at the meeting and even more on a call with Jake's new Jaywalker counselor. When I bring up Jake's angling for more spending money, he gently advises, "Why don't you give him the gift of 'no'?"

Okay, I'm listening. But I also fight the impulse to defend myself, to point out that I wasn't a parent who had trouble saying "no" when my kids were growing up, back then I wasn't living in fear. Now, terror of suicide, overdose, or brain damage has my decision-making askew. Dealing with addiction truly remakes parents. At the very least, I worry Jake will use this squabble as more fodder and continue to be stuck in anger and blame.

His counselor points out, "He's in a safe place to work through it."

And so, I tell Jake, "No."

————

Every once in a while, when he calls, we get a glimpse of Jake's life at Jaywalker. He's eating forty-nine eggs a week—he cooks up seven each morning for breakfast with toast and oatmeal, bent on maintaining his weight. *Jesus.* Clogged arteries might get him before drugs do. Is he being resourceful or just slyly retaliating against us for not providing enough money for protein powder? After only two weeks, Jake's no longer a newcomer—more than half the guys have now arrived after him—so he feels more settled in. The latest arrival is a friend from Cirque, who recently relapsed and is trying again. Jake is assigned as his buddy. They proudly keep track of the number of days they've skied. They're all going on an "expedition" to Moab for four days. Rock climbing and golfing.

When Bruce hears that he says to me, "Geez, *I* don't get to go golfing and rock climbing. How much longer do we want to keep funding this?"

Let's just hope he's doing the work, letting each guy's story sink into his bones, hearing words that snag in his brain, which will ultimately make the difference.

————

The date of Bopa's memorial happens to land on my own father's would-be eightieth birthday. A day for Bruce and me to remember our fathers; patriarchs gone. He and I, along with Alea, travel to Portland. Bruce's sister is hosting a brunch. When we arrive,

Bruce goes right over to give Gigi a big hug. She looks smaller. She's quiet. His presence comforts her but I can tell he wishes he could do more. All of us remain gathered around the table after the meal while Bruce reads one of Bopa's poems.

Hope to some may seem obscure
Like traveling to the stars in the skies

His voice follows the familiar cadence of many of Bopa's verses, then wavers. He presses his lips together, holding back emotion, then lifts his chin and finishes reading.

But hope is very visible
It shines in your loved one's eyes

He closes the book. Gigi pats his hand. Bruce's niece has written her own poem commemorating Bopa. Her sweet sentiments and effort to capture his essence cause most of us to pick up our napkins to wipe our eyes. As we talk and reminisce, Gigi listens but doesn't join in.

Despite a cold rain on this wintry January day, we don our coats and grab umbrellas. We make the short drive in several carloads to the edge of the overflowing Willamette. First Bruce, then his sister pour their father's ashes into the dark river as rain empties from the heavens above.

———

The following day, just after we arrive back home from Portland, Jake's counselor calls me.

"I'm concerned that Jake isn't at Jaywalker to find recovery."

Fear and anger hit like bombshells. "What's the alternative?" I blurt out. "*This is it.* Either he embraces recovery or he gets behind the wheel and starts driving that car to hell again."

The counselor says, "When I ask him if he believes he's an addict, Jake has no answer. The treatment team thinks he's in the program because he has nowhere else to go—because you, his parents, want him there and pay for it."

Bruce's sister was right; we don't have Jake's buy-in.

"Jake skipped an assignment *and* held on to his cell phone, which should have been handed over three weeks ago when he arrived here. We're giving him a couple of weeks to demonstrate that he wants to embrace recovery and do the work."

"Let's hope." I don't know what else to say.

I dump my darkness on our addiction therapist's couch when I walk in. She's like a candle flickering through my despair. She points out that every day Jake is at Jaywalker is better than him using out on the streets. Plenty of kids are in rehab and don't want to be there. She feels confident they won't ask him to leave. Based on my last phone conversation, I'm not at all sure they'll let him stay.

There's not a thing I can do. Bruce feels the same—we've done all we can, there's nothing more. I desperately want to shed this pure dread. Will Jake embrace recovery before the disease kills him? If I imagine him gone from this world, my insides turn to stone and my thoughts slam against a blank wall. I don't recognize what this devious illness is doing to my son, to his thinking. Where is he in his understanding of addiction? How badly does he crave? Does he feel hope? If he's afraid, will that fear lead him to recovery?

In the world of addiction, you either recover, go to jail, or die— often at a much younger age from drugs than from alcohol. You can also drag a lot of people down with you. Is Jake's addicted brain telling him not to accept that his drug use has caused his loneliness and failures? Does he connect that his addiction has put so many of his relationships in the shadows? Will his brain allow him to care? Twice now I've watched my son spiral down into skin and bones, hollow eyes, and an empty soul. The heartbreak, the powerlessness, the ongoing nightmare of being the parent of a drug addict is tearing me apart.

16
THE LAST TO KNOW

Addiction enters our lives with stealth and cunning. It disguises itself,
talking back to us in ways that make our heads spin. It tortures our
emotions so that we begin to believe that we are the ones at fault,
causing us to doubt ourselves, encouraging us to cover up, to protect
and defend, to run screaming with our hair on fire to the hills.

— KATHERINE KETCHAM

A YEAR AGO, my son fabricated a story, and I believed it. He
told me he and his friends were on their way out for ice
cream the night of the car crash. I had so many questions: Why
didn't the parents of the driver call us that night? Why didn't
they *ever* call us? What did the police report say? Should I have
tried to talk with the officers? Who was found at fault? Were
drugs and alcohol involved?

Parents walk a fine line; we want to trust our budding young
adults, and though we may pause when a question mark, like
a squirrel's tail, forms in our minds, denial can quickly shoo it
away. With hindsight, I can see that my inner voice was screaming at me that night. Instead of paying attention, I was simply
grateful that the boys were alive and well, with the driver of the
other car evidently at fault.

Seven months later, when I questioned Jake at Cirque, he admitted he and his friends had been on their way to buy drugs. The driver was his usual drug supplier, temporarily out of stock. At the time of the crash, it simply hadn't occurred to me that my son would buy drugs.

Might it have made a difference—might it have gotten Jake into treatment sooner, hurried along his recovery—if I'd pushed for more satisfying answers? Perhaps, but I was in denial, and I've come to understand that you can't hurry your way past it.

I don't want to believe that Jake will reject recovery. I can't comprehend that he wouldn't choose to embrace it. Is my mind still shooing away squirrel tails?

———

Jake's counselor calls when Jake reaches the end of his two-week probation period. "He's gaining an understanding of what it means to fully work at the program," he tells us. "He's responding to having been called out and he's now getting his assignments done."

"That's good to hear," I say, plenty relieved.

"However, when I asked him if he'd be in the program if he had his own finances, Jake answered, 'Probably not.'"

"He said that?" asks Bruce from the other extension.

"Yes. He's focused on how different he is from the other guys here, rather than how similar. There are guys who've done time in jail, seen friends overdose, have girlfriends with unplanned babies, and guys who've contracted Hepatitis C or HIV, or gotten DUIs. Jake's quick to point out that he's not like them."

"Not yet," I blurt out. The counselor doesn't comment, and I know what he's thinking: *Jake is the one who needs to acknowledge his addiction, not you.*

Jaywalker's next family weekend is in two weeks' time, during Alea's February break. Bruce will be traveling again for work, but she and I plan to attend. Alea just cut all ties with Ben, and she could benefit from getting out of town.

———

Traveling from Denver to Carbondale, my daughter and I put our lives at risk driving four hours through a snowstorm over 10,000-foot mountain passes on Interstate 70. Vail Pass closes—semis pull over to chain up. We wait. When the highway reopens, all I can do is chug along slowly and steadily, one mile at a time, in my midsize rental car. Following the grooves of chewed ice from chained tires, I try to keep from landing in a ditch. I push anxious thoughts out of my mind. How will I ever get back over this route in two days' time?

The hazardous conditions make the national news. Bruce sees it in whatever hotel he's in and calls just as we get to Carbondale, to make sure we made it safely. We quickly check into our own hotel, then hop back in the car and make it to Jaywalker in time for the welcome dinner. After pulling up to a three-story house right on the town's sleepy Main Street, we carefully pick our way over the icy walk and step into the entry hall, shaking the snow from our heavy coats. Jake is waiting for us in the large open dining room. He stands with a broad grin and strides over to hug Alea first, then me. It's as if everything is normal, my beautiful children inspecting each other up and down, together and smiling.

Jake's hair is buzzed short. He seems energetic. He has a different gauge in his ear—could it possibly be smaller than before? He unzips a new ski shell—did I pay for that?

Residents and family members all crowd in together at long wooden tables. It's a bit awkward, having just met, to try to start up a conversation with the addict seated across from you or the one next to you. "Uh...how long have you been here?" *No, that doesn't seem right.* "Is this your first treatment?" *Kinda lame.* So we talk about the good food, the storm, and the skiing. Alea is the only female under the age of forty in this room full of exuberant young men, and plenty of glances are directed toward her long blond hair and shapely figure. The atmosphere seems chaotic, and I have a hard time keeping names and faces straight. No one seems to be in charge, which the guys must like, but as a parent harboring hope and paying thousands per month, I find it a little unnerving.

During dinner Jake says the guys might play basketball later that night and asks me if I remembered his high-tops—which I brought from home and forgot at the hotel in the rush to be on time—and then mentions he wants to leave early on the morning of our last day to go skiing. A flash of exasperation jabs me. I want to shout, "I just got myself all the way here, first on a plane that was delayed, in high winds, then driving half a day through a treacherous snowstorm, and you want to go play basketball with the guys *and* lop off our last day?" Instead I stay silent, absorbing his words, observing his attitude.

Back at the hotel, Alea and I fall into our beds exhausted.

The next morning at breakfast, Jake leans over to tell me that his counselor wants to meet with us after the speaker meeting, because they feel Jake should move on. "Yeah, and it's annoying," he says, "because I love this program and all these guys."

I sit in stunned silence.

We file into a big room where everyone takes a seat in a circle. My mind is reeling, the tears are coming, and everything is upside down. Usually I sit glued to the speaker's words, absorbing everything I can, but now I'm trying to grasp that Jake is on his last few days at Jaywalker. What happened? Where will he go from here? Does he have to spiral down into another black hole? I'm sick with fear.

Just before lunch, Jake's counselor and Jaywalker's head counselor call us into their office. Together they explain that the treatment team feels Jake is not here for the right reasons; their program is for men who are desperately seeking recovery. I fight turbulent emotions, trying to keep my thinking clear. Turning to Jake I ask, "Are you an addict?"

He answers, "Well... I'm struggling with that..."

Alea lets out a small, exasperated sound and slouches in her seat. I want to crumble. I turn to the two counselors. "His answer says it all," I say, and they nod.

Jake doesn't fully accept that he's an addict. The disease is once again working on his brain, convincing him that he can do it alone, that it's not necessary for him to sustain sobriety, that he doesn't have to give up drugs and alcohol forever, that he's not as bad as the other guys at Jaywalker. I wish Bruce were here. Alea sits silently. I know she must feel the same anger and disappointment toward her brother that I feel. We all want this thing fixed without losing time to backsliding.

The harsh reality is, it might never get fixed, and I muster my courage to speak. I have learned that every opportunity to speak with my son is precious, because I never know when—or if—I may get the chance again.

I face him directly, trying to find my voice. "I heard from the speaker this morning that addicts are often unwilling to listen to the opinion of others. *I believe you are an addict.*" My voice becomes stronger. "I just finished reading every page of the *Big Book,* and parts of it describe you to a T. I heard you described again in this morning's lecture, and even jotted down the characteristics that jumped out at me: self-absorbed, secretive, manipulative, isolated, living in shame-based skin, in the shadows with relationships, entitled, broke, full of blame, lacking gratitude—it's a long list. These are not the qualities of the Jake I knew before active addiction. I know you don't have a long police record like Asher does. I know you didn't shoot up the town leaving three bullet holes in the neighbor-kid's bedroom wall like Kyle did. I know you haven't been found overdosed and rushed by ambulance to a hospital bed in freezing Denver like Clayton was, only to run back twenty blocks barefoot in nothing but sweat pants, driven by the need for a last hit of heroin. None of this has happened to you—*yet*. Your story isn't as shocking—*yet*. You're twenty years old and have this disease, and that sucks. I'll never truly understand what that's like for you. I wish you didn't have to spiral down again to be convinced. I want you to know I'm here for you. I will always be here for you."

There is a long pause.

His counselor gently adds, "Often the addict is the last to know."

"I don't want to use," Jake says, defensive. "I don't plan on using. I get the connection that my life is miserable when I do."

His counselor says, "Jake, I think you're holding on to the idea that when you first smoked pot back in high school, you could control it."

"Your use recently escalated from smoking Oxy to shooting heroin," I say, surprised at how calm I sound, considering how devastated I was by this news, just two months ago. "It's frightening how progressive the disease is."

"I don't totally buy the Twelve Steps," Jake says, changing the direction of the conversation. "I'm stuck on the God part, and this program focuses on it all day."

"Except when you're skiing," Alea says. Jake shoots her a look.

"Your dad told you a few months ago about his journey toward spirituality," I say. Jake knows his dad only as a complete atheist—he hasn't been around to see how our agony has catapulted us to new ideas, to seek help beyond ourselves. "He doesn't need a god for that. He's investigating mindfulness. Sometimes I find him sitting completely still, with his *Buddha's Brain* book in his lap. He's put away *God Is Not Great* and has *The Wise Heart* currently on his nightstand. All of us are changing."

"Huh," says Jake, surprised, then shifts direction again. "I liked what you said yesterday, Momma, about driving through the snowstorm one mile at a time. That doesn't sound like the mom I grew up with."

The head counselor says, "After listening to your mom and sister, Jake, it's clear they're further along in their recovery than you are."

She reiterates what we all know—Jake has to come to it on his own. Though his counselor and his peers have all been trying to get him to face reality, Jake still needs to be convinced he is an addict.

I'm the last to file out and Jake's counselor turns back to say quietly to me, "I have eight years sobriety myself and your words to Jake hit me in the heart."

That feels good to hear. Moms are always wondering what's the right thing to say. "I'm trying so hard to simply speak from my heart and let go of trying to control him," I say.

He touches my arm. "I can see how upsetting it is for you that we've asked him to move on."

I nod. Jake will have to let us know what he's going to do next. Maybe Jaywalker will help with the transition. It's not up to me to fix it or figure it out.

The afternoon processing group has started without us. Jake goes off to borrow the computer and make some calls. Alea is adamant that she won't go—she's had enough meetings. She heads out to walk the streets of Carbondale while I pull myself together then step into the room. Anton, a clean-cut guy, and both his parents move over to make room for me. Within minutes, the counselor has me processing my sadness and I'm in tears in front of everybody. Anton pats my shoulder. The beauty of these circles is that each person has deep empathy, having been there or been the one to cause such pain. One dad turns to his son and asks, "Michael, can't you talk to Jake? Try to make him understand?" As I think, *that's what we've all been trying to do*, the counselor voices my thoughts exactly, saying, "Jake has to come to it himself." Michael answers his dad while looking directly and clear-eyed at me, "I've listened to Jake these past weeks and told him he's exactly where I was three rehabs ago." Someone passes me the tissue box.

Lately, in meetings back home, I've been talking to newly-drained parents who remind me how shocked and angry I felt when I first realized addiction had invaded our family. Here I listen to parents who are further down this unending road, who empathize with me because they've been where I am now. Their concern and desire to help washes over me. I envy Michael's mother, sitting proud and calm as she watches her son. Michael clearly agonizes as he watches me struggle, knowing he has put his own parents through this same kind of pain for years. At the break, he follows me out and hugs me. These recovering addicts can be such amazing men. Will Jake ever get there?

I find my son. He has been researching sober houses in the area, and has discovered that only one has a bed opening up, but not until next week. Auspiciously, it's a block away from Jaywalker, which makes it less daunting for Jake. We walk over and meet with Charlie, a powerfully built man with an earnest expression. He runs the place and describes their six-month program. Guys there are expected to hold down a job, attend life-skills classes and counseling, attend meetings, and pass random drug testing while living in the sober house. Charlie wants a clear commitment so he structures payments with no refunds if a resident bolts before the first month is up. He speaks passionately about his work, offering support to men in early recovery. He, himself, lost everything to drug abuse—his wife, his house, his job. He understands how hard this is.

Guys from his program and Jaywalker all participate in the same AA meetings in this tight sober community. Jake could even go to nearby community college classes if he wanted. Walking back to Jaywalker, I pause in the middle of the road, and look into Jake's eyes. "We'd lose a lot of money if you walk out. We'll pay if you promise to stay." He's interested in the program, but isn't sure he's ready to commit.

Jake talks to Jaywalker's head counselor, who agrees to let him remain until the bed is available. When Jake and I talk again, he tells me he wants to go to the sober house, and assures me he'll stay. I begin to feel better. Maybe Jake can make it this way. If only he can make staying sober his top priority.

Alea returns from her walk, seemingly renewed, and the three of us go out to dinner. When we head back to Jaywalker to drop Jake off, it's still early, so I encourage my kids to go on in while I stay in the car to make a call to Bruce. He's not answering, so I sit, anyway, for half an hour until the car becomes cold. I know that time to talk alone with her brother is precious to Alea. She has a bounce in her step when she returns. Since this is my chance for a proper goodbye, I jump out to catch Jake alone.

"I'm so proud of your eighty-six days of sobriety. Transitions are never easy and you must be feeling anxious at this change."

"Yeah, a little," he admits.

"Jake, I've done my best not to leave things unsaid during this short visit. I love you very much." I give him a warm hug. Standing there in the freezing cold, I can see a sparkle in his eyes. Somehow the ordeal of getting to Carbondale, the emotional past few days, and the long road home are worth this ninety seconds with him. A mother goes forward on just a thread to fuel hope. Really, what choice do I have?

By morning, the storm has passed and the roads are snowplowed and dry. The return drive to Denver feels a lot safer, though I wonder if I will ever truly feel safe. At home, I hole up for a few days. Insomnia is back. I feel dried tears on my cheeks when I wake. I must be crying in my sleep—when I do get to sleep. I feel as though I've been gone a month and aged a year.

With addiction, nothing ever goes as expected. On my fourth day home, Jake's counselor at Jaywalker calls to tell me Jake broke the rules and won't be allowed to stay. He was two hours late for dinner. He also overslept and missed morning meditation. He's being discharged in a few hours.

Rules and consequences go by the wayside with Jake's hijacked brain. He seems incapable of looking ahead, and now he's facing three days and nights on his own before the sober house has a bed for him. As expected, he calls an hour later and asks if I'll pay for several nights at a hotel. I say, "No."

It does no good to bail an addict out. It feels like I've passed yet another exam on what amounts to a master's in addiction. I've done all I can do, but it doesn't mean my son is safe, it doesn't mean he'll recover. It breaks another piece of my heart to put down that phone, envisioning him homeless and penniless in freezing weather. How much does a mother have to take?

17
PAIN BREAK

If you don't let them fall, we can't catch them.
— ADDICTION COUNSELOR, to a parent

IN A SUPPORT MEETING someone says, "Every situation doesn't have to be a crisis." I understand this message in theory—we need to learn to practice detachment, for our own sakes as well as for our addicts'—but will I ever really take it to heart?

I get closer when I learn that Jake found a couch to bridge those three nights. I agonized the entire time, but he solved his problem for himself—an added challenge with an addicted mind. As far as I can tell, he's going in and out of acknowledging that drugs are his problem. I want to imagine him going forward without falling back. But if he slips and falls—a heartbreak to be sure and something to half expect—I hope I can step back and utter the words, "I support treatment." Period.

Ten days into Jake's stay at the sober house, Alea's eighteenth birthday comes and goes with no word from him. She keeps a picture of him taped to the dashboard of the car they've shared. Though the weight of addiction is crushing the structure of our family, Alea has not given up hope that Jake will rejoin us someday as the big brother she loves.

Jake has support from fellow recovering addicts in the sober house—to work, budget, plan, and develop his abstemious community as he strikes out on his own. After all the turmoil, he actually lands a job as a busboy at a midmountain restaurant at Snowmass. He says he's eager to get to work—he's tired of not having any money, plus he gets to ski, a perk of the job. Will Jake feel how delicious it is to work hard and delight in one's efforts? Growing up, he came to the conclusion that all his dad and I did was work, busying ourselves with house or garden projects during our free time. He didn't register the joy and satisfaction we got from it. He seemed to want to avoid work at all costs, as if it was a dirty word, making himself scarce so we couldn't draw him into helping us.

I want to let apprehension slip off my shoulders. Some days it's all I can do to sit hunched against more grief and disappointment, my rigid ribcage shielding and at the same time imprisoning my heart. My immobility alarms me so I add in more yoga, which seems to loosen things up. As Jake gains time in recovery, will my heart begin to unclench? Can we rebuild trust? Somehow, I sense that someday I will no longer get so lost in his squalls, or if I do, I'll know where to seek shelter.

It's taken me the last six months of focusing on my own recovery to be able to step away—to just let go and do something for myself. Our addiction therapist reiterates that many marriages are destroyed by this traumatic family disease, and encourages Bruce and me to take care of each other, not to allow addiction to slither between us. So we take a pain break.

We travel south to Indian Wells—palm trees and eighty-two-degree sunshine—as spectators of the annual ATP Tennis

Tournament. Alea stays home in charge of herself and Bella. I put Jake out of my mind for this three-day getaway, telling myself there's nothing he needs from me. As we enter the tennis center's main stadium minutes before Rafael Nadal is to make his way onto the court, my blood races with barely remembered exhilaration. From my tenth-row seat, I watch him stride in like a gladiator in full battle mode, music blaring. Wow! Bathed in desert air, I cheer and clap as Nadal crushes his opponent to a sweaty pulp. The packed, noisy stands pulse with life. Next up is the legendary Roger Federer; Bruce and I can hardly believe our luck. Pinch me. The crowd respectfully goes silent when Roger, wearing a royal blue Nike shirt and matching headband, fluidly serves up 125-mile-per-hour aces, masterfully executes drop shots, and bounds to the net graceful as a gazelle. Peace and joy have been dormant for so long that I feel like a queen now, magnificently entertained, sitting on my throne, the best players in the world at my feet. My husband's warm shoulder presses against mine as the sun shines down on us, and I feel what he and I were before. Where I want to be again.

Three hours after we arrive home, still basking in the glow of our brief escape, Jake calls to get our medical-insurance information. "Someone parked this truck just outside the gate," he says, "and I was taking out the trash in the pitch dark and I rammed my shin into the trailer hitch." Like a bullet, *relapsed* lodges in my brain—I can't help it. But no, he's being drug tested every day, it's nearly midnight there, and Charlie has driven him to the emergency room in Glenwood Springs to get seven staples and some stitches to cover the bone back up.

Jake's tone turns indignant. "Can this be a lesson that I need my own insurance card in my wallet?"

I'm taken aback. I only have one card—it's not as if I've been denying him his own card with the intention of treating him like a little kid.

I'm also irritated. How hard would it be for him to say something like, "Gosh, I'm glad you guys have coverage for me for this type of accident, I'm sure glad I don't have to shell out all my earnings as a busboy to pay for it"?

At least I control myself not to react. I read him the numbers from the card. The fact that I can employ calmness is progress.

Later I talk to Charlie about Jake's comment and he succinctly puts it into perspective.

"The root of Jake's arrogant entitled tone comes from his shame that he has to call his mom late at night for medical insurance, which feels to him like spotlighting another screw-up. It's embarrassing. It's uncomfortable to have to call home. Many addicts do the same thing—they cover up their humiliation with bravado."

"Oh." I'm quiet while this rolls around in my head.

"It took me about nine months of sobriety to build confidence just to be able to call my parents and say hi. Jake doesn't call you because for a long time he's felt like he's had nothing good to show for himself."

"Okay, that helps. More patience. Got it."

As if I'm not already evaluating Jake's voice enough whenever I call—his tone, his energy, even the background noise—I'm on red alert a few days later because he sounds so distracted and quiet, almost fragile. I've been wondering how it's going, getting to work with his injured leg. I can't conquer the temptation to monitor him. "Letting go" is the slowest process for me. As he talks, my gnawing intuition growls at me. Am I getting better at interpreting my inner voice?

I finally ask, "Is everything all right?"

Silence. My heart contracts hard; is something coming I won't be able to handle?

Slowly, reluctantly, he starts up. "Well, there've been a lot of relapses. Remember my friend Kirk? He got kicked out of

Jaywalker because he sniffed nitrate. And three other guys smoked weed. And, well...Anton is dead."

"Oh, god." I close my eyes. Anton. That polite guy I sat next to last month.

"He went out on a pass to Denver and overdosed..."

It can't be true. His parents were both there supporting their son. I visualize them now, getting this dreadful news.

Jake's words start to come in a rush. "And today I heard that the guy who left here whose bedroom I moved into overdosed—and when the paramedics finally found him he was blue. He was airlifted to Denver Hospital but they're saying he doesn't show any brain activity."

I gulp air. A parent's nightmare. You can have a hundred and ten days sobriety and then you don't. You can be alive and then you aren't. "Oh Jake, this must be so hard for you to hear. This is all so tragic." My voice cracks.

"Yeah," he says. "They're alive and doing well and the next minute they're dead. You hear about it, but this is the first time it's someone I know."

I can't imagine what this is like for Jake. I stomp back visions of it being him who overdosed. I fight my urge to lecture, to voice that Anton's death should remind him and all the guys in the program of the fatality of this disease and the fragility of their early recovery, to proclaim *You can protect yourself if you don't use, you can save your own life if you believe you can't touch it, even once,* to repeat what he's heard over and over, that when drug addicts get clean, then go back to using what they once did, their bodies aren't accustomed to that dosage, and they die. I bite back those words. I just convey my sadness, how awful...my voice shakes in empathy. Cradling Jake in my mind's eye, I tell him how glad I am he's alive and well.

All week, I struggle with images of Anton, his parents, this senseless devastation. Why isn't there more discussion of the huge numbers of people dying from drug abuse? Deaths from overdose have been rising steadily for the past two decades. In 2010, the Centers for Disease Control and Prevention reported 38,329 drug-overdose deaths nationwide. Contrast that with the number of American troops who have died fighting the wars in Iraq and Afghanistan—a *total* of 6,802 as of April 2014.

Drug technology produced the much heralded pill OxyContin, which came on the market in 1996 when Jake was just five years old. He's been taken down by something younger than himself. Opioids are pain relievers derived from the opium poppy or synthetic versions of it and there are plenty of choices—hydrocodone (Vicodin), oxycodone (Percocet, OxyContin), fentanyl (Duragesic, Fentora), methadone, and codeine. Of the 22,114 deaths related to pharmaceutical overdose in 2012, 72 percent involved opioids.

Abuse of opioids is driving the epidemic of overdose deaths. Some pain doctors who promoted the drugs are now saying they made a mistake by understating the risks. Some admit that the growth in their opioid prescribing has contributed to the soaring rates of addiction and overdose deaths.

With clear perspective, the public might register these shocking statistics. In order to get past the myths that cloud understanding of addiction as a chronic disease—addicts are just being irresponsible; they should just quit—we need a massive public-education campaign. We need to progress toward treatment becoming available for all. Otherwise, we might be looking at a lost generation.

Part Four

THE
SPRING
RUN

18
SPIRALING DOWN

> When decision-making functions are corrupted... addicts
> fail to learn from past mistakes and don't shift strategies
> when things are going wrong.
> — JEFF AND DEBRA JAY, *Love First*

BRUCE HAS NOT SEEN our son in nearly seven months, so at Jake's invitation he goes to visit. On the first day, Jake asks Bruce if he'll pay for him to move into an apartment with a newly recovering friend in Southern California. He's eager to try some classes at a community college there. He would consider going to an outpatient program. When Bruce calls to tell me this latest idea, I feel furious. Jake is a master manipulator at work. What about the six-month commitment to the current program? What about the opportunity to take college classes right there in his established sober community? His request does not come with any solid details, sensible explanations, or a substantive plan.

Jake resisted the time commitment of his wilderness trek. At Cirque Lodge he was convinced he should finish in thirty days instead of ninety, and walked out after forty-five. At Jaywalker, he didn't like focusing on the Twelve Steps all day and was told he had to leave. Now in sober living, working as a busboy feels like drudgery and he complains about his roommates.

Addiction is ever at work on the mind, convincing an addict he's fine, that he doesn't have a problem, that he can do it alone. Here we are again. *Not one* of the many counselors along the way has ever said, "Hey, Jake, you're not an addict! What're you doing here?" Instead they tell him, "I was just like you." The truth of addiction is a bitter pill and swallowing it is so painful that Jake wants to run. Our paying for reputable programs has provided him with precious information, chances at recovery, and at the very least some periods clear from drugs, but he doesn't sound ready to accept his powerlessness.

Bruce needs time to think about his response so he puts off Jake's question, telling him he didn't come to make decisions but to enjoy spending time together. Meanwhile, I fall back on my scaffold of support to deal with my frustration and discouragement, and to figure out my own response. I read Al-Anon literature, watch the Bill Moyers' addiction series, call Jake's prior counselor, email his current one, go to a meeting, and talk to an interventionist for advice. I keep hearing the same thing: decide on your boundaries, communicate them to your addict, and hold them. If he doesn't respect them, let him go. The interventionist, a no-nonsense gal, listens then bluntly asks me, "How long do you want to do this dance?"

My lips form an O shape, but no words come out.

"Sounds like Jake's in the habit of wearing you down. Have your script by the phone. If he mentions you paying for an apartment—or any program other than the one he's in—just say, 'No, and don't bring it up again.'"

"But when I say 'no,' he perceives me as trying to control him."

Without missing a beat, she says, "You get to control your boundaries. And maybe it's time for your son to take on complete responsibility for his life—including financial responsibility. You've paid his way at three great programs. He's heard what the experts have to say. If he walks out again, he's on his own."

An email arrives from Charlie while Bruce is en route home. Though Jake is keeping up with the assignments and engaging in their sessions, he's missed some. He's focused on moving to L.A. and disregarding some house rules, swiftly sabotaging himself. Rather than trying to read between the lines, I call Charlie to get a better understanding of what's going on.

He says, "Jake is maneuvering to see what he can get you to pay for. I really love Jake. When he's on top of his game and in a good mood, there's no better buddy. I see myself in him. But you need to realize that Jake's promise to participate in an outpatient program in L.A. is the carrot to get you to bite."

"I'm not interested in supporting yet another program in L.A. My husband's been saying for months that Jake's in treatment because he's got nowhere else to go, *not* because he truly believes he belongs there. Now that he's got a little money plus his tax refund, I guess that gives him some confidence to leave."

"He's not ready."

When I pick Bruce up at the airport, he gives me a quick hug but his irritation is apparent. There's nothing like spending a few days with a struggling addict to become enmeshed with the problem firsthand. He climbs into the passenger seat and we drive in silence for a couple of miles. Then he says emphatically, "We need to see Jake prove that he can complete a program. I think we should continue to support—and pay for—his participation and completion of the program *right where he is,* and nowhere else. It makes no sense for him to move to L.A.—I won't pay for him to live in an apartment with some friend *or* for outpatient treatment there. Jake can choose to stay with Charlie or go out on his own." He's echoing what I've repeatedly heard these past few days and have come to believe is the right course. My husband and I are on the same page.

Then a second call from Charlie. Jake has told him clearly that he doesn't want to stay and is arguing he isn't an addict. Charlie feels that all of us are standing in the way of Jake's descent, which is something they learn in AA never to do.

"We can't cheat him out of his pain," he says. "Jake told me he can't learn from my past mistakes or from the other guys here— he needs to feel the pain himself."

For a moment, my resolve crumbles. I want to save Jake. I want to save my son from pain. But what if trying to save him keeps him sick? Does he really need to sidle up to death, to get well? The stakes are so high for a parent when you let your addicted child descend down...down...again. You hope and pray that powerful love can be the successful counter-pull against the devil of addiction. You hope and pray your child returns from the abyss.

In an often told story, a man stops to watch a butterfly free itself from its cocoon. It seems that the butterfly is struggling and stuck, so the man decides to help by snipping away at the cocoon to let the butterfly emerge effortlessly. He waits for the butterfly to fly away but his help has interrupted the butterfly's natural struggle, which would have prepared it for flight. The man's good intentions crippled the butterfly. I think of the story's lesson as I literally sit on my hands. I don't want to rob Jake of his necessary struggle. Allowing him to feel the consequences of his actions, the consequences of his addiction, has been our guiding light this past year. I cling to that now.

Charlie calls again. The situation is deteriorating at the sober house. He has given Jake three days; after that, he needs to leave.

Jake doesn't wait. In his next call, Charlie tells us that as soon as Jake heard he would have to move on, the guys in the sober house observed him slipping out intending to score with a known drug dealer in Carbondale. They notified Charlie, who confronted Jake. Jake told Charlie yeah, he'd thought about using but he wouldn't actually have done it, it was just because he was mad. Charlie drug tested him.

"It's too soon for results," Charlie says. "I asked him, 'If you don't have a drug problem, then why did you think about drugs the minute you were kicked out and angry?' He didn't like *that* question."

Bruce and I remain silent, taking all this in.

"He threw a bunch of stuff in a duffel—he didn't even grab all his clothes or shoes—and stormed past me out of the house. I asked him if he had some place to go and he ignored me. It was freezing, but he absolutely wanted out of there. I hollered after him that we could put him up in a motel for the night, but he turned the corner and disappeared."

It's Jake's thirty-first day of the six-month program.

We set the receivers down. Bruce and I are at a loss for words. I sit in my warm living room picturing Jake walking off into the cold night in the little town of Carbondale ringed by frozen mountains.

19
SAME COUCH

Without a family, man, alone in the world, trembles with the cold.
— ANDRE MAUROIS

JAKE SABOTAGED HIMSELF so quickly my head is spinning. What just happened? Bruce was having a nice time visiting him yesterday morning and now we don't know where he is. I call his cell and leave a voice message in the calmest voice I can manage. "Hey, Jake, I haven't talked to you in a while and wonder what's going on. I'd really like to talk—give me a call." I'm compelled to keep communicating love and understanding, believing I can counter his denial. My journal brims with thoughts and feelings from Alea's and my visit to Carbondale. Was that just last month? Would it help Jake to hear my perspective?

A puff of wind could knock both Bruce and me over when, about an hour later, Jake actually returns my call.

"Hey, what's up?" I say.

"Not much. I left the sober house and I've just been walking around."

He laments about being kicked out and the more I empathize—"That's so tough"—the more he talks.

"After I left Jaywalker, they asked me not to hang around so much."

"That must've felt like rejection," I say.

"Yeah. That really hurt."

I expect him to be angry about L.A., but he doesn't even mention it. Straightaway I wonder if he's high.

"What are you going to do?"

"I think I can spend the next couple of nights at a friend's. Then I'll get my skis and tie up some loose ends. I can catch a bus to Boulder to Paul's house."

Shit. Same friends, same town, same denial.

I'm beside myself with worry—so many overdoses happen fresh out of rehab. With the phone pressed to my ear, I pick up my journal, walk into Jake's bedroom, and sit on his bed while Bruce listens on the other line. "Jake, I want to read to you from my journal...from when I just came to visit. Do you have time to listen? Are you in a place where you can hear it?"

"Yeah, okay. I'm just leaning against a building where it's warmer."

Imagining him shivering, but listening, I spread my story all over him. I'm determined not to get choked up, even though I want him to hear the emotion in my voice, my viewpoint, my love.

When Alea and I walked into Jaywalker after getting through the snowstorm, we saw Jake standing, smiling, strong with clear eyes. We felt so hopeful. Then he told me he'd have to leave and suddenly if felt as though my legs had been kicked out from under me.

I pause. He doesn't say anything. I don't know what his head is telling him.

Hope began to slip away when I listened to him talk, when he said he was not as bad as the guys there. Outside the sun was shining on the snow, but it felt dark inside listening to his self-absorbed addicted thinking. Then he broke the rules, and it broke my heart...

Jake starts to speak but it sounds like he's close to tears, and he goes silent. I no longer trust my own voice, and it's all I can do to wish him well.

Bruce says softly, to help end the call, "Jake, we love you. We hope you'll find recovery."

I suffer the emptiness of his bedroom. I don't notice the rows of his soccer, baseball, and basketball trophies high on a shelf, or his prized Harry Potter and Artemis Fowl collections gathering dust, or the mementos from various family trips grouped together on his desk, or even the faint odor of smelly socks. I just cry hard as a coldness creeps in. Bruce comes in from the other room and wraps his arms around me.

He whispers in emotion, "You've saved Jake."

I cry harder. I understand his optimistic words. He thought he heard surrender in our son's voice, and he wants to believe that Jake's willful façade has given way to reason. I know he's amazed at how calmly I've been talking with Jake. I'm surprised, myself. But I've had similar conversations before and later learned my words touched my son only in the moment. This past autumn, when he was lonely in Boulder and depressed, I felt like I'd reached him, like I'd caught the end of a balloon's string just before it floated away. I later learned he went right back to using heroin.

Finally, I'm cried out. Bruce and I sit together for a few minutes in our sadness and worry, then drag ourselves up and do our best to carry on with our lives.

I've communicated my deep love and concern, but Jake walked out of the sober house so suddenly that Bruce and I didn't have the chance to communicate our new boundaries. So the next day I send an email clarifying where we stand. I also once again share my understanding of his disease—you never know when or where an addict might hear a phrase that triggers a moment of clarity. I want my words in black and white on his screen. If he checks a screen, that is.

> *Dear Jake,*
>
> *We hope you will keep in touch. We believe you will find recovery for yourself in your own way. You have heard all the information about addiction. If you go back to using, then I guess you have your answer about yourself and powerlessness. Using is what happens to addicts on their own despite their best intentions. The question is...what will you do if you slip? Will you think, "I've blown it anyway, so I may as well keep using for a while," or, "I'd better get right back to recovery before it gets much worse"?*
>
> *You get to choose what you do.*
>
> *Addicts can die little by little—they can cycle in and out of jail, grow more and more separate from family and friends— or they can overdose and be gone in an instant. This terrifies Papa and me. We know that Oxy and heroin overdoses are happening in epidemic numbers and often because young people think, "Not me, it won't happen to me." I wonder what were some of Anton's last thoughts. Addiction is one wound that time cannot heal, and you can't outrun it. Jake, I can't know how hard this is for you. This is not the life you ordered. I wish it were different.*

Papa and I need to do what we believe—and what the professionals tell us—is right, knowing that we have done all that we can for you in love. And we have come to believe that we need to set new boundaries. We will not finance your destruction. We have stated this all along. But we've now come to recognize that we may not be helping you by financing your recovery.

To be clear, nothing means more to us than for you to find recovery, but you will need to find and finance it yourself, which will probably mean a free or publicly-funded program. We need to see the behavior of healthy decisions, not hear promises. We get to choose our boundaries and we have limits.

We have always planned to help finance your education. If you embrace recovery—if you prove that you can complete a program on your own, if we hear a professional treatment team say you are ready to move on—we can talk about college.

We have to use our best judgment to decide what is right for us.

Love,

Momma and Papa

My heartfelt words are all I have left to give. Any assistance interferes with Jake's struggle by easing his pain. He needs that pain to propel himself toward help—yet every day he's out there using, he could die. He needs to feel the penalty of his choice to walk away from recovery, to experience sinking to the inevitable low—yet he must also survive. I want out of this nightmare as much as my addict does. If it were easy, there wouldn't be millions still suffering and there wouldn't be ever-growing self-help groups like Al-Anon. So we wait, hoping the pain of living in active addiction becomes greater for Jake than the perceived pleasure of using drugs, that pain will lead him to choose recovery. And hoping that happens soon.

Dina Kucera writes about losing her addicted daughter piece by piece until she becomes someone else. "The person you knew just isn't there anymore, and all those years of their descent are lost forever. She may recover—you pray she recovers—but she will come out on the other end a different person. You never really get back the person you lost."

I'm mourning my smart little boy. I'm grabbing at the pieces of his goodness that are scattering in the wind. A week goes by. Ten days. Is he shooting heroin? Is he once again telling himself that he can control it? Heroin can turn a healthy brain into a smaller one, full of holes like a bowl of Cheerios, turning reasoning and decision-making into haphazard events. *Your brain—you only have one. What are you doing to it?* My emotions get depleted while his brain cells get seared. Addiction is a disease, not a learned behavior. *You can't choose not to be an addict.*

Standing back and doing nothing is killing me.

———

Alea's dragging herself around. She quit gymnastics and water polo and spends increasing amounts of time in front of the television. She's been working on her senior thesis for her English class—*Addiction: A Family Affair.*

"Didn't you tell me you were going to the mall and then dinner with some of your girlfriends tonight?" I ask one Friday afternoon.

"I changed my mind. I'm not going."

"That doesn't sound like you. Are you okay?"

She shrugs. "All my friends are so happy high school's almost over. There's lots of parties and things going on. But I don't feel like they do. I feel like something's pulling me back from all that."

"Do you want to talk about it?"

"No."

———

What would it take for Jake to choose recovery? From our addiction therapist I know what it's taken for other addicts—divorce, jail, losing kids, a job, a house—but what would it take for Jake? Many believe an addict has to hit bottom before he or she will be ready for help. That's an unchallenged myth that stops us from dealing with a fatal disease. Just as many people coerced into treatment find recovery as those who walk in on their own. Bruce and I have not given up that treatment will work, though Jake is proving that it almost always takes multiple attempts. We've removed the safety net he has always relied upon in the hope of spurring him to take up the fight himself—the battle only he can fight. Unfortunately, he might still need convincing the net is no longer there.

———

"Say goodbye to the old me," Bruce says a tad nervously as I hug him goodbye at the airport curb. He's carved out a week to do his own personal-growth trek. He's on his way to meet Lorri and her husband. The three of them will head out to the Gila National Forest, exactly where Jake and I each were last year.

It's mid-April. Bruce will be warm in New Mexico, but the snow is just melting in Colorado. Still no word from Jake. If something terrible happens, will someone know to call me?

After a fortnight of silence, he calls. I hear discouragement in his voice. He's sitting on the same couch in the same house saying the same words as last September, "I don't know what to do, Momma." He can't find a job and can't afford the security deposit of a place he wants to sublet. He regrets the way he left the sober house. Does he register his actions as impulsive now? He admits to using. I don't ask what. Does it matter? My anxiety is soaring already. He seems to want to talk.

"I thought being content with myself, working, and the last four months of treatment would be enough. But I'm amazed how fast things fall apart when I try life on my own. I want to get out of my head—I'm combating a pessimistic voice. All day long I listen to this negative self-talk and again when I go to bed at night and it's still there when I wake up in the morning."

"What would your sponsor or your counselor say right about now?"

"Go to a meeting," he replies quietly.

"Sounds like a good idea. Maybe you could speak up at a meeting and say, 'I need help.'"

Since he's reflecting on his actions, I pepper him with more questions. "Did you knowingly sabotage yourself?" "Did you think you could handle it with your old friends?" "Do you think the people and the place contribute to how you're doing now?"

He answers no, yes, and yes. "I never thought of it that way but I can see the sabotage and the lack of impulse control now."

When he describes his frustration with his failures I read him some facts about drugs and brain damage. I'm still trying to penetrate denial. He listens.

"What will have to happen before you accept you need recovery?" I ask him.

"I don't know, Momma."

"Addiction affects our family. It causes me to suffer, too. I worry and wonder—what will it take? Will it be more time passing, will it be the end of friendships, will it involve police, jails, and hospitals? Will it be a personal tragedy?"

"I don't know," he repeats almost inaudibly.

I struggle with aggravation and compassion. Expecting his addicted brain to think like a nonaddicted one is useless. After we hang up, I'm still reminding myself it does no good to get angry. He's an unwell twenty-year-old trying to navigate life with a brain that's emotionally delayed. My kid is trying. He's doing the best he can. He isn't racing off to L.A. high as a kite. He has growing awareness that he can't yet put his life together, even though his acceptance of his disease seems tentative—"Well, *I guess* I'm an addict." We are communicating—as long as he answers his phone. Is he secretly hoping I'll take action? I honestly don't know what the next step is. I have no idea. The experts tell me that is exactly where I need to be— not in control. *Get your Al-Anon telephone numbers out and start calling; that's your life raft.*

Five hundred times a day I have a primal urge to lead my cub to safety. His relapse rocks my conviction that he will recover. I feel the universal energy of all mothers who've come before me—motherhood is screaming at me to help my child. Every fiber in my being is fighting every minute of doing nothing. More days go by. Is he alive? No word. I console myself that he needs time—the same time that tortures me—to steep in misery, exactly what all the counselors said he needs to do.

I want to break into his thought process to help him glimpse the truth of his situation. Do I have any power to affect what he does? Can I abandon my cub? Though my body and heart want to carry him to safety, my brain insists that I work toward listening to him, educating myself, avoiding moral judgment, and striving to detach with love.

Bruce arrives home from his week in New Mexico. Alea and I listen as he describes how simple life became out there in all that quiet. "You can really just sit and think. I can't remember a time without distractions." Bruce looks straight at me. "I want to set in motion balance in my life."

I smile at him.

"What's Lorri like?" asks Alea.

"She's incredibly insightful; she's great."

"How many hikes did you go on?" Alea's curiosity is aroused. She's the only one now in our family who hasn't gone on a trek.

"We went every day...*and* I've never written so much in my life. Lorri gave me lots of assignments. Do you think you'd go, Alea?"

"Maybe," she replies.

The first of May comes and goes. It's now been a month since Jake walked out of the sober house. What is he using? How much? His voice sounds several notches lower in wretchedness when at last he returns my call.

"This must be a disease, because I can't seem to be able to do anything. I know what I need to do, I just can't."

Listen, I remind myself. *Detach with love.*

"How do you spend your days?"

"Going from one distraction to the next."

"How are things with Paul? What does he think?"

"We just goof around, we don't talk about life."

I remember Jake telling me last year that Paul was the greatest friend and they frequently had long deep conversations about life.

"Jake, you sound awful. It might feel uncomfortable to call someone, but if you did, who would you call?"

"Charlie." Even though Jake's last interaction with Charlie was storming past him out of the sober house, he knows how much Charlie really wants him to make it. Charlie's been in Jake's shoes.

"I think your intuition is good. He really cares about you—he'll understand, no judgment."

"I can't believe how fast I can go from feeling good to so bad."

"I remember you said that last fall, honey. How did you feel five weeks ago?"

"Really good, skiing, making money."

"And now?"

"Terrible."

"What's the difference?"

"Being alone. No support."

I don't press him to admit that the difference is drugs.

"You can't do it alone. You need a recovering community. I wish I could be the person to help you, but I can't be." I hear him crying in the silence.

"I guess I'll call Charlie," he whispers.

Will he make the call? When I hang up I wrap my arms tightly around myself, rocking, trying to banish the image of him sticking a needle in his arm, ignoring the consequences of his behavior, not picking up a phone.

Jake, drugs are slowly but surely taking your life away.

We all try to keep hope alive. Alea is hesitant but goes with me to a meeting. She's curious because she's seen the impact this group has had on me. When we get to the church, I suggest the Alateen meeting next door but when she peeks in and sees three "fifth graders" she decides to stick with the adults. "No way, Momma. I'm not going in there with those little kids."

She listens intently as we go around the room, parents introducing themselves by first name, each telling what brought us in. "My thirty-year-old is a meth addict. I don't know where he is." "I'm the father of a nineteen-year-old alcoholic in detox." "My twenty-two-year-old daughter is a pothead in denial." "I have a twenty-six-year-old son currently five years in recovery from heroin." The sheer number of parents in the room is staggering.

I wonder how listening to the stories of the other parents affects her but Alea is tight-lipped on the way home. She does tell me the following afternoon after school that she delivered her oral report for her senior thesis on addiction. It's a courageous way to let her pain out, to speak before her peers. She tells me her teacher—who was Jake's teacher, too—wept.

It isn't long before an acquaintance, walking her dog past our house and glimpsing me through my kitchen window, motions to me and waits for me to open the front door. She launches into a heartfelt, "I'm so sorry—is it true Jake is a heroin addict?" Her words cause me to step back. I've hated to think our story is out there in the community, and now it is. She mentions a classmate of Alea's, who heard the speech, who told her mom, who told so and so. We chat a few minutes and I try to succinctly relay some of what I know about this awful disease, yet her parting words are, "Well, at least Alea will know better." Slam. There it is—the judgment. My words sailed right over her head. Addiction is mired in myths, gossip, stigma, pity, and judgment. Jake is not here to defend himself against the myths—addicts use because they want to. My son not only has to battle a disease; if he gets into recovery, he'll be up against judgment, too.

Though Alea has continued to keep a distance from her ex-boyfriend, his parents are having a harder time letting her go. His dad calls to tell her he's taken Ben to the hospital for another three-day psychiatric watch. Ben's threatening suicide. He won't talk with his parents and will only agree to talk with Alea. They broke up nearly four months ago, but she goes and convinces him to enter the offered two-week program and to take the medication the doctors are recommending. She returns home glum to find me sitting on the couch only able to go from breath to breath.

20
FRANTIC MOTHER

Addiction has caused us repeated heartache and disappointment.
It has robbed us of our dreams of how life should be. It has put
our loved one's life at risk and strained relationships
within the entire family.
— BEVERLY CONYERS, *Everything Changes*

MOTHER'S DAY IS A WEEK AWAY and I'm one frantic mother.
Am I sending Jake e-mails merely to make contact? That
contact feels so important.

> *Jake,*
>   *Addiction is robbing your brain of the ability to make the
> decision to get help. It affects your brain and your soul. You
> may be fearing that you will fail if you try to get your life back.
> Addiction wants you to think that, so that you will continue
> using. There is a beautiful person in there but addiction has
> a stranglehold. Your current problems, loneliness, confusion,
> anxiety, fear are all because of addiction. Only in recovery can
> you begin to get yourself back.*
>   *Momma*

Should I quit leaving emails and voicemails and somehow wait? Is he breathing? What about harsh truths? *Jake, your continued drug use is causing heartbreaks that your mind is rationalizing away. It'll be so hard for your sister not to have you there at her graduation.* Or straight facts. *You are extraordinarily smart, and your judgment is severely impaired. If all you can think about is getting high, get yourself to an AA meeting because you can't trust your judgment right now.* Should I find someone in Boulder willing to talk to him, and offer only that phone number if he asks for help? I can't imagine Jake calling and saying, "I give up." Can his brain register that he should?

It's a source of solace to call and speak with his past counselors. Charlie predicts Jake still needs to feel more despair. "If he comes right back to the sober house because he doesn't have anywhere else to go, he'll be no further down the path."

Charlie gives me his own mother's mobile number because he recognizes my frenzied state. Though we've never met and probably never will, I call her, awed that the recovery community is so vast and so giving of time and compassion.

She says kindly, "I know how dreadfully painful this is. Are you taking good care of yourself?"

I let out a deep sigh.

"That sounds like a good breath," she says, "It's good to just breathe and practice being with this pain. When my son was in dire circumstances, I came to a point where I finally truly let go of the outcome of what he might or might not do."

"How? What'd you do?"

"I told him I didn't think he was going to be one of the ones that makes it."

"You actually said that to your son?"

"I did. He'd lost so much, but still kept using. The hell had gone on for so long I wasn't sure I was going to make it, myself.

When he finally realized I was absolutely done, something seemed to spark in him. A short time later, he got himself off the streets and into recovery."

"I know what you mean about not believing you'll make it. I feel that way now."

"You'll make it. You've gotten him treatment. You're holding boundaries. He'll get there."

For several days, I feel comforted as I turn her story over in my mind. Charlie got himself into recovery without his mother's help.

But soon my agitation returns, full force. I call Jake's old counselor from Cirque. I want a clear-cut answer. Is it wise to leave our son to choose recovery? As we allow him to feel the consequences, his brain is *actively ignoring those consequences.* Can he get so dysfunctional, depressed, and stuck to his same ineffective strategies, that he can't make it? Is he at risk for suicide as well as overdose? Some people are no match for this disease and die. Other's lives are saved because they were initially forced into treatment. What should we do? The counselor says, pray, meditate, and follow your intuition.

Bruce too is wavering on our boundary, wondering if we should intervene. He's concerned Jake might kill himself. He's haunted by his friend's son overdosing. I am, too. He worries about what Jake is doing to his brain. Jake isn't answering his phone. Is he on a binge? Despite his Soltrails resolution to seek more balance, Bruce throws himself into long hours at work.

Six weeks ago, when my son was safely working away on his recovery, I agreed to be the speaker before a packed Al-Anon parent meeting. Now I try to set my agitation aside and speak from my heart. Bruce and Alea come to sit beside me for moral support.

"I don't know where my son is tonight. He's found people who will ignore his addiction, party with him, and let him sleep on their couch. He's most likely convinced those 'friends' that his parents don't love him because we won't allow him to live at home and won't pay for him to continue in college, either. He keeps walking out or getting kicked out of rehab. We've begun to realize that we're contributing to that cycle, so now we're leaving his choices to him. Other addicts have found recovery without their parents spending tens of thousands of dollars. AA is free. Or maybe the best thing would be if he got himself to the Salvation Army's treatment program—I know that's free, too—just because it would mean he did it himself. 'Helping' turns into enabling, and when he doesn't feel the consequences of his behavior, nothing changes—so we've set what seems like a harsh boundary *because* we love him. It's truly bleak sitting in limbo not knowing if holding this boundary is the right thing to do."

When I look at all the faces surrounding me, something like a taproot goes down and I feel myself grounded in support. This rootedness bears fruit. A serene woman whom I've never seen before speaks up and tells how she lost track of her alcoholic son after sending him to several treatment centers. She had no idea where he was for months. Later, she learned that while he was wandering around perpetually drunk, homeless, and sleeping in a park in Berkeley, somebody—whom she likes to refer to as an angel—took him by the elbow and walked him to a treatment center where he began a six-month residential program. He went on to live in their sober house, participated in the outpatient program, and worked full time to support himself for that year. Gradually he took a few community college classes as well, and then transferred to UC Davis where he's finishing his college degree. He reports to his mother that he's surrounded by college kids who drink like fish. She doesn't appear worried about his every little step; she truly seems to have handed all responsibility over to him. I live for encouraging stories like hers.

People come up to me after the meeting with lots of warm support. An elderly woman, thirty-five years in Al-Anon, comments that when she and her husband at last realized that money didn't make things better, they said to their addicted son, "Well, there won't be any more of *that*." But then a newcomer overhears this remark and says, "If you're ready for that kind of resolve and can do that." It's an awful struggle. Will Jake get himself to an AA meeting? What are the chances he'll make his way to the Salvation Army or some other rehab with a sliding scale down to zero? On the drive home, I argue with myself; someone led that mother's kid to rehab, he didn't walk there on his own. Who will lead my son?

The next day I track down her phone number to ask her more about the program in Berkeley. It turns out that New Bridge Foundation has a six-month residential program with a focus on behavioral modification. It's an hour's drive from our home, and in certain cases residents can obtain funding from the county. She tells me it's a tough program but she believes it made the difference in turning her son around.

I call admissions to ask whether Jake could somehow qualify for funding, figuring I could give him their telephone number and hope he'd make the call. I learn that Jake would first have to participate in their short program, which lasts a month, at which point he might be able to qualify for the long program. Nothing is ever crystal clear in the field of behavioral health services, but I get the impression that New Bridge works hard to help clients stay if they desperately want it. I keep the number handy.

Each minute I ask myself *what can I do*? Since I know Charlie drives in to Boulder from Carbondale several times a month, I call to see if he'd consider offering to take Jake to an AA meeting. I convince myself that he might just be Jake's angel. Am I trying to control things? At this point, I don't care. I haven't heard from my son in nearly two weeks and I'm mad with worry.

The hoopla for Alea's prom night has escalated to fifteen young couples and their parents gathered at her girlfriend's house for the pre-event. A friend asked Alea to be his date; no romance tonight. Parents are milling about with cameras, enjoying this "once in a lifetime" photo opportunity. The girls have spent the day trying to out-do each other—the highest heels, the most dazzling dress, the sexiest hairdo—and now are posing every-where, enjoying angling for the cameras, finally ridding them-selves of the day's stress. The boys, stiff in tuxedos, stand uncom-fortably clustered around the expansive food table.

All the girls compliment Alea on her smoky eye makeup; I watch her light up at the attention. But then, as my statuesque daughter pivots in her elegant turquoise princess gown, the plunging V down her back faces me, and I notice the tip of a blu-ish curlicue peeking out from her skinny strap. That there is a *tattoo*. Suddenly, I can't see my gorgeous daughter for who she is. I'm seething that she has secretly gone and done it.

Bruce arrives straight from his office and can't figure out why I look like I could explode at such a beautiful event. Like a rain-bow, all the girls position themselves next to a sparkling pool with a backdrop of climbing red roses.

Alea waves at her dad. He waves back, admiring her. Then he looks around. "I don't know any of these parents," he says, nearly but not quite as ill at ease as some of the girls' dates.

I swallow and say nothing. Let Alea have her night. How won-derful to postpone that conversation until tomorrow, Mother's Day. Bruce heads back to his office. It's Saturday night, and he'll be there until midnight at least. He's worked the last twenty-one days straight. I go home alone dragging my heart.

While I wallow between anger and tears, Jake calls. I grasp at this unexpected Mother's Day gift.

"I'm journaling, which is making me feel better." Could it be that he's made a shift? Or are his words aimed precisely at a susceptible mother? "I even prayed to God and felt some spiritual awareness. I'm gonna make it, Momma."

He says he knows recovery is the way but he's not ready to take that step. He admits his friends are enabling him. I can recognize empty words and no action toward that recovery.

"So what're you going to do?"

"I need to feel the gift of desperation, Momma."

"If someone were to knock on your door and offer you a ride to a meeting, would you go?"

"Yes."

"Do you feel like your brain is telling you that you have lots of time?"

"No."

He's getting there slowly, but not ready yet. The next morning, I dig up the name and number of a local man in Boulder who escorts kids to rehabs. When I briefly sketch the situation and tell him how worried we are, he empathizes that his own son went through this and he offers to be of any assistance. I add his phone number to the growing emergency list on my desk. His name is Don. Maybe *he's* the angel.

The next morning, when I sit down on Alea's bed and ask her if she got a tattoo, she breaks down in tears. It turns out she got it six months ago, when she was still seventeen—underage, even. Holding the secret must've been awful.

"Alea, I've always said if you want me to fund your college, don't do drugs and don't get a tattoo."

Tears turn into defiance. "You never said that to *me*, just Jake."

No remorse. I could use a proud moment from either kid right about now. I know tats are more common by the minute but asking my children to wait until they're financially independent gives their prefrontal cortex time to mature. As an adult, Alea can decide to decorate her entire body if that's what she wants.

She shows me the tattoo—her brother's name in two-inch letters. *Damn this disease.*

"I thought he was going to stay clean when he went back to Cirque and I got it in celebration."

"Oh, Alea," I say, putting my arm around her.

I leave her wondering about her fate. I'm wondering, too. Does it make any difference that it's the word "Jake"? To her, the tattoo represents her love for her brother. Not paying for college seems harsh now. Absorbing her sadness and dashed hopefulness compounds my own sadness.

During our first conversation about it, Bruce and I scratch our heads trying to remember if, technically, we sat Alea down and made the same request we made of Jake before he left for college. We're not sure—but shouldn't she assume?

"She should contribute to her college bill," Bruce says in frustration, entertaining a compromise. "In fact, Jake should've contributed to his tuition, even without a tattoo. I paid for mine."

"Or she could do a gap year, after all," I say. As with Jake, we suggested to Alea that she take a year off between high school and college. Like him, she declined. Might a gap year have made a difference for Jake?

When we discuss it again the next day, Bruce says, "Let's give her the choice to defer college a year, or contribute ten percent toward her tuition bill. That's a significant portion of her net worth."

"That'll sting. We should've insisted on Jake contributing; he didn't have any skin in the game."

"Let's hope this helps her make better choices in college."

Alea's been keeping a low profile for the past two days. When we all sit down together, she looks both eager and solemn. Bruce lays out the choices and she stiffens for an instant, looks at each of us, then immediately chooses to contribute. She breathes out in relief that she's still going to college in August. "That tattoo just got really expensive," she says.

She doesn't linger. As usual, she wants to process her feelings alone in her room, but she allows me to give her a hug as she turns to go. I tell her I love her.

———

Nearly two weeks go by. Isn't Jake out of money by now? My intuition tells me he's getting more desperate.

Midafternoon on the Saturday before Memorial Day, the phone rings like a gunshot and I jump. Over the line a garbled voice says, "*Momma, I need help.*" *Jake*? I tremble. I panic. I'm going to faint. Then my son's tiny voice says, "I need a reason to live." I want to race to him, to speed him straight to detox but I'm a thousand miles away.

"Jake," I say, my voice unsteady. "I love you more than anything, and I'll do everything I can. Is anybody there with you?"

He mumbles he's alone.

"I'm going to get someone to come. I'll call you back as soon as I can. I love you."

Bruce by now is standing anxiously beside me. I fill him in quickly, then call an Alcoholic Anonymous number in Boulder. That guy calls eight numbers, but it's a holiday weekend and no one is answering. He gives me the phone number for a welfare check, which means the police would come to determine if Jake needs to be admitted for a 72-hour psychiatric watch or take him voluntarily to an alcohol/drug recovery center. But I don't have an address for where he is.

I call Jake back. He's scared of the police coming but agrees to go to a Narcotics Anonymous meeting. I give him the telephone number of the escort, Don. Jake agrees to call Don to give him his address.

Bruce and I know full well that Jake could be poised to kill himself after hanging up the phone. We've lived that possibility every day, but this feels acute, and I'm having trouble breathing, trouble thinking. Should we try to get Jake to tell us where he is, then call 911 and report that our son has threatened suicide? We decide to sit tight. It's a horrid gamble.

The phone rings. It's Don. He tells us Jake called and agreed to go with him to the meeting. We breathe. Four hours later, Don reports that he took Jake first to get a meal—"He's *really* thin"— and then to a meeting. He tells us he and Jake talked openly about the local ARC, Alcohol Recovery Center. Jake asked a lot of questions about the center but resisted Don's urging him to go right then. He's back on his own.

Bruce and I are shaken, faced with the risky uncertainness of our son's condition, left to stand by our words that he'll have to get himself to recovery and figure out how to pay for it if it isn't free. We've crossed swords with the powerful foe of addiction. The next day—supposedly a relaxing Sunday with my husband— I worry, cry, call parents from my Al-Anon list, and worry some more.

Finally I text Jake:

been waiting to hear from u. Thinking of calling welfare check if u don't call. Worried.

He fires back that he's with friends. That he's better and will call back tonight. Impossibly, he's not ready to leave the party yet.

Three more days go by.

21
DETOX

No matter what we do, no matter how we agonize or obsess, we
cannot choose for our children whether they live or die.
— DAVID SHEFF, *Beautiful Boy*

"MOMMA, THEY WON'T ACCEPT ME." Jake's voice is shaky on
the line.

First, a flicker of relief, then confusion.

"What? Where are you?"

"Sitting on the curb outside the ARC in Boulder."

We've been desperate for him to walk into a detox center and
now he's sitting outside?

"They won't take you? What's happening? Are you okay?"

"Momma...I'm starving, I can't think." His voice quavers. My
skin contracts and I shiver, reliving the moment he came to me
as a little boy, cradling his right arm, which hung limply at an
odd angle after he fell off a trampoline.

"I told them I've also been using Xanax."

"Also…" I know what he means, though I've been praying it wasn't true. My son has been shooting heroin, probably this time for nearly two months.

He manages to explain what the problem is. This particular detox center is not set up to handle Xanax—benzodiazepine—because of possible seizures, so he needs to go to a specialized medical facility.

"Are you someplace where you can just sit? I'll make some calls and get back to you."

I spring into action. I'm desperate to find an alternative fast. I call Bruce; he's back in his work world, and I hear in his voice his refusal to go into crisis mode. "I'll call ARC," he says, "and get more information while you call Boulder's AA numbers. Maybe someone can pick him up."

By the time I get back to Jake with some information, he's called a friend to fetch him, and they're about to arrive at the medical detox center recommended by ARC. He's done just what we hoped—gotten himself to detox without our direct intervention. He even saved our insurance information from his emergency-room trip in Carbondale and provides it to the facility. After a forty-five minute intake interview, they admit him—chemical dependency and suicide watches are precisely what they do.

Our relief that Jake is in detox is swiftly undercut by what will become a five-day mental-health quagmire lacking continuity, information, and solutions. No one returns my calls questioning cost or insurance coverage. I deal with a social worker who is useless, with no pertinent information. I'm repeatedly denied permission to speak with Jake. And I learn that a doctor has started him on the controversial drug, Suboxone.

At first Suboxone—buprenorphine and naloxone—sounds like a miracle drug, helping addicts keep their craving for drugs at bay. But I remember some parents at meetings speaking out strongly against it. Here's one more thing I need to read about, to try to understand.

Bruce and I are depleted from fighting addiction from a different state. We're like marathon runners who somehow need to find another gear. To complicate matters, Alea has decided to attend CU Boulder, starting in less than three months. If Jake is still there and back to using, it would be asking a lot of Alea to turn him away.

I telephone New Bridge Foundation in Berkeley to see if a bed is available. There was a time when I would have gone to check out the facility, would have worried if it'd be a good fit, but I've shifted my perspective. These programs, wherever they are, offer counseling, help, a way out. This one has the tremendous advantage of being close to home. Whether Jake will benefit from this particular rehab is much more about the timing and his receptiveness rather than the feeling I'd get from taking a look.

When I speak to the admissions director at New Bridge, I learn they are in-network for our insurance plan, which is amazing news. I've already learned that our plan will cover thirty days of residential treatment per year, but at only 80 percent. Bruce and I are willing to soften our stance and cover the 20 percent. Jake did, after all, get himself to and through detox, and a facility like New Bridge sounds less frightening to us than the Salvation Army.

The director explains that the long program is hard work—roughly 50 percent of those who enter it finish it. Still, it sounds like a new approach, and nothing has worked before.

I also learn that New Bridge's philosophy about Suboxone clashes radically with that of the detox center in Boulder. The director explains that Suboxone is a drug developed to prevent withdrawal symptoms in a person who quits using an addictive opiate. It is intended to block the euphoric effect of the opiate.

However, a thriving underground market exists, and Suboxone has become yet another prescription drug to abuse. Additionally, Suboxone used with Xanax can suppress breathing to dangerously low levels. Everything he tells me makes sense, and the doctor in Boulder has told me nothing.

"If your son seeks treatment here at New Bridge, he can't stay on Suboxone."

"Oh. Okay. I'll explain that to him."

That afternoon, I'm finally able to get Jake on the phone. He tells me he's feeling better, eating a lot. He sounds so much stronger than he did three days ago.

I ask him about the Suboxone.

"The doctor says I'm a poster boy for it, that it'll keep me from craving. He says I'll have to be on it for years, but it'll really help. So I said okay."

I find myself thinking, *Of course you said okay—the man offered you pills!*

"Jake, there's a rehab in Berkeley I want to tell you about."

I explain that New Bridge is a nonprofit treatment center, unlike Cirque and Jaywalker, which are both private-pay facilities.

"The state allocates money to nonprofit county programs that are in compliance with healthcare laws. If you complete the short program, the month you'd spend there might qualify you as a county resident, and then there's a chance the county might reimburse New Bridge for you in their long program."

"Okay," Jake says softly.

"The admissions guy says that based on what I told him you're a good candidate for their six-month program, but they need to speak directly with you."

This is not the right moment to mention that the admissions director described the six-month program as a combination of the military and a monastery, and predicted that Jake will hate the first month as he gets used to the behavioral-modification aspect of the program. I do, however, explain that they won't take him if he stays on Suboxone.

He says weakly, "Okay, Momma. It sounds like a good place."

I give him the number to call, and go to work getting insurance preauthorization. Jake manages a call to the admissions director, completes an interview over the phone, and agrees to enter their thirty-day program. We agree to pay for his one-way plane ticket once he's discharged in two days' time—another departure from our stance, but it's the only way to get him to California—pick him up, and drive him to treatment. He'll need to spend the night at home since the rehab can't take him until the following morning. We expect he'll be in bad shape, yet we're hungry as bears to reconnect.

Alea has hoped these past months that somehow her brother would get himself to her high-school graduation. She interprets his absence as rejection, that he doesn't care. Our family drama casts a shadow over her limelight; she suffers me running around focused on Jake's crisis instead of her accomplishment.

I'm so sorry, Alea.

Instead of feeling joy for my daughter on the day of her graduation, I fear I won't get through the morning. The phone is glued to my ear as I grapple with various insurance-company representatives and the detox social worker. Each attempt to speak directly to the Suboxone-prescribing doctor becomes more futile. Some mothers have described to me how things turned nightmarish when their kids became addicted to it. I want to hear what this doctor has to say but I can't get him on the line.

I hurry to a noon meeting to help fortify me. After that, I drive straight to an appointment with our addiction therapist. Sitting in her office, my agony feels as big as Niagara Falls, and it spills over. The therapist wipes away her tears. She comments on my extremely depleted condition and gently reminds me that addiction can cause loved ones to be in a state of high vigilance for so long, operating from a fear-based place, that our brains adapt to the rushing adrenalin. Like a taut rubber band stretching, stretching, I am about to snap. Addiction is taking over. Old thoughts are squeezing in; I know that I didn't cause it. Did I cause it?

It's been ten months since Jake's been home. I yearn to cook his favorite dinner, savor watching him eat. I want to be reunited, watch him roll around with Bella—a glued-back-together family. We can keep him safe for twenty-four hours, can't we? What if he has an old stash in his room? A few months back, I angrily went through his drawers and ended up washing just about every stitch of clothing in his closet. I'm fairly certain there's nothing in there. Jake must look terribly thin and hollow, yet I see him strong and healthy in my mind's eye, not wanting to face what he's done to himself.

Bruce has worked until midnight all week but has promised to get home in time for the late-afternoon graduation ceremony. Some of Jake's high-school classmates have younger siblings in Alea's senior class. I dread hearing parents speaking of their child as a brilliant snowflake. I fill my purse with tissues, knowing I'm likely to cry.

Mobs of people file onto the football field where hundreds of white chairs have been set up. The band is tuning up for Pomp and Circumstance. As I gaze over the crowd, I recognize several faces from Al-Anon. One woman sends me an air high-five over the boisterous throng, then pastes on a smile and sits next to her actively alcoholic ex-husband, her graduating son's father. Another catches my eye and blows me a kiss. Bruce and my mother sit next to me, Jake's seat is empty, and all the optimistic graduates sit facing us. After speeches full of hopes and dreams, Alea is swept up in the celebration, surrounded by her jubilant friends. They all traipse off—their tassels now on the left, arms linked together to form a swaying chain—toward buses that will whisk them away to a secret location to celebrate grad night, all night.

———

Instead of the doctor deciding when Jake is ready to be discharged from detox, the insurance company determines that four days of acute care is all that they'll cover:

> Our Medical Reviewer has determined: We cannot approve the request for continued hospital care as of June 4, 2012. The information your provider gave us does not show this is medically necessary. You were admitted due to having thoughts of suicide. At this time you report having thoughts of suicide off and on but no intent or plan to act on them. You have shown good control of your behavior. You have thoughts of self-harm that you are able to cope with and not act on. You can be safely treated with outpatient service...

Their reply doesn't mention a thing about the medical necessity for detoxing from heroin and Xanax. I hope there won't be a problem about thirty-day coverage at New Bridge—theoretically, that's a completely different claim. It sounds as if the insurance company is saying, "Now go out and be a good boy, Jake." If anyone needs to be in residential drug treatment, it's my son.

On his last day, Jake is not discharged in time to catch the airport shuttle they've arranged and he calls us in a panic. At the last minute, they get him a taxi, but Jake's agitated they haven't given him any pills to taper off Suboxone. The current health-care system in this country seems to have no real interest in solutions for addicts. Piecing together help is unnecessarily complicated, particularly if resources are limited. A parent is left to lead the charge under complete duress with limited information learning as fast as she can.

———

Bruce, Alea, and I—even the dog jumps in the back of the car—head to the San Jose airport at one in the afternoon to pick up Jake. Alea squeals, "There he is!" He's dragging what looks like a half-empty duffle bag toward the curb. We all jump out and hug him. He feels awfully thin within my embrace. He's withdrawn but looks relieved and glad to see all of us. On the drive home he wants to stop at In-N-Out. Showing a spark of determination, he says he was down thirty-five pounds but gained back nearly ten eating nonstop the last five days. At home, we all pile out as he's finishing the last bites of his burger. He begins at once to unpack his stuff and do his laundry; initial avoidance probably feels better than struggling with shame. He asks if I'll cut his hair but ends up going to get a cheap buzz cut accompanied by Bruce and Alea rather than risk a butcher job from me.

Though we would all like to imagine Jake merely coming home after being away at college, he's here straight from detox and a dreadfully dangerous past several months. When he and Alea propose that the two of them take a long drive to talk, it's tempting to say, "Of course—go!" We want to show our beloved son respect. But Jake has not earned the right to jump in the car and go for a drive. I have to remind myself with every breath that the addiction that lives inside him is looking at these moments as opportunities to manipulate us. What boundaries will we hold? What openings are there for negative behavior to sneak back into his life as well as ours? Like prairie dogs, we need to stretch up tall from our burrows, scanning the horizon for threats. Our clan has to be vigilant. A sentinel has to be on guard for manipulation. If he receives a perk, will it turn into entitlement? We can't trust Jake.

He and Alea go for a walk instead. When they step back into the kitchen, I see Jake lift his head to savor the smell of roasting pork. He sees that I'm stirring a huge panful of his favorite crispy potatoes, but he doesn't say anything. At the dinner table, it feels bittersweet seeing Jake sitting in his place, knowing that tomorrow his chair will be empty.

Early the next morning, I drive Bruce to the airport. Before we knew Jake would suddenly land at home, Bruce arranged to visit his mother, who's been agitated about her finances and wanting him to come. He's torn now because he'll miss taking Jake to New Bridge, but he goes. At breakfast, Jake is ill-tempered, kicking Suboxone cold turkey. Alea gives him a hug and heads out the door. She's dressed in her red lifeguard shirt and navy shorts with a whistle around her neck; today's her first shift at her summer job.

Jake gathers up his clean laundry, stuffs half of it in his closet and the other half in a much smaller duffle, and climbs into the car. He seems alternately jumpy and sleepy. I've been around my son so little this past year that I ache to talk with him. But it's clear he doesn't want to engage with me, so we travel the whole hour in silence.

I park in front of New Bridge's offices. On the one hand, I feel like I'm about to open the door and step into a void. On the other, if I can accept that my role is simply to drive him here, drop him off, make whatever advance payment is required, and then go home and focus on my own life, I can imagine fifty pounds of worry lifting off my shoulders. I'm not at all sure what Jake's thinking. I open my mouth to offer encouragement—I don't know when I'll see him next—but Jake shuts me down, saying tersely, "Mom, I don't need a pep talk." An addict's irritability can really bite.

On the other side of large doors, a mountain of paperwork greets him. I learn to my surprise that our insurance has only preauthorized seven days. I've read the policy carefully—it specifies thirty days coverage of residential treatment—and confirmed all the numbers with the insurance woman on the phone, so I tell myself it's just a matter of sorting things out. I write a check for 20 percent of the first week, ask a few questions, give Jake a hug, and tell him I love him. He goes back to his pile of forms as I walk out the door. I don't shed a tear. If a monitor were hooked to my heart it would show a flat line. I have no confidence that Jake will stop looking for a way out and start looking for a way in, but at least he's back in treatment, and close to home.

Glancing in my rearview mirror, I ask myself, *Was this a rescue?* Jake *did* ask for help and *did* get himself to a detox center. My head bats these thoughts back and forth all the way home until my fortress is sealed back up, solid, protecting me from another deep hurt if Jake once again rejects recovery.

Part Five

SOBER
SOLDIER

22
ADDICTION'S NEW BEST FRIEND

Some people change their ways when they see the light;
others when they feel the heat.
— CAROLINE SCHOEDER

SLOW IN MOTION, days creep past. New Bridge holds a family education session each Tuesday night. When the first one rolls around, Alea won't leave the house. Some new acne medication is just not working for her. Ten minutes before we need to go, she bursts into tears. "I am *not* going. Jake can miss *me* for once." I can't help thinking this is more about the hurt of her brother's disease than about her skin. I can't convince her to change her mind, and Bruce is away, so I go alone. It's hard to distinguish residents from family members in the crowded room. Unlike Jake's past two programs—which were specifically for young men—the residents of New Bridge are women as well as men, of all ages and a wide-ranging racial and economic mix. I take the seat Jake has saved for me.

A young heroin addict, Tristan, speaks to his dad with power-ful words of sincere apology. The father listens, his eyes brim-ming, as his twenty-year-old son courageously takes up his fight, such honest emotion pouring from what seems like the depths of his soul. Tristan is waiting to hear if he'll get into the six-month program next door and wants his dad to know he's willing to do whatever it takes. Each of us sitting next to our loved one has a kind of darkness hanging over us, weighing on us, crushing us, and this father looks as if a wind has just blown his darkness right out of the room. I'm glad for him, and can't help feeling envious. I don't dare believe Jake will express that change in atti-tude. He's very quiet, and his demeanor seems unchanged from the morning I drove him to Berkeley. After the meeting wraps up, and a quick hug goodbye from Jake, the counselor hands each of us a letter of guidance as we walk out the door.

Advice to Friends and Family:

Treatment at New Bridge may not be an easy process for many clients. While it is often easy to recognize why it is necessary when they first arrive, in time many clients might start to think that they don't really need to be here, or that the program isn't the right kind of treatment for them. We find that in many cases this is often a conscious or even at times unconscious move to return to using.

We ask that family members try to understand and be supportive of the overall process, and that you support the clients in dealing with aspects of the program they might not like or simply are resistant to. Your loved one may call or write in sadness, anger or other emotional states. They may try to convince you that things are suddenly better, that they realize the error of their ways, or that they will "never do this again." We encourage you to uphold your support of their recovery by not helping them change their initial commitments to the program. While success is hard to guarantee, we have seen our clients do better in life with the more time they've given themselves in treatment.

Jake's proximity now to my extended family and his friends worries me. It would be tempting and easy for him to call someone to come pick him up. His aunts and uncles, his cousins, and my mother are clamoring to know more, and any one of them could innocently sabotage him out of ignorance, so the next morning I send an e-mail to his seven young adult cousins and cc their parents, too.

To all my nieces and nephews,

Jake is an incredible person with an unimaginable brain disease. Those of you in the area may be wanting to visit him; however, the program is strict about visits and limits calls. You can't just show up; they won't let you in. I want to pass on guidance from New Bridge.

Deep down Jake knows he needs to be in the program, yet the addiction wrapped throughout his brain works to convince him to search for those of you who might enable him to escape the work of recovery. If you are thinking, "Wow, this is all over the top...sounds way too strict," then you have yet to realize how formidable a foe addiction is. In order to put his disease in remission, Jake must be sober the rest of his life. He can never drink a beer. He cannot use drugs of any kind. He will need to stay away from triggers—certain music, places, even people—until he is more solid in recovery. This is so hard for his brain to accept and the disease can lead him to fight recovery to the death. Or he can accept it and learn to live joyfully in a sober way. I know how hard it is not to give him

money, a ride, or a place to stay. Don't give him an excuse to
leave. The only people who can help him are the professionals
and those in recovery. As difficult as it might be for you, you
need to urge him to stick with it. He may not have many
chances left.

Love, DD

Right before bed, I show Bruce a copy of the letter. He too
feels relieved having this message go out. We've been so accustomed to resistance from Jake that Bruce expects more. He says
to me, "We should figure out what's on the table for negotiation."

"There is no table anymore," I say and lay my head down on my
pillow.

In the past, I would have already called Jake's counselor several times and followed up to check that he was on course. But
my battle-worn self can't quite get my heart to pick up its normal
beat. I lie still, willing sleep to come.

———

After the first week of coverage, we manage to secure another
week's authorization from the insurance company. Then they
refuse to pay more and the quagmire deepens. Jake has no money.
Bruce and I have agreed to pay the uncovered 20 percent for the
short program, but we are not budging beyond that. Bruce does,
however, go to bat for Jake, taking the argument up the claim
chain. He's the purchaser of health care for the employees of
his small business, and this bit of clout should help him reach
somebody with decision-making power. Part of the problem, we
learn, is that we haven't adequately documented Jake's history
of unsuccessful rehab treatments and relapses. We're working
on that, but for now our claims seem to get placed on an aim-
less conveyer belt in an empty insurance warehouse. Meanwhile,
addiction tightens its hold on Jake, whispering in his ear to avoid
sobriety at all costs, and he shows signs of bolting.

I dump all responsibility in Bruce's lap while Alea and I fly to Colorado for her college orientation. Instead of a relaxing reprieve focusing on an exciting time with my daughter, I receive a steady stream of calls from Bruce, Jake's counselor, the insurance company, and even my mother. As Alea and I are checking into our respective dorms, my cell rings. My mother, who has not spoken with Jake in over a year, rattles off that she was pleased and surprised to get a call from him asking if he can stay at her house for a while. *Oh, no.* While New Bridge tries to channel Jake into what they know to be the surest way toward recovery, addiction's new best friend, the insurance company, is now calling the shots, dictating that Jake can only complete the thirty-day program as an outpatient.

Jake's commitment is already wobbly, and he's probably lunging at the chance to quit living at New Bridge and maybe avoid the long program altogether. He's thinking that sleeping at grandma's house and driving an hour and a half each way through rush-hour traffic to a day program sounds less daunting than residential care. Minor detail that he doesn't have a car. I'm trying to let go of as much of this as I can—if Jake *wants* recovery, if his attitude changes, I need to trust that New Bridge will help him find a way to stay.

The next morning, while I sit on a low reddish sandstone ledge in the middle of the stunning campus, I field calls and watch the college kids in summer classes come and go. One looks just like Jake, the same casual clothes, Vans, same dark hair—how hard it is not to howl for what might have been. My eyes drift up to the rugged Flatirons that seem anchored today against a deep blue sky. Few parents send their second child off to the precise place of destruction of their first child, and with that comes enormous fear and worry. Many friends are in disbelief when they hear Alea has chosen CU Boulder. I've asked a handful of PhD counseling professionals along the way, "Are we crazy?" All responded more or less the same; Alea has earned the right to choose. My favorite reply came from the director of Jaywalker—"Oh, tell them all to be quiet." Alea has been determined to go off this fall to the same college her brother went to and prove herself.

Back in my bare dorm room, it's late at night. My alarm is set for the crack of dawn so I can meet Alea for the joint parent/student session. Just as I'm drifting off, my cell rings again.

Jake's agitation lands in my ear. "Momma, I want to be true to myself now so I don't fail again at something I don't want to do. I don't want to do the long program. I didn't want to go into those other programs and I failed."

I am beyond exasperation. I bristle at his excuses. I say sharply, "You are looking to the left and then to the right, trying to find a way out rather than going straight at it." Then more gently, "I know you're scared. Anyone would be."

"Something's wrong with me that I don't feel inspiration or motivation when I hear people like Tristan apologizing to his dad. I have no feelings."

"Jake, *you have the disease of addiction*, and avoiding that truth is one of the symptoms of the disease," I say forcefully. "You've been *numbing* all your feelings, but they'll come back."

He's floating in and out, pumping his life raft full of air then letting it all out, believing he's okay then knowing he isn't. There's no logic to be found in what he's saying. As he glimpses the truth he's kept hidden from himself, it seems to only intensify his fears. It's probably a good thing he hears my vexation.

———

When my daughter and I return home, Bruce—unshaven and irritable—unloads about the fucking insurance company and goes to bed early. The kitchen looks like a war zone. The dog eyes me dolefully. Bruce has experienced my reality these past three days.

Usually he's distracted by work or gone on a business trip, so secretly I'm glad he's been bombarded. He has made progress by initiating an appeal process.

Even so, the insurance company's refusal to pay has given Jake an excuse, and he appears teetering on the verge of walking out. He's now been in the thirty-day program for twenty-two days. I write him a letter hoping to be able to hand it to him, if he's still there, the next day at the family session.

> *Dear Jake,*
>
> *If I had the disease of addiction, I would want my family to stand up to help me fight it. I certainly would not want them to enable me. I would want them to do what they could to fight the disease and be supportive to me in life going forward. I would want them to learn everything they can about it so I would feel better understood. This is what we have tried our best to do.*
>
> *You are at a crossroads. I see and hear your addiction fighting as hard as ever to win, to get you to avoid the long program. My hope is that you don't truly believe those excuses: "The program is too strict, I might fail, I don't have a three-year-old son like Tristan to motivate me, I can do it on my own." That is distorted thinking. I have to stand against this disease and say that bluntly.*
>
> *My wish is that you trust those around you and take a leap of faith that the long program is stretching before you like a lifeline. One day at a time. Living in active addiction is the road to death. Here is a chance to live.*
>
> *Love,*
>
> *Momma*

In the morning, fairly refreshed, Bruce decides to write one too. It'll be powerful for Jake to receive one from both of us.

Dear Jake,

You've walked a long and troubled road these past few years, and now you've arrived—yet again—at a fork in the road. One direction is the status quo—it's the same tough path you've been traveling. The other direction is new. It, too, is a tough road to travel, and it's daunting because you haven't walked that road and you don't know what it's like or where it will take you. You have a difficult decision to make. And to make the choice even harder, you've got a disease screaming at you to continue the status quo.

I heard you talk last week about what you don't like about this program—it tells me that you're not here because you want recovery. You, unfortunately, have a brain disease. It's not your fault. You didn't do anything to deserve it. You just got it. What's important now is: What are you going to do about it? Will you allow it to destroy your life, or will you fight for the life that you want and deserve?

You're not the only person in our family who has had to overcome a disability or tragedy. Your great grandfather, Gigi's dad, was born with only one hand, and as a young boy lost an eye in a tragic accident. Despite these adversities, he didn't give up and instead fought to overcome them and, as a result, enjoyed a long and fulfilling life. His road wasn't easy either, but he fought for what he wanted and he found his path. And Bopa lost his mother, father, and sister by age twelve. Imagine that—losing your mother, father, and sister so early. Imagine the pain he must have endured his entire life. Yet he didn't give up. He, too, fought for what he wanted and he, too, enjoyed a long, successful life.

It is terrible having to deal with the disease of addiction, and living a life with the disease will be a struggle. You'll always be able to find reasons why this program or that

program isn't right for you. Don't go looking for such
reasons—they'll only cheat you out of living the life you want.

My wish for you is that you'll set your sights on recovery
and that you'll commit to yourself "I'm going to complete
this program no matter what happens, because more than
anything else I want back the life this disease has stolen
from me." That for the next six months you'll put on blinders
focusing only straight ahead at that finish line where you'll
find that life you want.

I love you.

Papa

By means of an all-out offensive, Bruce has finally spoken with someone higher up the insurance company's chain, and he fills me in as we drive together to Berkeley.

"They've denied coverage for thirty days because of 'no medical necessity.'"

"For god's sake," I say, "even Jake knows it's life or death at this point, at least when he's thinking clearly."

"I know. I haven't given up yet—I'll keep pushing."

We arrive at New Bridge and make our way inside. Jake will be finishing this short program in exactly a week. *Then what?* Before the residents join us in the big room, I pull a counselor aside and spill my frustration about the insurance hassles. It doesn't help to hear her say that this sort of fight is commonplace, that many addicts simply walk off and use while waiting for a green light that never comes. But, she reminds me, "Jake is still here. He's agitated, struggling, but he's still here."

To those of us who've witnessed Jake's past year and a half, it's ludicrous to think he could recover as an outpatient, that he could go off and live somewhere and show up bright and shiny like a Boy Scout every morning eager for a day's work in groups.

During the session, Jake fidgets in his chair next to me while I try to focus on taking deeper breaths. When it's time to say goodbye, Bruce and I each give our son a long hug and place our letters in his hands.

In his documentary *The Anonymous People*, Greg Williams spotlights the widespread problem of getting insurance companies to reimburse treatment nationwide. His film is about the struggles of 23.5 million Americans living in long-term recovery. Williams believes it is time to change everything about our current health-care delivery system and that we can start with small steps. In his work assisting youth and families as a peer recovery coach he came across an opiate-addicted man desperate for treatment. Williams writes, "…because his insurance report said he hadn't failed enough detox/rehab treatments, he was denied any recovery supportive services. The system's actions basically said to this young man, 'If you go out and relapse and come back, *then* we can help you.'"

Where's the sense in that?

23
RELEASING TEARS

You cannot create a statue by smashing the marble with a hammer,
and you cannot, by force of arms, release the spirit or soul of man.
— CONFUCIUS

A N ADDICT CAN BE COMPELLED to blame or disappear when
he feels cornered. Jake still seems poised to disappear but
tries blaming first. On day twenty-six, we meet with him and his
counselor.

In a tiny conference room with mismatched upholstered
chairs, Jake says angrily, "You guys won't let me get back to
college. Rules like a minimum 2.75 GPA, Mom, are ridiculous.
I don't ever want to be under those rules again."

Can he really have convinced himself he would've been fine
continuing on at college? Keeping my voice low, I remind him
that *he* was the one who lost his scholarship when his grades
dipped down.

He tries another tack. "I'm thinking of joining the military
because they'll pay for school."

Gulp. Not a wise choice for an addict. When we step on the snake, addiction's venom shoots out of his mouth, wounding us.

Jake's current roommate is fresh from his second tour in Iraq. He's a twenty-three-year-old muscular marine with a wife and young child. Two of his best buddies were blown up right in front of him. He's been at New Bridge for the past forty-five days fighting his urge to drink, and in the process has come to learn that he also suffers from PTSD. He's been given an additional month to get treatment for that and has orders to ship out again for a third tour.

Jake's counselor speaks up. "You don't want to go that route, Jake."

Bruce and I remain silent.

Maybe the military seems like a way to feel pride, but it's terrifying to imagine an active addict, minus impulse control, with a gun. If he believes our boundaries are tough, wait until he encounters the strictness of the armed forces. Surely when he comes right with his thinking that idea will fade. His addict-self has been holding on all this time, seemingly getting stronger, lasting through days of rehab. What if his thinking never comes right? Would he have a fighting chance within the military's structure, following orders with a firearm?

At the end of our session, the counselor asks Jake, "Just to be clear, what's your understanding with your parents, if you were to walk out of here? What'll your parents offer if you leave?"

"Nothing," he replies.

Although he sounds bitter, he understands exactly where we stand.

"Have you ever been out on the streets?" she asks. "I have, and it's not a place you want to be."

The end of Jake's thirty days approaches. I wait and wonder what he's thinking—what he'll choose to do, whether his attitude has changed, whether New Bridge has helped him find a way to stay if they believe he's committed. That day finally arrives. Bruce, Alea, and I, full of apprehension, troop in to the now familiar meeting room. Every week at the family session, the residents who are leaving the thirty-day program have a chance to speak.

The counselor motions for everyone to quiet down. Jake volunteers to speak first, and stands up. He says he wants to do things differently. Sitting on a hard wooden chair, I lift my chin a little higher and blink as he offers a bit of his history and experience to the group. Then he singles me out, and everything for me suddenly goes out of focus except for him. I believe I've stopped breathing.

He is speaking clearly. "You can never count on your dealer to pick up the phone when you need him, but my mom was always there. Sometimes she just sat silently on the phone with me. Sometimes she offered me encouragement and hope."

His eyes are shining with honesty. I have to squeeze mine shut, as if a sand storm has suddenly blown through, transforming the landscape. When I open them, through spilling tears, I see that his whole body exudes relief as he announces he has stopped debating it, stopped trying to escape it, that New Bridge has offered him a place in the six-month program next door— even helped him figure out the funding—and he's going to take it. Wasn't it just a few weeks ago he told me that nothing inspires him, that he has no feelings? Wasn't it just four days ago that he was fighting this tooth and nail? He looks flooded with emotions now and even uses the word "inspirational" several times. He goes on to talk about eighteen-year-old Zeke, who is graduating from the short program today, too. Zeke has no family here. "He's like a little brother to me," Jake says. "We've shared so much, and I'm so proud he stuck it out." When Jake sits down, all the residents whoop and enthusiastically pump their fists in support of their "New Bridge family."

Zeke speaks up next. He's sweet, funny, and tattooed from head to foot. Just the little he shares of his abused childhood, and life as a dealer in gritty circumstances, causes my heart to squeeze. He thanks Jake for "saving" him from walking out the door his first week. I shoot Jake a proud look. Even at his tender age, Zeke appears to be quite the lady's man. He's made a point of sitting next to my daughter. Unlike Jake, he won't be going into the six-month program; he plans to move in with his grandparents, who've offered him a place to live and get work in Kentucky. I sincerely hope he'll be able to maintain his sobriety.

On the drive home, I mull over my pride, relief, and exhaustion. I know better than to sing from the rooftops because so often when I've carted my hope up high I've only gotten hammered right back down again. Sometimes just in the blink of an eye. It's safer to stay down and allow myself back up, inch by inch, as trust is gained and actions become clear.

A ringing cell phone from the back seat startles me. Bruce asks, "Who's that?"

Alea smiles and says, "Zeke."

———

I have to keep bringing my focus back to myself, to let my son do whatever he will. With Jake safely settled in a long-term program, this could be, for me, a time of healing. Or as Anne Lamott suggests in *Help Thanks Wow*, at least a second wind, "when even though what you want is clarity and resolution, what you get is stamina and poignancy and the strength to hang on." But I drag myself around. A hot bubble bath does nothing to ease the twisting of my stomach. The muscles around my ribcage clench in spasm, leaving me short of breath. Nurturing myself back to normal—back to common sense, back to sanity—is like trying to unsqueeze in slow motion. I book myself a massage. In the semi-darkness I lie back, listen to soothing sounds of a babbling brook, and hear the masseuse oiling up her hands. Even before the first touch, a rush of emotion surprises me and tears just start flowing, strong and steady as they haven't before. Deep vats of sadness begin to siphon off. The hurt has chosen this quiet moment all on its own to spill. I can't seem to summon this release at more convenient times. If I could, I would climb to the top of the nearest mountain and wail.

Pema Chödrön, the Buddhist nun who has inspired millions, shares her teachings in books and on CDs. Her calm comforting voice—reading from *When Things Fall Apart*—washes over me whenever I'm driving.

Things falling apart is a kind of testing and also a kind of healing. We think that the point is to pass the test to overcome the problem, but the truth is that things don't really get solved. They come together and they fall apart. Then they come together again and fall apart again. It's just like that. The healing comes from letting there be room for all of this to happen: room for grief, for relief, for misery, for joy.

I've been certain I could solve this problem—that I could fix it. All my life, I've been driven to avoid uncertainty, to solve problems. Taking charge makes things neat and tidy, predictable, well ordered. Jake is not the only one who needs rewiring.

Carolyn Ball, psychotherapist and author of *Claiming Your Self-Esteem: A Guide Out of Codependency, Addiction, and Other Useless Habits* writes how the powerful introspective work that happens in Twelve-Step programs creates awareness of behavior patterns that are dysfunctional, which results in emotional healing. It's true. Listening to people who have risen from the wreckage, who bravely share their courageous true-life stories, baits me to get up. Slowly, as the weeks go by, I feel I might just be able to take on change. As if Carolyn Ball is aiming words directly at me, she writes,

> When we decide to do what it takes to improve the quality of our lives, we are taking the courageous step to stop putting our energy into trying to make others be different.

24
ONE MORE TREK

Letting go of the fixed self isn't something we can just *wish* to
happen… It's something we predispose ourselves to with every
gesture, every word, every deed, every thought. We're either going
in the direction of letting go and strengthening that ability or going
in the direction of holding on and reinforcing that fear-based habit.
— PEMA CHÖDRÖN, *Living Beautifully*

THERE'S STILL ONE LEFT in the nest. Alea has decided to go on
her own two-week wilderness trek. Last summer, she adamantly refused. But having experienced her brother's absence
and her anger at being left behind to watch her parents suffer—
and suffering herself—she now sees it as an opportunity to let
out her pain, to get clearer about herself, to think about relationships, and to figure out what direction she wants to go in college.

Our family is discovering that one of the best antidotes to
being torn apart by addiction is to piece ourselves back together
in the solitude of nature. Alea is the last of us to go. Since it's July,
she'll be in and around the lakes of Minnesota and the boundary
waters with Lorri.

When Lorri asked me to write an impact letter for Jake's
trek a year and a half ago, it took me days and many revisions.

When she requests one for Alea, I'm able to crank out a five-pager without input and I know I've communicated just what I hoped to, even before Lorri tells me it's heartfelt and just right. Alea will receive it a few days into her trek.

Change is creeping in. But not so much that I don't stress about Alea getting herself packed, through the airport, and to the hotel in Duluth by herself. Bruce just says goodbye and goes off to work, not a shred of worry. Is that because I take care of things? She nearly forgets her hiking boots. Do I do her thinking for her? Sparks begin to fly between us as she sits on her bag and we try to zip it shut. Yet at the airport curb we hug and she flashes me a genuine smile. I'm thrilled she's agreed to go *and* she's elated to be on her own. So why worry?

I worry because I've absolutely perfected that skill. I can even do it in my sleep. My brain never rests. I've cracked another tooth clenching my jaw. In the dead of the night, my thoughts jolt me wide awake. Then my mind zigzags with zillions of what ifs, going from zero to catastrophe in a split second. Worry cements me in misery. Is trying to stop worrying a thousand times a day what resisting craving is like for my son? I relapse every five minutes. I want to cast off worry and emerge shiny and new like a snake shedding its skin.

By focusing on myself and allowing others to take care of themselves, I am striving to replace fruitless worrying with positive change in my own life. My son is working diligently in his own program taking responsibility for himself. My daughter is striking out on her own, exactly as she should. My husband and I are in agreement for the most part in dealing with addiction, and especially since his trek he's engaging more in family life. Yet I need a fresh sword every day to slash away at worry. *Will this ever get easier?*

Lorri forwards Alea's first letter from her trek.

Dear Momma and Papa,

The first twenty-four hours out in the woods has not been glamorous. I learned how to tie a Fisherman's Double, a Daisy Chain, and a Trucker's Hitch and they've already come in handy. The forest that I'm in looks different from the ones in California. The trees are all tall and skinny with white and gray bark. The mosquitoes are incredibly annoying and I squished one in my hair and blood came out. I hope it's not mine. Lorri was so excited to finally meet me. She has already picked off a tick that was crawling up my neck. It's only the first day and I have successfully mined out all the M & M's from my bag of trail mix.

Thanks for the little notes in my hiking boots.

Love, Alea

I read her sweet note twice on my computer screen, then roll back my chair to gaze out my window. These last two years of high school, as her brother got sick, I clung to Alea longer and harder than I should have. We went round and round, her rebelling and me controlling. We're doing so much better, but each time we interact it still feels as though I'm peeling my fingers off one by one.

When she returns, we all plop down on couches in our living room. Bruce and I are eager to hear all about her trip.

"What'd you think of Lorri?" Bruce asks.

"Honestly, she's such a natural-born counselor, just the way she talks. I liked her right away. She taught me a lot about communicating."

I immediately take an opening. "Alea, I want more than anything to share in your life, to listen to what's going on for you, to be there for you."

Her beautiful smile lights up. "I want that too, Momma. I'm tired of keeping secrets from you and even my girlfriends. I've kept myself disconnected."

I lean over to put my arm around her and give her a squeeze.

"I've been so sad about Jake," she says, then pauses. "I feel like he picked drugs over me...and he hasn't been there for me. I could always ask him stuff...we used to be like teammates. Now it's like I'm the one always there for him."

"Yeah, it's been hard, for all of us," I say.

"I'm glad you got to spend time with Lorri," Bruce adds. "She's helped all of us see things more clearly."

"She was great. She helped me look at some unhealthy behaviors...I feel more prepared to start college, and I'm proud of all the introspective work I did."

Bruce and I look at each other, then back at her, witnessing her new and tremendous self-awareness. Then her eyes meet each of ours and she smiles. "Thanks for pushing me to go. It really was a gift."

She takes herself off to another shower to work on those dirty fingernails.

The following week, we once again put into action our new and improved communication skills so Bruce and I can voice our concerns about Alea living away at college and she can share her own thoughts about it. At a time we all agree on, we sit down together, implementing a rule that you can't talk unless you're holding the special painted rock that Alea brought home from Soltrails. We each speak as long as we need, then pass the rock to the next person who wants a turn.

Past "discussions" never lasted more than three minutes, but more than an hour slips by and each of us feels heard. Clearly it's hardest for me not to relapse into old patterns, lectures, and arguments—"Wait, you don't have the rock," Alea reminds me. I try simply to keep listening, and as Alea expounds on her goals and plans for college, my fear lessens and some of my worry dissipates.

———

From my book tower, I pick up *Buddha's Little Instruction Book* and read, "Every life has a measure of sorrow. Sometimes it is this that awakens us." Sorrow has pressed me to work on changing my mindset and to replenish myself at the same time. Jake is immersed in a long residential program, so I should be able to lay that burden down. Alea has just taken a big step for herself. Yet I remain exhausted, as if I'm holding myself in a push-up a few inches from the ground. My children keep me drained of energy to go forward with my own life. I seem to allow that.

Bruce's sister suggests that I consider spending time in her Rome apartment. While my heart responds *Am I ever grateful to have a person like that in my life*, my self-talk whispers *That's frivolous, indulgent*. But I get a little bit excited. Would it be selfish to escape to Italy? Would travel shake me up, or better yet restore me? Would it cut the strings—if only temporarily—that keep me psychologically bound to my children?

Then once again, I take up my yoke and resist.

25
ATTRACTED TO AN ADDICT

We are not born all at once, but by bits. The body first, and the spirit
later; and the birth and growth of the spirit, in those who are
attentive to their own inner life, are slow and exceedingly painful.
Our mothers are racked with the pains of our physical birth; we
ourselves suffer the longer pains of our spiritual growth.
— MARY ANTIN

EARLY AUGUST, ALEA ANNOUNCES that Zeke has been calling her and they've been having lengthy conversations. He's sweeping her off her feet long distance. He invited her to come visit. She wants to buy herself a ticket to fly to Kentucky this weekend. *What? You mean* Zeke, *the eighteen-year-old now sixty days clean from meth? That Zeke?* I use all my strength not to go screaming out of the house. Will any of this *ever* get better?

The realization that my daughter seems undeniably attracted to the addict personality, and has posed this ludicrous proposition, causes me to see red. Couldn't Alea go off to college and find a nice stable business major or shy engineering student? In just a few weeks, she could choose from over ten thousand guys on campus. Instead, she's talking about pursuing a wildly risky relationship halfway across the country. *No, no, no.*

And then the flip side strikes me: Will some mother, someday, feel alarmed for her daughter when she falls for my son?

The evening when he and Jake finished the thirty-day program, every person in the room responded to Zeke's sweet, fun, attractive energy. When we learned his stepfather had horribly abused him, that he only had a seventh-grade education, our hearts went out to him; we leaned forward, realizing he was doing the best he could without much, wanting to help even as our lesson for the evening was to learn that an addict needs to do things for himself. At the end of the meeting I hugged him sincerely, sad for him that his own mother wasn't there. I wasn't, however, extending an invitation to join our family.

Bruce and I diffuse our feelings by talking to each other first; our teamwork gets me calm and clear. We all agree that we'll talk on Tuesday, when we're home together before heading to New Bridge for the family meeting.

We gather in our living room. Bruce says, "Alea, you are more informed than most kids your age about the world of addiction, and you've seen bad things happen firsthand."

Alea lets out a long slow breath then presses her lips together. I notice she didn't bring the talking rock.

I speak up next. "Thinking about beginning a relationship, or encouraging a spark, should be a good thing. Unfortunately with an addict—especially someone in early recovery—it might be hazardous."

Alea crosses her arms and looks off in the direction of the ceiling molding.

I forge on. "We've all heard the counselors advise addicts against getting involved in relationships for the first whole year of recovery because of the vulnerability of those emotions— they risk relapse."

Bruce says, "Zeke doesn't have the support of a place like New Bridge, carefully screening visitors to keep him focused—he's living with his grandparents."

Alea still doesn't say anything but she juts out her jaw.

"Zeke's sobriety needs to be his primary focus for months," I say, "just like for Jake."

I can hear Lorri counseling Bruce as he continues—*Pose questions, so Alea can think through the situation for herself.*

"There are consequences to choices, Alea. What is a safe choice for your heart? How do you think your choices might influence Zeke so early in his recovery?"

She doesn't answer. I jump back in, working hard not to fall back on old patterns of control. "You have a right to your feelings, and you can't help those feelings, but you don't have to act on them. There are consequences to precarious actions. You can be intentional."

Like many teenagers, once Alea hears "no" she quits listening—she's angry. She stands up abruptly and stomps off, flinging her first and last comment over her shoulder, "Well, I guess I'll just have to wait a month and go visit him from college—when I get to *make my own decisions.*"

I'm incredulous that she's willing and enthusiastic to make this leap, and I desperately want to head off the wreck I see coming. Zeke must feel like a connection to Jake, someone she can talk to about her brother, someone who has been through what her brother has, someone who has recently been connected with him...someone who can fill the emptiness within her.

Alea can't hole up in her room for long; this is her last chance to see Jake before she leaves for college, and we need to get going to Berkeley. In the long program, the counselors hold monthly family sessions, rather than weekly. Loved ones are first screened, then invited in to learn how the residents are working hard at recovery. The real prize is the twenty minutes saved at the end for a visit with our recovering addict.

Just as we're walking out the door, the phone rings. It's my neighbor offering to walk Bella. She remembers that the first Tuesday of the month is the evening we visit Jake, and knows how guilty I feel leaving our energetic Labrador shut up in the house for so long. I burst into tears at her unexpected kindness. And then, like the swish of a horse's tail, I decide I will go to Rome, travel, put physical distance between me and this mess.

In the car, there's no further discussion between the three of us. Alea's ears are connected to her iPod and she's expressionless staring out the window. A purple dusk stretches across the sky. My stewing in traffic melds with my simmering powerlessness over my daughter, but as we finally near the treatment center, my emotions begin to shift toward eagerness to see Jake.

After the families-only meeting, in a room crammed with fifty people all talking at once, the four of us sit clustered on metal chairs pulled tightly together. Jake's cheeks are plump. He's wearing a pressed dress shirt and necktie, his dark hair buzzed short. The hole in his ear from his gauge is beginning to close up. He talks a mile a minute—something he hasn't always been able to do—describing his daily routine, his job requirements, groups, the counselors, and various clients. His eyes are animated, steady, and he looks directly at each of us. Not once does he say, "Get me out of here." All too soon, visiting time is over. Jake gives Alea a huge hug and wishes her well for her freshman year. His expression is tinged with bittersweet regret but he turns to his dad and me and hugs the two of us at once. When we climb back into our car, Alea sums things up succinctly. "Damn, that's the old Jake."

There's extra emotion spilling over as Alea packs up her bags a couple weeks later. She still intends to visit Zeke after she gets settled at college—an addict in early recovery, a guy she spent only a few hours with in a room full of people—which has me extremely anxious. Worry does no good, yet there it is again. I tell Alea I can't control her decision to go see Zeke, but I don't have to agree with it, either. Trying to leave a side door open on this train about to barrel down the tracks, I say, "You can always change your mind about going to see him. Think about what's right for you."

Three years ago, wrapped up in the natural parental emotion of sending a child off into the world, I hugged Jake in front of his freshman dorm. I had no suspicion of substance abuse, yet I felt an underlying uneasiness. An involuntary sob materialized the moment I hugged him, as if somewhere in my depths a part of me was afraid of what lay ahead.

Loaded down with her duffle bags, Alea and I arrive on this same campus with its red roofs of clay-barrel tile and walls of native sandstone. She's been assigned to the dorm next to Jake's old one. Bruce and I have asked ourselves if we're doing things differently this time. We regret that we allowed Jake to return to college after he failed two classes freshman year, and Alea knows there will be no second chances for her. We've all agreed she needs to achieve the minimum GPA or better each semester to keep her scholarship in order for us to continue paying for school. She's on a tight budget, our money as well as hers. She agrees to make use of the counseling department and to find an Al-Anon meeting to build a support network. She's seen how easily college ambitions can be curtailed, which we hope will produce caution and focus in her. Above all, we want to keep honest communication going, so we plan on weekly Sunday phone calls.

It's time for my daughter to take the wheel of her own life. I hope to continue transitioning to a supportive parent who sits quietly in the back seat. I want to be part of the journey but I don't want to tell her how to steer. Shifting away from being in the center of my children's lives is much harder for me than for Bruce. I want to be square in the middle of my own life yet I keep relapsing by taking over and "helping." Thinking of this behavior as relapsing helps me understand Jake's challenges. Just as he convinced himself that drugs were not his problem, I can easily persuade myself that inserting my solution—even before Alea realizes she has a problem—is my motherly duty. I want to intercept pain for her just as I did for Jake.

She and I spend two days hustling around in ninety-five degree heat, up and down four flights of stairs moving her stuff in, buying bedding, setting up her room, and meeting chatty floormates, until we're both worn out. I want to leave her organized, confident, and happy to start the new semester. While she crawls under her dorm bed to untangle computer cords from extension cords, a thousand excuses for her not to go visit Zeke rattle around in my head. My "practical" inner voice argues that this is my last chance to convince her, face to face, that she's crazy to pursue such a risky relationship. *Don't stay silent.* Stupidly, I listen to that voice instead of my budding mind-your-own-business one. I launch the Zeke conversation because I just can't leave it alone. Relapsed again. We're both on overload—perspiring, emotional, and not particularly rational. A few hours earlier, I made the mistake of entering Target holding an endless list, truly hungry, which resulted in me having a meltdown over the price of a desk lamp Alea wanted, and miserably weaving an overflowing cart around hundreds of overwhelmed college students and their parents. I resorted to being passive aggressive until we finally got some food.

It's lousy timing to voice my thoughts about Zeke. An argument ignites and we both end up upset. Then my best idea of the day finds its way to my lips. "Let's go find a quiet place outside on this beautiful campus and just sit." Tearfully, she agrees. After the shopping malls, buzzing dorms, and the pressure from all the new faces, we find solitude and spread out a plastic bag to sit side by side on the watered grass under a spreading tree.

Like a reassuring friend, the rocky Flatirons are a quiet presence. We get calm watching the pattern of light and shadow play on textured masonry walls. I'm wondering whether I should leave her—she seems so emotional, uncertain, vulnerable. I try to steady myself to think. Trembling and pulling out what I hope are words of comfort and connection while tears I can't stop spill down, I tell her, "Honey, you're building such muscle for yourself in starting your life here, changing nearly every aspect of it, and figuring it all out, little by little. Remember all these freshmen are going through similar emotions. Most are scared and excited. They're anxious and exhausted. Savor your accomplishments. It's a lot you're figuring out."

Gusts from nowhere start to pick up and the temperature begins to cool. We're not used to how fast the weather can change in the mountains. A minute ago I was sweaty; now I shiver. She's quiet but listening.

"Alea, take time to be kind to yourself. Tackle one thing a day to figure out. Instead of saying 'yes' to your new neighbor to walk all the way back to the crowded bookstore when you're hot, exhausted, and already have your books, you might say, 'How about getting together for dinner later?'"

"What if I don't like it here? I don't have any friends. I feel all alone."

"It feels that way at first. Be patient. You'll make good friends."

Suddenly it might rain. Just as unexpected as the darkening clouds, Alea pours out how she misses her brother, how she hoped to join him here, how she never thought college life would take him down.

We're both a mess of heavy emotion.

"We have to be patient," I say, my voice quavering. "It'll take time for him to recover. He's in a safe place. It's hard on all of us."

I desperately need to set down the world I've been trying to hold up. I miss Jake terribly, too. I'm dreadfully sad that he's not here. Like a weary Atlas, I can't hold up any longer under this weight.

Silence. A few raindrops splash our legs and shoulders as fresh tears wet my cheeks. Love—a sharp lance—twists in deep.

My big exhale soars out, swirling into the wind now whipping the tree branches over our heads. "What sounds good to you right now, Alea? What do you need?"

"Listening to my music on my bed, taking a shower and drinking some hot chocolate."

"Sounds wonderful. How about I drop you off at your dorm and then go buy you some stamps and envelopes so you can write to Jake? That's all we can do to connect with him right now."

When I return from my errand, I see Alea striding across the parking lot toward me, long blond hair blowing behind her. She's changed into fresh clothes—shorts, leg warmers, and her Ugg boots. She doesn't notice she's turning guys' heads. As she marches past one boy standing with a cluster of his friends, he actually clutches his heart and feigns falling over. Since she's taken some time alone, I witness a huge energy shift in her. Both of us are absolutely dry-eyed as we're at last ready to say goodbye. We give each other a bear hug and separate, smiling.

26
EMPTY NEST

Don't judge each day by the harvest you reap,
but by the seeds you plant.
— ROBERT LOUIS STEVENSON

ENVIOUS OF MY TRAVEL PLANS, Bruce has cleared his calendar.
We cash in miles for air tickets, borrow the key to the Rome
flat, and sleep upright in coach.

Landing in Zürich, we train first to a tiny village in the Swiss
Alps and hike during the pleasant September days. Each morning we set off in a different direction, rambling along incredible
trails close to glaciers then into high meadows dotted with cows,
the bells strapped to their necks tinkling merrily. The Eiger,
Mönch, and Jungfrau—each spectacular in its own right—
tower magnificently three in a row.

In the days after returning from Boulder without Alea,
I moved as if through molasses in my empty quiet clean house.
Way up in the shadow of the Eiger, I want to send out a mighty
gush, to blast sadness and deadness from my life. I want to leave

it all here. But the coldness—solid like this glacier—isn't ready to be dislodged.

Instead of thinking about heroin addiction, codependent behavior, and the dysfunctional boys in my daughter's life, I try to keep my mind on my feet traversing miles of footpaths. I'm mesmerized by the fortitude of climbers who scale this rugged North Face. Along crisscrossing routes, we eat delicious cheeses and sausages served in the open air from tiny family huts and watch paragliders—brave souls suspended from brilliantly colored kite-like wings—leaping off ridges to ride air currents, spiraling lazily toward a distant landing spot in the valley below. At night, we hungrily devour savory soups, crusty bread, salads, local rosti and pork. We drink wine from the steeply terraced vineyards along the shores of Lake Geneva planted hundreds of years ago by monks. We read novels—addiction books are banned on this break—and fall into bed under downy duvets. The physical distance from home is restorative. Some perspective sprouts. This beautiful world is one that gives back as well as takes.

It seems a world ago when our family lived in Rome's historic Jewish quarter. Memories flood back as we arrive. We're swept into the commotion that is Rome, jarring at first, but we leave all the noise behind when we climb three flights of stone stairs and turn the heavy metal key in the lock. The slightly sloped hardwood floor squeaks as we step in. This is a different apartment from the one we lived in seven years ago but the stone, wood, and centuries give it the same familiar smell.

For our first meal, we head to the family-run pizzeria that our kids loved best. The waiters used to tease Jake because he wanted his gnocchi without parmesan and his bruschetta without tomatoes. Bruce orders what he knows will be a mouthwatering pizza margherita and I repeat Jake's best sentence in Italian, *"Gnocchi*

al pomodoro sensa formaggio e bruschetta bianca, si?" I swear I see a
flicker across the waiter's face; his eyes seem to be asking me, *are
you that American kid's mom?*

For days we alternate between soaking in the complete still-
ness inside our comfortable refuge and strolling through Rome's
bustling streets, avoiding the tourists as much as possible, walking familiar routes to touch a favorite fountain, to say "Buon
giorno, signore" to Attilio, our old neighbor who has just turned
eighty-six, to gobble a mouthwatering dish of Rome's traditional
carbonara, and to taste some new gelato flavors. We try to get
back to what it's like to be a couple not in crisis. The lines on
our faces soften. Life flows again. Our time together reminds us
that we have each other to lean on going forward, though neither
knows what's ahead.

————

The last week of September we settle back into our routine at
home. With Alea away at school, our nest seems especially empty.
I'd hoped for a letter from Jake, since we missed this month's
rehab visit, but nothing is waiting. I doubt he'll call, either. He
doesn't like the process for phone privileges—first you sign up
for a reserved time slot for a five-minute call, then you go down
to the basement to wait your turn, finally you put the telephone
on speaker so your call can be monitored. He usually only calls
when he needs something.

A couple days later, just as I'm dashing out, my phone rings.
Jake sounds upbeat and full of life.

"I wrote you a letter but it got stuck in the no-communication
shutdown, so it should be coming any day. The whole house's
been on restriction."

"What does that mean, 'on restriction'?"

"Basically, since the residents do all the jobs, we run the
house. If the counselors notice that not everyone's being one
hundred percent forthright—like we aren't holding each other

accountable—the staff steps in and takes over. Then there're no visits, no passes, no calls...nobody going out, nobody coming in."

"How long was the shutdown?"

"Fourteen days."

"Well, I look forward to getting the letter."

He quickly tells me in the minute he has left, "I've put on thirty-five pounds so I've outgrown three out of my four dress shirts."

"Thirty-five pounds!"

"Yeah, I'm working out."

"Do you have to wear dress shirts much?"

"Only every day, all day, with a tie. So could you see if I have a few more in my closet, especially any large ones, and bring them to the next visit? *And* bring my other pair of dress shoes?"

I don't mind at all that he asks for something; he sounds great.

His letter arrives the next day. He describes getting lots of practice in juggling different responsibilities, learning patience, and practicing time management. No complaints. I feel like I've been crossing the Sahara carrying him on my back, and his engagement in this program has arisen like a shimmering oasis. I call New Bridge to see if I might be allowed to bring him a small birthday gift next week when we come for the October family visit. His case manager says I can leave the present, but that Jake won't receive it for two weeks, because he's on restriction. He won't be permitted a visit, either. My buoyancy pops. How quickly things change. I don't comprehend the specifics of the infraction because I'm so disappointed that we won't be able to see him for yet another month—something about Jake being warned about an inappropriate conversation, and not heeding the warning.

Rules have unwavering consequences at New Bridge. This sometimes seems harsh, but the counselors have explained that an addict needs to learn to pay attention to warning bells because a slip out in the world could happen lightning fast. Listening to their supportive friends is a skill they need to develop.

I consider slogging through hours of rush-hour traffic to the family lecture next Tuesday, to drop off the clothes and gift even though I won't get to see Jake. Then Bruce and I realize we'll be traveling that way for a dinner this Saturday, so I gain permission from the rehab to drop his stuff off then.

As we enter New Bridge carrying several ironed button-down shirts, a new wallet, and two ties wrapped up in a bow, Jake is standing tall in an adjoining room. I'd truly wished to catch a glimpse of him and here he is. I blow him a kiss and he beams. After we sign in, the guy keeping track of who comes in and out kindly asks us to sit on the waiting couch. Jake walks right over and gives us hugs. I keep expecting someone to shepherd him away, to not allow him to speak to us, but no one does. Surprised, we enjoy ninety seconds together.

"How're you?"

"Jake, you look so good!"

He glances down at the box tied with red ribbon in my big bag. Then he's asked to step back across the threshold and we're left just cheerfully looking at each other across the busy room. The place is humming with activity. Some residents are eating a meal in the next room, and others are carrying dirty dishes back to the kitchen. One is standing pondering a huge white board attached to the wall. It looks like he's redoing a complicated schedule. Another is sitting ignored and silent in a chair next to our couch. Looks like he's been sitting there all day.

Jake mouths, "I'm a hundred and ninety pounds!" and turns profile like a proud expectant mother to display his brand-new potbelly. We all smile some more. The residents are in motion coming and going, except when they stop to cross over the threshold into the next room. Then each pauses and asks, "Permission to cross over?" and the guy who signed us in responds, "Permission granted," and they continue on their way. Everybody appears focused. A woman calls us around the corner where I deposit the bag I've brought so they can search through it. She reiterates that Jake can't receive it, nor any mail either, until he's off restriction.

When we come back, Jake is gone. I ask if he's around the corner in the dining room, and could I wave goodbye, but he's gone downstairs. *Oh well, that was nice.* My feet barely touch the floor as I float out with a light heart. When Jake's twenty-first birthday rolls around in three days—a day that will pass like any other for him—I'll know that he's alive and well and that eventually he'll get a little present and a cute homemade card. He may not realize he has given us a gift in return—continuing on in rehab. We are grateful that he's working on his self-sabotaging tendencies and doing battle to shrink his disease down to size. It's like when my lime tree unexpectedly drops and rolls a lime onto my patio. After waiting months for one to ripen, I come upon a perfect unsolicited gift.

The behavior-modification component of this therapeutic community appears to be motivating Jake to pursue recovery. There's an AA saying, "If you always do what you always did, you'll always get what you always got," which the program seems to be pounding in. Jake is surrounded by really down-and-out people, just like him, fighting for another chance at life. I know to keep my expectations low and my hope from soaring.

27
STAY OUT OF IT

I've always lived as if finding (and holding on to) the answers
was the point of life. But it suddenly struck me that true
enlightenment consists in being empty, not full, of answers, that
people who are full of answers must drag them around all day like an
over-packed suitcase, with no reason for anything new.
— Phyllis Theroux, *The Journal Keeper*

ALEA REFUSES TO CHANGE her mind about missing a week of
school to visit Zeke. Bruce is livid that she would jeopardize
her success in her classes by being gone. There have been emails
and calls back and forth trying to keep the dialogue open. I want
to say something that will get her to give up the plan. But she
goes. My beautiful baby girl...so reckless. I tell her, "You have the
responsibility of your happiness and pain squarely on you." It is
several days before I realize the same goes for me.

Sadly, Alea has a great time. Her long-distance romance with
Zeke continues; she even schedules another trip to Kentucky,
after the first of the year. If she wants to pursue a relationship
with a newly recovering addict, and doesn't want to hear how
painful that could be from me, I hope she gets herself to Al-Anon
to hear stories from others. Last week I heard a speaker share

how three times she met, married, and divorced husbands—all three alcoholics. It took those marriages and divorces to finally gain awareness of her painful pattern. "If there's one alcoholic in a crowded room, that's the person I'm drawn to," she declared. Her increasing understanding of her behavior helps her at least to be intentional about her future relationships.

The first Tuesday of November, after the family lecture, we finally get to visit with Jake. He tells us he heard about Alea and Zeke because Alea wrote him a letter. "I'm *shocked*. I still don't know what to think. Zeke's a sweetheart of a guy but that's risky. I never thought *that* would happen."

Jake looks vibrant. He switched from laundry detail to the "greeter" job over in the next building where the new guys come in for the short program. He says he can remember how scared and unsure he felt when he walked in five months ago. He gets up at 6:30 a.m. and finishes at 10:30 at night. Sundays are luxurious because he gets to sleep in until 8:00 a.m. New Bridge is hosting an upcoming Thanksgiving meal on the day after the holiday since the program does not allow clients to go home. That should help make up for these frustratingly short visits.

Alea arrives home for her Thanksgiving break. After dorm living, she's eager to luxuriate in her own bedroom and bathroom and to enjoy some home cooking. She tells us all about school but avoids the subject of Zeke. She, Bruce, and I vote on how we want to spend Thanksgiving Day. It doesn't feel comforting to any of us to gather with relatives without Jake. I stand firm with my mother that we're celebrating this year with just the three of us, though I'm met with raised eyebrows and questions. On Thanksgiving morning, we help a charity deliver turkeys. Then we go for a hike and each cook a dish for our little table for three. We are thankful Jake is getting stronger, thankful to think of him as safe, thankful he is six months clean and working hard.

The following evening, in a large room in a senior center, Jake and thirty-five other residents from New Bridge—two thirds of them men, the rest women—wait for family to trickle in. All the men look sharp in their dress shirts, ties, and short haircuts. Women are in dresses or skirts; makeup is not allowed. The room is set up with round bare tables and folding chairs and our family is assigned to one of them. One client, Joe, sits at our table, too, because he's currently not in "good standing" and his family hasn't been allowed to attend. There's time to get to know him as we wait our turn to get paper plates, plastic forks, and knives and then line up for the buffet turkey dinner.

Families have been assigned to contribute a dessert, and I point out my homemade pumpkin pie to Jake among the assortment of sweets. Alea chatters away to her brother. How does he feel, listening to her talk about her first few months at college? She imagines him back to normal, busily showing him pictures on her phone of places in Boulder, off-campus parties, and Zeke. I want to reach over and throw that dumb phone out the window. If I were Jake, I would indulge in a little self-pity right about now. Despite his strong physical appearance and wonderful progress, I sense fragility following him like a shadow.

As he finishes seconds and Bruce chats with Joe, I ask, "What are your thoughts about where you'll go from here?" and his shoulders go up.

His answer is evasive. What's clear is his anxiety. Upcoming change and the long rocky road ahead scares me, too. He talks about wanting to get back to college full-time, as soon as possible.

He asks, "Would you be willing at this point to finance it?"

"Hmmm." I think of the guidelines we set out back in the spring—that we would talk about college if he completed a program, if his treatment team confirmed that he was ready to move on. But shouldn't he take other steps first, find a job, get established in a sober house, become a regular at AA or NA meetings, get a sponsor? Shouldn't he figure out the basics of stringing a life together, public transportation, grocery shopping, cooking?

"We'll have to think about that."

I worry that Jake won't have enough support when his six months are up, in a little over six weeks. It seems like he still has a long way to go. When dinner is over, I speak briefly with one of his counselors.

"Sometimes," the counselor says, "they need to stay a little longer."

How should we respond to Jake about college? For several days, Bruce and I go back and forth discussing it. Not long ago, I asked a woman in Al-Anon to be my sponsor and I seek her wise counsel now. Her advice is to keep any answer simple and avoid spelling out any steps in detail, which helps Bruce and me come to agreement. I'm still writing down scripts in case Jake calls.

Jake, you have done an amazing job getting yourself through this program. What a great opportunity that they offer continued support at their sober house and an evening aftercare program. We hear how impatient you are to get back to college classes. We would pay for one community college class for now. It makes sense to talk about any more classes further down the road.

When I finally get Jake's primary counselor on the phone—Dr. Coysh—he lets out all the air I've just pumped into my tires.

"Do you need to tell him anything?" he asks me. "Is that script for you or for him?"

"Huh?"

"You're in Al-Anon, right? You know the answer."

I still don't quite grasp what he means.

"Picture this," he says. "Jake recently got kicked out of a group because he wasn't participating. He just got invited back and now he has to come before a large group of his peers and explain his aftercare plan. They will hammer him with questions. *This is hard.* He won't get through a paragraph without tears. He'll have to come back again with a revised plan, and perhaps do that many times. The hope is he will eventually come to a solution on his own. He may need to stay a few months longer; he's not showing he's ready."

"Ohhhh." *Now* I get it. Jake doesn't need to hear anything from me. But wasn't it a fair question for him to ask, and for me to answer? I sink deeper into my chair. There's always another degree of staying out of it that is not immediately apparent to me. His peers have all kinds of questions, just like me, about how Jake would protect his sobriety while starting right back up in college—*and* it's not my problem to solve. Jake needs to work it out with his recovery people, not me.

Having been reminded that my job is simply cheerleader, I rewrite my script:

Look how far you've come! Take the time you need to build your support system. There's no rush. It might be hard to be patient with yourself. I know I struggle with that. If you need a sounding board for your ideas or plans, I'm here to listen.

———

It takes all the way to the end of the semester for things to fall apart between Alea and Zeke. As we're standing around talking with other parents after an Al-Anon meeting, Bruce switches on his phone and it instantly rings. I can hear our daughter wailing into his ear. He passes the phone over to me. Alea, stricken, has discovered that Zeke has been with another girl. I keep reminding myself: *Name her pain, empathize with how terrible she must feel and how difficult this is, don't try to fix it.*

"Oh Alea, this must be so hard." I walk over to a quiet corner in the room.

"How can I go through this *again*, Momma?"

"Honey, I know when Jake sends me down the hole, I can get back out faster than I used to. It doesn't hurt for as long. Remember how you told me recently that even though it really hurt when Ben kept breaking up with you, you were glad you finally made the decision to break up with *him,* and you don't care a whit about him now?"

She sniffs. "Yeah, he's a jerk."

"Can you imagine a time somewhere in the future when you might not feel anything for Zeke? That he can't hurt you? Try to imagine that now as you channel your energy into your finals."

She blows her nose.

"In five days you can bring all your pain home in your suitcase and I'll put my arms around you."

A couple hours later I call again to check on her. She's sitting in the hallway of her dorm because she doesn't want to cry in front of her roommate.

"You're not thinking of anesthetizing the pain are you? Pain is part of this—you have to feel the pain."

"Why would I *want* to feel pain, Momma?"

"Because feeling it is the only way through it. You've got support for yourself deep inside you."

"I don't feel like I have any right now."

"At this moment it seems that way. Each day will get better."

"Momma, can you cancel that flight I made to Kentucky?"

"Of course I can. Good night, honey."

"Good night, Momma. I love you."

I set the phone down gently. My daughter is beginning to recognize her attraction to addicts, and how much it can hurt. She manages to get through finals week and onto the plane home for winter break.

Zeke, we later learn, relapses after the first of the year and his grandmother kicks him out.

Another Christmas looms without Jake. At the mall, "Joy! Joy! Joy!" jingles from every doorway. I look around at people Christmas shopping—shoes on sale surround me, jewelry looks dull, piles of pawed-through clothing seem useless—and a terrible sadness settles upon me. Retail therapy has never worked for me. I can't seem to find a gift to suit anyone. I cry all the way home.

My phone is ringing when I step into the house.

"Momma, I've decided to go to New Bridge's sober house and get a job and take a class at the community college."

That's one phone call you don't want to miss.

"Jake, that's wonderful—that sounds like a great plan!"

"I'm going to need to extend my stay here an extra month at New Bridge because it's going to take some time to find a job over the holidays. Actually, I don't have permission yet to look for a job, but they'll give it to me soon."

We both know it will cost $350 a week to extend. I pause at his pause. More silence…and then he does it.

"Will you and Papa pay for me to extend my time here?" Jake is *asking me directly* for support for his clear plan. He's not just assuming; he's not showing entitlement.

My heart beats faster yet I calmly say, "Thank you for telling me your plan, and for asking me for what you need. Yes, we'll be glad to pay their weekly fee as you search for a job."

"Thanks, Momma. My time's up, gotta go."

His voice—I hear the shift in attitude in his voice. I have waited these past dreadful years to hear that tone in his voice. I'm filled with fresh hope and don't need any other Christmas present.

Part Six

NOT KNOWING

28
A LITTLE BIT OF JOY

Christmas for me was about as good as a Christmas
in rehab can be, which is about mediocre.
— JAKE

FOR A LONG TIME, I've been climbing up a mountain, longing for all this to end, wanting to begin the journey back down. I'm tired of picking my way around boulders and gullies. I'd like to throw uncertainty over the cliff and come upon something familiar, to rest upon level ground, but I know I may have to scramble up again. I don't know whether I'm on a lone peak or surrounded by an entire range because the view is shrouded in clouds. I've built strength and resilience, but I just don't want to climb anymore.

It's not easy to remember what we were like before, what I was like. Memories of a good mother don't sally forth—it's as if she never was. Is it like that for Jake? Doubt is ugly. The blackness of addiction erases sweet memories as if a claw has reached out and snatched them away.

I remember baking chocolate chip cookies in our apartment in Rome when we'd been there only a few months. Bruce and I stumbled on an international market that sold brown sugar and chocolate chips, a real find. At the bus stop, we waited with our heavy bags, impatient to return home. When the crowded bus pulled up, we squeezed into the stale humid space.

I began mixing up the dough as soon as we unloaded the bags. The kids were still at school. The oven smoked a bit whenever I first heated it up so I opened the big kitchen window. I cracked an egg into the batter, stirred—and heard English words. *Someone around here speaks English?* An American voice seemed to be floating up from a skinny window across a narrow space between buildings, about ten feet over and down a bit.

When our children burst through the door, Alea tipped up her nose and sniffed the air. Jake searched my face for confirmation that the delicious aroma was, in fact, chocolate chip cookies, his favorite. I nodded and they both dropped their backpacks and scrambled into the kitchen to find the full plate, still warm.

"I have another surprise, too," I said. "Listen!"

As they munched, more English words glided in. All of us stood still like Bernini statues.

"It sounds like a girl," said Jake.

The ancient buildings surrounding us were a warren of apartments—not exactly easy to walk over and knock on the correct door.

Bruce suggested, "Why don't you guys write a note and send it over as a paper airplane?"

"Yeah, Jake—c'mon," said Alea excitedly.

They spent the next hour experimenting, folding the best plane and practicing with it so that it would be sure to fly straight. Alea announced that she would write the note—introducing herself and all of us—and elected Jake to throw it, since he had the most consistent results in their preliminaries. It landed in the flower pot on the ledge and hung precariously on a fern. Alea checked every half hour to see if the English-speakers would discover it before it fell or blew away. By bedtime she couldn't stand it any longer, so she rewrote the note, wadded it up, and threw it like a baseball into the open window.

The next morning, as the kids hurried to get out the door to catch the early school bus, a return baseball sailed through our window and landed next to Jake's breakfast plate. He uncrumpled it to read that a family from California had moved in but were only staying a month. The aroma of baking chocolate was driving them wild.

"Later," I said, "when you get home from school, you can send over another note offering them some cookies and explaining it's a *long* bus ride to buy those ingredients. Hurry up now, *your* bus won't wait."

———

Jake calls on December 30. I often have to guess what he's thinking or wanting because addicts can be anything but direct.

"Hi, Momma, how're you?"

I pause. I'm not used to him asking.

"Fine, how're you?"

"Good. Are you still working on the steps with your sponsor?"

"Yeah. I just finished step one. What step are you on?"

"Step two." When we commiserate that steps two and three will be challenging, he says, "Step one is the one you need to do perfectly."

"Progress, not perfection," I say, reminding him of one of the slogans. Side-by-side recovery—who would've thought Jake and I would connect over "recovery speak"?

"But Momma, what're you doing the steps on? Not alcohol or addiction, right?" There's a brief silence as he thinks it through. "Oh," he answers himself. "Me."

"Yeah," I say, smiling. "But actually I'm powerless over your sister, your dad, and everyone else too, so it works for anything."

Whoever is monitoring his call must prod him because after what sounds like a moment of reflection he says, "Well, the reason I'm calling is I'm wearing out my shoes here. Could you buy a pair of original authentic black Vans, size eleven, and bring them? I'll pay you back."

"Okay... I'll try to get them this week"

"Thanks, Momma."

This conversation astounds me. My son has stepped outside of himself and asked how I'm doing. Addicts are not normally out there worrying about the folks at home, but he's made a big leap to think of me. And he couldn't have been more forthright in his request, down to the precise description of the shoes he needs.

Over a simple phone call, you can be joyous as Rudolf Nureyev standing ankle deep in a pool of flowers absorbing a standing ovation. You can forget about the parents who boast about their kid's A+ grades and full schedule of AP classes, or their son scoring all the goals in a season-ending game, or their daughter volunteering in a remote corner of the earth before being accepted to Harvard. When your kid goes down the dark hole of addiction, you just have to step away from the comparison game that rages in Silicon Valley. It's beautiful to realize you don't want to play that game, anyway. Who you are comes into focus instead of what you do. Addiction, like a needle trailing a long thread, weaves itself into your life, binding you to those with addiction in their lives, too. It feels good to be around them, to see and hear of their progress, to understand their struggles because you have those struggles too. Cutting out the extraneous leaves truth, honesty, and responsibility. Those are the achievements you want. Is your kid alive today? Yes? Okay, you're good for the next twelve hours or so. You spend more time reading, reflecting, paying attention, listening—and one day you look up and notice that things are a bit better, you've figured out a way to move forward, to keep your nose out of the nest of bees, to lend a hand or an ear when it's asked for, to focus on the present moment, to notice the beautiful sky. Life becomes more satisfying. Your daughter calls and asks for your advice. Your son, formulating his early recovery plan, asks if Sunday evenings work for family dinners. You decide to play Scrabble in front of the fire with your husband on New Year's Eve.

——

Like letters sent on a ship across the ocean in the old days, interactions with Jake are slow. Alea, when she pulled out pen and paper to write him from college, waited months for a letter in return. We discover we can be intentional with what we write because we are regularly left to reflect, to let our thoughts wander the old fashioned way. We develop patience; we learn that waiting is painful. Alea will only have one chance to see Jake over her winter break, in a crowded room at New Bridge after the Tuesday lecture. The few minutes we've had face to face with him can fit into my two cupped hands. We are joyous over any connection—a letter, his face, a five-minute call.

Jake is struggling with impatience. All through December he hoped and prayed to be put on "job search" status. He doesn't want his time in the residential program to extend any longer than necessary, but he needs to be earning a paycheck to cover the rent before he can move a few blocks over to the sober house. The treatment team is intentionally frustrating Jake, not giving him what he wants, seeing how he handles his impatience and desire for instant gratification. During these six months, he's held various jobs at New Bridge, including Head of the House, an honor and a responsibility. Recently, however, he laughingly told us he is now Head of Maintenance and manages a "crew of three." Not many people vacuum and clean toilets while sporting a tie, but the head counselor believes Jake is not used to putting real effort into anything—doors have always opened for him, and he could use more practice with humility, which is not uncommon with this disease.

The longstanding program at New Bridge has a strong self-help ethos. Its clear structure, expectations, rules, and consequences force clients to confront the daily behavior that is intertwined with behaviors of drug and alcohol abuse. After months of raising their awareness of destructive conduct and practicing alternative solutions within residential treatment, clients—when they are deemed ready—move on to the outside world. The treatment team at New Bridge knows how crucial this step can be to staying clean, so those who move ahead are encouraged to reach back a hand to those coming along behind, creating a mighty chain.

The counselors are tough on residents with excuses. They know that people who've lost their sense of purpose need to be part of something larger than themselves. The power of service is pounded in; the gift is in the giving. After all the badness of addiction's symptoms and behaviors, service is simply goodness. If you're doing something for others, you're less likely to be thinking about yourself. You're presenting yourself as a role model, a potential leader. You feel the eyes on your back of those coming up behind you. Small steps made with effort lead to big change. When you move to the sober house, staying connected to the residential house with your time and energy—and especially your heart—is central to your transition.

Jake needs to prove he wants the opportunity to live in the sober house and the chance to continue on with aftercare. Dr. Coysh, his counselor, tells me to think of it like this: Jake's genuine-self atrophied to a weak puny state while his addicted-self mushroomed into a strong giant. The result of the work Jake's been doing all these months has shrunk that addiction monster down and increased the strength of his true-self, the one we all know and love. The monster will always sit on his shoulder but now, at least, it's a fair fight. His lifetime work will be to "take his medicine," which means to stay connected to a strong sober recovery community. By the first week of January, Jake still hasn't been allowed to search for a job. On a call, we hear his growing frustration. He sounds about ready to explode.

"I'm having to really advocate for myself," he announces. "I asked Dr. Coysh if he could sit at my table for dinner last night— that I needed to talk to him."

"What'd you say?" asks Bruce.

"I told him I'm *not* going to let anything they throw at me wreck my chances of going to the sober house since I've put so much into New Bridge already," he declares. "The only way I'm going out is from the red chair."

"What's that?" I ask.

"It's the seat reserved for people who complete the residential program and 'cross over.'"

"You mean for graduates."

"No. Graduation happens at least a year after that. They do a big ceremony once a year." He explains that first you have to complete requirements like supporting yourself, attending out-patient groups three nights a week, paying a small back-debt for funding support, participating in the New Bridge community, and complying with commitments like curfews and urine testing.

Full of pride, I listen to him. It all sounds so logical, so structured, each step perfectly laid out. I can practically hear his fortitude growing like Jack's beanstalk stretching to the sky. Outwardly, he demonstrates unwavering belief that moving on to the sober house is a privilege that he's set his sights on. Inwardly, I know he's trying to cope with it taking so long.

The first Tuesday of January falls on New Year's Day, so the family meeting is delayed until January 8, a couple days after Jake begins his "extra" month and the day before my birthday.

Parents are encouraged to pull back and allow addicts to feel consequences. When Jake asks me to bring his black North Face fleece to the meeting—he doesn't have anything for the cold weather—I search, but it's not in his closet. Bruce and I disagree over what to do.

"Clearly he's lost it—or possibly hocked it—and doesn't remember," I say, trying to remain firm, like Dr. Coysh has counseled us. "When he feels the cold, he'll feel the consequence."

"It must've been a pretty empty Christmas. Couldn't we buy a new one as a gift, to keep him warm?" says Bruce, appealing straight to my heart.

I hate that I struggle over this. My friends give their children presents and don't have to agonize. Yet the parents of addicts must take a different stance on unconditional love. How will our children change their behavior if we always pick up the pieces? I have come to understand that the coldest "No" is often the most loving response.

But Bruce can see me melting. He already has one foot out the door to go purchase a new fleece jacket. I'm grateful Jake's in a place where they hold the line.

Bruce, Alea, and I make the familiar drive to Berkeley. As always, the visit is too brief, but Jake appreciates his gift, and I receive a wonderful one of my own: Jake has remembered my birthday and hands me a letter as we hug goodbye.

I read it as soon as I get home.

Dear Momma,

I have to say in the beginning I did not think I would be able to make it six months at a program like this. I came here thinking everything was looking pretty bleak. This has been a giant lesson in patience, acceptance, and humility. I find it surprising the grace and serenity that I can use to deal and cope with situations that would have been unacceptable to

*me maybe eight months ago...I am grateful to you and Papa
for finding New Bridge for me and really making me work
for my recovery this time. I feel like I would still be going in
circles if I were someplace else. It's funny how more expensive
treatments don't equate with more success. I think all the
places before were necessary parts of the process because
I never would have been ready to do this program if I hadn't
gone through everything leading up to coming here. I want
you to know I am thinking about you as your birthday
approaches, and while it's unfortunate I am still in treatment,
I am counting down the days until I can make up for lost time
with you.*

   Love,

   Jake

The warmth of pride spreads through me. This has been ago-
nizing work for both of us and it is truly remarkable to hear
grateful words from my son. I'm proud of both of us for enduring, persisting—surviving. When Jake calls to say he's nice and
warm in his new fleece, I tell him his letter meant so much to me;
a heartfelt gift.

Every once in a while I reclaim my sense of joy. I dutifully tend
to my brand-new yoga practice and begin acupuncture weekly—
things I thought I would never do, yet they help me begin to
reclaim my life. Reading continues to soothe me. Phyllis Theroux,
an essayist, teacher, and author, speaks to my heart when she
writes of "a contentment that is like an incoming tide, sliding up
the sand, filling in the holes, leveling the surface." I know, despite
all my best efforts and deepest desires, that I can't guarantee a
happy, healthy, and successful path for my children; still, once in
a while, I feel the tide touching my toes.

29
DISMANTLING BEHAVIORS

If we didn't have faith in the promise of a better future for ourselves
and our family, we wouldn't put ourselves through the
hard work and pain involved in recovery.
— *The Life Recovery Bible*

O N THE FIRST OF FEBRUARY, we scoop up Jake at New Bridge
along with his "little brother" Carl, who's fourteen years
older than Jake and outweighs him by sixty pounds. Jake still
hasn't been allowed to search for a job and needs to extend his
stay a second month, but he's earned a six-hour pass to be with
his family. He submitted a proposal to New Bridge detailing how
we would spend those hours, and we're on our way.

Winter can be glorious in California. While other landscapes
are brown or buried in snow, Tilden Park in Berkeley opens up
to sweeping views of emerald hills brought forth by December's
rains. Bruce, Jake, Carl and I along with our dog climb to a van-
tage point. To the west, San Francisco is bathed in sunshine,
sailboats scoot past Alcatraz, and a freighter steams in under
the Golden Gate. To the east, a full reservoir is fringed in more

green velvet. Jake bends down to scratch behind Bella's ears—he knows the exact spot—and she leans into him lovingly. He looks up, breathing in the warm spring air. "Man, it's gorgeous up here. This'd be a great place to bring a date," then adds wistfully, "in about two years."

We walk and talk unhurriedly, and in the natural world our spirits relax in camaraderie. Carl grew up in nearby Richmond. Tragically, his sister was murdered on those same rough streets. He became a football star in college and was drafted to the Cincinnati Bengals. His girlfriend got pregnant and three more kids quickly followed. Like his mother, Carl is an alcoholic. After his last DUI, the court ordered him to rehab for a year. He's been at New Bridge for five months. Now on this hilltop, Carl gazes around in awe, thumps his chest like Tarzan, and exclaims, "I live in such a beautiful place!" Jake told us recently that he spent two days helping Carl draft a letter to a judge requesting that he be allowed to spend his second six months in a facility where he could be freer to see his kids.

Bruce and Jake, quicker hikers, pull ahead. Carl falls into conversation with me. Missing his kids just pours out of him—it's the hardest thing about being in rehab. It's been eating him up that he wasn't there for his twelve-year-old son's birthday two weeks ago.

"I complained to Jake that I'd probably have to make up my absence to my son by spending a thousand dollars on him, and you know what Jake said?"

"What?"

"He said, 'When you get out, why don't you spend a thousand *hours* with him instead?'"

"Jake said that?" I stop in my tracks.

"Yeah, he did. I never would've thought of that myself, but it's a good idea." Carl pauses. "Jake's exactly right. My son would love that...I would love that."

I swell with pride that my son gave such insightful compassionate counsel to this huge warm-hearted father. My smile lasts the rest of the hike.

In the nick of time, we all sit down at the last unoccupied table in a busy Japanese restaurant. Jake and Carl look in wonder at the intricate spicy sushi rolls that the waitress sets down before us; neither has set foot in a restaurant for months. I check my watch—we need to stay on the prescribed timetable, to return to New Bridge on the dot.

We devour the sushi. In just these few hours we've enjoyed precious time with our son and gotten to know another person with this disease. There's no pity here, only heaps of compassion. What's the difference? Negative and positive. Enmeshed and free. Sad and happy. Pity seems wrapped up with hopelessness, compassion with love and hope. In pity there's a feeling of I-will-do-it-for-you-because-you-can't, and in love there's the capacity to stand back and encourage.

Our last stop is an open AA meeting not far from New Bridge. I'm surprised when Jake speaks up—he's usually so quiet.

"I feel proud to be eight months clean," he says, "and grateful to have spent a spectacular day with my parents and my 'brother.' Even my dog came along. I'm dealing with impatience to find a job, and hope to transition to a sober house soon. After eight months in a residential program, I'm kinda nervous about finding a home AA or NA meeting for support on the outside."

I'm nearly levitating above my metal seat. What a miracle that my son views joining the legions—those who soundlessly march on, dismantling their addictive behaviors and cravings, and retraining their brains so they can continue forward—as power. Like an army of ants, recovering addicts and alcoholics must band together in colonies for strength. One little guy, all alone, can be smashed in a minute. Clustered together in fellowship, persisting against a cunning opponent, addicts in recovery have the common purpose of reinforcing each other in their war. Though nobody is in charge, experienced soldiers use their rank to organize and mentor newcomers, leaving a trail of guidance so that their social cooperation results in preservation. A stray is shepherded back into the fold. Quietly, like they're not even there, they do the hard work that comes with keeping their common disease in remission.

———

"How's Jake?" Alea asks, calling from school.

"We had a great day with him—he got a pass and we went hiking and then out for sushi."

"Really? I wish I could've been there."

"He still doesn't have permission to look for a job and he's frustrated about that. He has to extend a second month."

"Do you think he'll be in the sober house by spring break? I was hoping I'd get to spend time with him without all those restrictions."

"We don't know yet."

Bruce and I have gladly agreed to pay for Jake's second extended month—he's making such great progress. I do hope he'll move on in March, but I find myself doubting it.

Alea changes the subject. "You know that guy who's liked me since the first day of school?"

"The cute one who helped us carry your bags up all those flights of stairs?"

"Yeah. Well, he's never stopped pursuing me...and well, lately I've been seeing him a lot..."

"Alea, that's wonderful!"

"Yeah, he's really great," she says dreamily. "In all my past relationships, I've been the one to make things happen. But he takes me out to dinner, he bought me chocolates, and he even planned a day at the Denver Botanic Gardens because he knows how much I love flowers."

"That's so nice for you to experience a more balanced relationship, honey. I'm glad."

Two days later, when we walk into New Bridge for the February visit, I'm surprised to see Tristan sitting in the entry hall. I thought he'd already moved to New Bridge's sober house. Jake tells me Tristan went out on a pass with a couple of guys and they went into a liquor store. He ended up buying some chewing tobacco and then returned to "tell" on himself.

"He's been going downhill this last month because he's been job hunting for two months and hasn't found anything. His felony makes it hard to get hired. His consequence is to sit in the entry hall chair and journal."

"Why'd he do that the minute he was outside?" I blurt out without thinking.

"I don't know, Mom," Jake fires back. "We're addicts and we do stupid things."

His retort is a quick reminder that they can never let down their guard and things can change in a minute. *And* I realize it's the first time I've heard Jake refer to himself as an addict.

Before my eyes, my son is changing. I'm still not used to his healthy round cheeks, short buzzed hair, and strong muscular shoulders. He's exuding joy today and proudly tells us that after requesting it for eight long weeks, he's finally been given permission to search for work. He can practically taste moving on.

He calls just three days later, frustrated because he hasn't found a job yet. Not only do addicts struggle against impulsiveness, they also wrestle with lack of patience. "I haven't heard back from any of the places where I sent my resume," he says.

"This is a process that takes time," I say. "Another opportunity to wait patiently."

All the practice I've had stopping myself from jumping in and trying to solve Alea's problems this past year comes into play now. *Don't inflict help,* I remind myself.

"Finding a job takes persistence and staying power. All you can do is keep searching, putting resumes out there, following up, and one day an opportunity will present itself. There's no rush; it'll happen."

Three more weeks pass, and Jake still hasn't found a job. I'm finding it easier to say, "Whatever happens, happens." I don't want to be sucked into anybody else's life. Staying in the center of my own life takes all my commitment. When I'm not enmeshed in Jake's and Alea's, there's so much more time for my own.

The first week of March, on our Sunday phone call, Alea describes how she woke up on her birthday to her room filled with balloons. We've already heard about the roses on Valentine's Day.

"Nick must've got most of my floormates to help him blow up hundreds of balloons and I guess my roommate let him in. I didn't hear a thing. I was blown away when I opened my eyes."

My daughter is nineteen and in love.

Then she casually drops a bombshell. "The other day I bumped into Scott, you know, Jake's old roommate. Apparently Jake invited him to come to Berkeley over CU's spring break. So I was surprised when Scott just tossed out that he may be visiting my brother in a few weeks."

Bruce and I are dead silent.

"Are you still there?" Alea asks.

Questions, like fireworks, ricochet against my skull. Is Jake thinking he's cured? That he can handle seeing an old party buddy? Or even worse, is he hiding this precarious idea from his counselors at New Bridge? I remind myself that I can't control what Jake does, that I can allow him the freedom to consider his own recovery.

Somehow my words come out calmly. "Thanks, honey, for telling us. I may need to mention this to Jake because I want to stay completely honest with him about what I know. Are you okay with that?"

"Just don't make it sound like I'm squealing on him, because I'm not. I'm just telling you what Scott said."

"Thanks, Alea."

All afternoon I try not to stew over this. It would be so easy to fall back into old behaviors—monitoring, manipulating, and worrying. The past two years, in the face of threatening situations, these behaviors became necessary coping skills, but now they're a burden. I want to break free of them, and if I can, I may be helping Jake more than I realize. It's a waste of a perfectly beautiful day to pester myself with what if Jake does this, what if he's thinking that? Do I want to spend my life bird-dogging him?

At dinner I ask Bruce, "How many times today, if any, did you think about what Alea just told us?"

"Huh?" he says. "Just the one time you brought it up. I've been busy fixing the sprinklers and cooking dinner."

God, I want to be like that, to be able to let things go. In the past, I might have interpreted Bruce's reaction as not caring— and resented him for it. But that's not true. He has a different way, arguably a healthier way, of dealing with things. He can assign the problem to whom it belongs—in this case, Jake—and not concern himself with any second-guessing. Will this ever get easier for me?

Observing how others handle troubles while remaining open to change, I feel as challenged as a golden-robed monk upholding a strict monastic code of discipline. Pema Chödrön writes in *Living Beautifully,*

> I realized then what it means to hold pain in my heart and simultaneously be deeply touched by the power and magic of the world. Life doesn't have to be one way or the other. We don't have to jump back and forth. We can live beautifully with whatever comes—heartache and joy, success and failure, instability and change.

Instead of jumping back and forth, I concentrate on sorting out facts from fears. Most troubling to me is Jake thinking that getting together with Scott is a good idea. Was Jake's anticipation of seeing a college buddy over his spring break the source of his recent impatience? Once again, my sponsor advises me to keep things simple, to mention just the facts to Jake, then say no more. Trying to mother, manipulate, and monitor him has not worked before, so don't go back to that behavior.

Tuesday evening, the usual meeting room at New Bridge is full of families anticipating visits. First, Dr. Coysh leads an hour-long discussion focusing on behavior that might point to relapse. Bruce and I glance at each other. *Is this guy a mind reader?*

Dr. Coysh says, "Nobody walking out of here can say, 'I beat this thing.' The hope is that they tell themselves, 'I'm in the process of controlling this thing.' The disease of addiction produces world-class liars and manipulators and so I ask you, the loved ones of our clients here, what behavior would point toward relapse?"

"Lies and dishonesty," says one.

"Isolation," says another.

"Reconnecting with drug-using friends," says a third.

Dr. Coysh nods and concludes with useful advice. If we're concerned about a certain behavior, we need to be forthright and ask our loved one, "Is this decision or behavior in the service of recovery or in the spirit of relapse?"

All the New Bridge clients push forward into the room, a herd at first, then self-selecting, turning this way and that to become enfolded within each family's embrace. Jake's fairly bursting with the news that he got a job at Staples. He feels glorious, giddy with relief. In a week, he'll begin a week-long training period. Then he'll be fully employed and hopefully can move to the sober house. Bruce and I light up, happy and excited for him.

And yet, we've just been reminded how crucial it is to confront behaviors that might lead to relapse. I wrestle with the need to change the subject in the few minutes left. We won't see Jake again for weeks until after any potential visit from Scott. It feels like I'm about to dump ice water, but the moment is now.

"Alea mentioned she heard from Scott that you invited him to visit. That makes me feel scared for you." I've just erased all our smiles.

Jake's animation is gone.

I stay silent.

"I didn't invite him," he says, trying to minimize. "I just asked him to see what his dad would say about flying him out."

In the ensuing silence I think to myself, if New Bridge's tough director, Angela, were sitting right here with us, she would say, "*Bullshit.*" Jake has told me Angela has an uncanny ability to ferret out the truth and the residents respect her greatly for it.

He adds, "I don't want to give up that friendship."

"You don't have to give it up forever, but should you see him *right now*?" Bruce says.

"Have you discussed it with anybody here?" I ask.

"A coupla guys."

"Your counselors?"

"No," he says, and I see his jaw tensing.

"Getting together with Scott really makes me concerned for you," I say, looking directly into his eyes. I don't have any idea whether Scott is sober or an addict or something in between, but I take my sponsor's advice and say no more.

Bruce brings the conversation back around. "Jake, it's really great you got a job. What a big accomplishment!"

Jake's only half listening now; most likely his mind is reeling. When we leave, I give him an extra-long hug. He's in a safe place to deal with any guilt, annoyance, or frustration with his parents, and he can stop and question if he's being honest with himself.

On the long drive home, I make an effort to let my concern about Jake drain away. From behind the wheel, I look over at Bruce who's already dozing. There's a lot of road still ahead.

30
SPIRALING UP

True sobriety is much the same: it's not ordinary life with the drugs
and alcohol cut out. It's a new way of living, or relating to ourselves
and the world. It's not a different version of the life we are living;
it's a completely new life, one that can't be imagined until
you are there. And it is both appealing and frightening.
— KEVIN GRIFFIN, *One Breath at a Time*

"I FELT SO OUT OF PLACE, standing there wearing this oversized
Staples uniform at the copy center. I didn't know how to work
anything." Jake is telling me about his first day of work. When a
customer asked him a question, he felt awkward telling them he
didn't know. He felt anxious the whole day.

"I was relieved to get home to New Bridge and feel safe again."

"The first day is always rough," I say.

"Yeah. One good thing, though, is that one of Staples' star
employees is a New Bridge graduate—Andrew."

He tells me that Andrew graduated from Stanford and received
a Master's from MIT in computer science before coming to New
Bridge as a meth addict. He's been putting his life back together
the past two years.

"I'll bet Staples is thrilled to have Andrew's recovering brain running their tech department."

Jake lets out a puff of air. "Yeah. He looks out for me."

Once again I'm impressed by the sturdy chain New Bridge has linked together, with the guys helping each other. And Jake has become a role model for newer guys trying to get through the program, watching to see how it goes for him.

"Momma, they've scheduled the 'crossover' in two weeks. It's on April fifth."

He explains to me again that this is not called graduation. That's a bigger milestone, still a year away. "Tristan and two other guys are scheduled to cross over, too."

"Can't wait, Jake." My heart beats faster thinking about this upcoming marker for a new kind of normal.

———

Spring break doesn't coincide with a monthly meeting, so Alea can't see her brother. There's no visit from Scott, either.

I check in by phone with Alea after she gets back to Boulder. She seems stressed about several tough classes. She tells me Nick has been acting coldly toward her, and she doesn't know why.

"He was really mad when I got back to the dorms an hour late from the airport. A guy from one of my classes was on my flight. He gave me a ride but we got talking and weren't paying attention so we got lost. We ended up having to backtrack on the freeway. It was no big deal but Nick was really worked up."

"Hmmm. How's the new therapist?"

"I've seen her a couple of times and I just love her. She's really good, Momma."

"I'm glad. Your dad and I are going to the Tuesday meeting at New Bridge this evening. It's our last visit with Jake there. This Friday he 'crosses over.'"

"That's so great—tell him I said congratulations!"

Later, as we're idling in traffic on our way to Berkeley, Bruce jokes, "What'll we do without these long Tuesday drives?"

"Don't even say that."

Jake looks so confident when he enters the room, and we can see he commands respect from the other residents. I could weep at the difference from ten months ago, when he first stepped into the short program. He's bubbling with excitement at the upcoming transition.

We only get twenty minutes at these visits so he jumps right in, telling us that there's been a problem with Tristan.

"There was a girl here a few months ago who was flirting with a number of guys, including me. She kept doing it so she got kicked out. Turns out that Tristan had sex with her back then."

My eyebrows go up. Bruce's too.

"With his crossover about to happen he didn't get discharged, but his consequence was to sit in the entry hall chair loaded with writing assignments that'd take days to finish. He didn't want to jeopardize his new job 'cause it took him so long to get it, so he walked out."

"Oh *no*," I say, feeling his crushing defeat in my own body. "He was so *close*." The choices of recovering addicts put them on such a razor's edge.

"I could've made the same dumb choice." Jake swallows and speaks more slowly. "When she was focused on me, I flirted back...at first. But it started to bother me, so I spoke up about it in group. *That* got me the support of the whole house. So whenever she came to sit by me, someone would swoop in and usher her on." He pauses. "I could've easily been out like Tristan."

"Wow, Jake. I'm glad you made it through," says Bruce.

"There'll be a big hole with Tristan missing at the crossover," I say.

"Yeah, there'll only be two of us, Landon and me—the fourth guy was mixed up with that girl, too."

Jake will soon be allowed to have his iPhone and iPod. Both have been in my desk drawer these last ten months. Wondering if his phone will even work after so long, I plug it into his charger and set it on my kitchen counter. Unexpectedly, it rings throughout the day. The same number keeps appearing on the screen. I figure out the caller is Scott. I want to grab the phone and block the number. Each ring jangles my spine. It feels like tattling, but I let Dr. Coysh know, figuring Jake can get support from his recovery community just like he did with the temptress. Certainly I don't want to get into an argument about it.

When we arrive at New Bridge, I hand the phone over to Dr. Coysh. He mentions he had time to ask Jake, "How does Scott know to be calling you?" But we're interrupted because the ceremony is about to start. We're shepherded downstairs. It's just as well—it's not my problem. Monitoring Jake will land me back at square one.

In a huge room where everyone is gathering, a guy stands like a sergeant barking out orders. I realize he's a resident reading off weekly job assignments military-style. Others are seated listening intently for their name and new job. This house meeting, run by the clients themselves, is just finishing up and the counselors filter in behind us. The only two sitting in the special red chairs are Jake and Landon, beaming and justifiably proud. The estimate that roughly 50 percent make it to this point proves accurate.

One by one, the counselors stand and speak to the difficult process Jake and Landon have come through. One says Jake came in as a boy and she witnessed his transformation into a young man. Another says that after the first thirty days, he worried that Jake still had the mindset of not being done with drugs and he's full of pride that Jake made it to this chair. A third explains that when they realized Jake was somehow coasting through the six-month program, the staff decided they needed to really piss him off. Dr. Coysh says, "I saw lots of resentment and resistance lurking under this boy's quiet compliant shell. Our eight weeks of denying Jake 'job search' was the cornerstone of his program—he really had to go after what he wanted—and the last three months were where changes really happened." I sense their truthfulness and affection for Jake.

The counselors speak with equal passion and pride about Landon. Unlike our son, Landon has no family here to witness his transition. Some graduates arrive and speak up—they've rushed here from work to congratulate Jake and Landon. Bruce and I see that many people at New Bridge care deeply about our son. Their words feel like balm on my roughened soul. My heart is warm, my throat is tight, and my eyes swell with tears.

It's as if Jake's been on a hellish train ride while Bruce and I have traveled another, equally desperate route. Now both trains are coming into the station—converging, reconnecting. Tentative trust is part of this new track. We're excited to be able to see more of our son. He's excited to have more freedom. Could there be normal times ahead?

As they cross New Bridge's threshold into the great outdoors, each young man is handed his phone and iPod. They haven't been able to listen to music in ages and on our way to a celebratory dinner with both, I hear from the back seat, "Hey, listen to this one." My shoulders tense up. Electronic music, associated with raves, pulses out of their ear buds. They're simultaneously checking their phone messages. Counselors caution addicts in early recovery about strong associations with music from drug-using days—and what about those texts from past buddies?

As we step into the Italian restaurant, Jake stops and draws in a big whiff of simmering sauces and roasting garlic.

He sighs. "This is the second meal I've eaten at a restaurant in a year."

Just then, my cell phone rings. Alea's calling. I motion to Bruce that I'll take it outside while they wait for our table.

"Momma, Nick just dumped me and I don't understand why," she wails, drenching me in her sadness. "*I want to come home.*"

"Oh, honey."

"He told me this afternoon that he wants to break up. Everything was fine and then a couple times it's like a curtain drops and he goes completely cold. When he's like that I'm miserable—I don't even want to wake up. I just don't know what to do."

Her emotion pours through the phone line. I stand flattened against a brick wall, away from the line of diners streaming out the restaurant's door.

"He's probably out at a party tonight hitting on some girls," she says, keeping herself twisting in misery.

I recognize a behavioral pattern of my own—assuming the worst, creating a negative story without all the facts—behavior I've been working hard to change. "I doubt that, Alea," I say, trying to pull her back from worst-case scenarios. "Most likely he's hurting, too. That doesn't sound like the guy who gave you red roses on Valentine's Day or filled your room with balloons on your birthday. You just don't have answers yet."

Bruce signals to me that they're being seated.

"Alea, when do you see your therapist next?"

"Tomorrow. Last time she said she thought I might be in new territory with a stable boyfriend. She said he might seem boring compared to the high-risk guys of before, and that might be okay..."

"I guess neither of you saw this coming. I'm glad you have an appointment."

"Yeah."

"Talking with her should help a lot. Maybe you could schedule a couple of extra sessions for the rest of the week."

"I guess… But I still want to come home." The level of pain and panic in her voice seems to be dropping.

"You've got less than a month before finals. You've worked so hard. Don't let him wreck your semester, Alea."

"I feel so alone."

"What would help?"

"I guess I can hang out with a girlfriend."

"And then let's talk more about it tomorrow."

"Okay," she says in a small voice.

"Love you."

I lean my head against the brick wall, thinking back to the tough times Alea had with Ben. She holed up then, told me nothing. Now she's calling me, much more open. It feels good to have Alea seek my support. She feels safe trusting me with her feelings. I was able to respond to her with empathy, to resist reacting to fear, hers and mine. She's showing she's better able to cope—she's not running away. She's talking about her unhappiness and suppressing her impulses long enough to think ahead to possible consequences and better alternatives. And as children do, she's giving me umpteen opportunities to practice holding space for her to do that.

I draw in a big breath and slowly let it out. I will be available for Alea tomorrow. For now, I rejoin our little group inside. At the table, Jake is just digging into a plate of bruschetta brimming with tomatoes and basil. No more *bruschetta bianca* for him. He looks up at me. "Momma, I like tomatoes now, you know."

There's so much about him I don't know and I'm looking forward to slowly discovering who he's become. Bruce looks at me questioningly, but I smile and shrug. There'll be plenty of time later to fill him in about Alea. Now I want to switch gears and enjoy our evening together to honor Jake.

I wait until the following afternoon, until after Alea's classes and therapy appointment, to call. Sitting in a comfortable chair in my bedroom, my feet up on the ottoman, I punch in her number and she picks up.

"I feel better after talking with my therapist," she says. "I've decided I'll stick it out. I don't want all my work to go to waste just because of *him*."

Good. I hear a bit of Alea's characteristic defiance. That'll help carry her through. "Would it help to make a dorm room change? Having him right there must be awkward." Damn—I'm trying to fix things again. *Put that cape back in your closet.* It's progress to recognize my impulse, but catching my words before they roll out feels like a monumental challenge.

"I don't know. Maybe. I'll think about it. I just wish I knew what happened. I really care about him and I'm sure he did about me. Then all of a sudden he wants to break it off."

"Maybe he's not ready to talk about it just yet."

"Well, meanwhile he's broken my heart..."

When we hang up, I sigh. Though this current boyfriend trouble is terribly hard for her, she's showing such growth in regulating herself. If I can stay out of it, Alea can pick up her own responsibilities and grow into the accomplished young woman she's destined to become.

Several times over the next few days, she calls me weeping.

"Momma, why does every guy end up abandoning me?"

"It must feel terrible," I say softly.

"I talked to him. He thinks he might be bipolar and he's going to see a psychiatrist. He said he doesn't want to drag me down."

My first thought—*Are there any healthy boys out there for Alea?*—whizzes through my head before I think to say, "It must help to have some feedback from him about *why*."

"Yeah, I guess. I don't know why it took him three days to tell me that."

"I'm sure it's hard for him, too."

"I'm seeing my therapist again tomorrow. I've decided it's too much of a hassle to change rooms and I wouldn't know anybody over in the other dorm. *And* I've got a lot of studying to do."

See, she's figuring it out on her own.

"Good for you, Alea. Focus on taking care of yourself. Don't forget about your girlfriends—they care about you, and remember I do, too."

———

Jake's transition is emotionally exhausting both for him and for me. I work overtime letting go, resisting monitoring, keeping my mouth shut. After such long anticipation, he's merely moved a few blocks away to a shared one-bedroom with a Spartan kitchenette. The sober house is actually an apartment complex. Women share second-floor apartments and the men live below. All of them come from the New Bridge program. Jake is paired with Andrew—his mentor at Staples—and Landon's with a guy who's a year ahead of him.

After Jake's first week there, Bruce and I visit. There are fewer rules now and plenty of free time. The beds are made and everything looks neat and tidy. The guys have learned that an organized living space equals orderly thinking. I open a few kitchen cupboards to see what pots and pans they have. Completely empty.

"Jake, what do you use to cook with?

"There's a frying pan in the drainer."

"Oh...but how do you cook pasta?"

"In the frying pan."

"And a colander?"

"We don't have one."

"Oh."

Bruce asks, "So what's it like being out of the treatment facility?"

"It's kinda disappointing," Jake says. "I just want to have some *fun.*"

Worry stabs at my heart. Will he find healthy outlets? He and Landon seem like guarded lost souls. Transitions are never easy, especially when your life has been tightly scheduled and now you have to figure out every hour. Jake keeps himself busy until he's required to be at work, a meeting, or aftercare—a delicate balance.

He's only working thirty hours a week at minimum wage, which isn't much to live on. I offer to buy a few groceries as a house-warming present, and he's appreciative. Even the ride to the store is a luxury, since usually he has to use public transportation or walk. While Bruce finds parking, Jake and I stroll the grocery aisles. I share some tips on tasty economical one-pan dishes. He listens carefully, and seems glad not to have to carry the full bags all the way back to his apartment.

The next time he calls, Jake tells me he bumped into a high-school classmate near the UC Berkeley campus. They decided to meet later for lunch. She's graduating from Cal next month, as are many of Jake's peers.

"What was that like, seeing her?"

"Well, we met at a pizza place. She told me she's going to Yale for her Master's because it's more prestigious than Berkeley."

"Hmm."

"Kinda like she was answering questions at a job interview promoting herself."

"What'd you say?"

"I told her things for me didn't really go as planned. And I just said... I'm an addict, but I'm doing much better now."

"How'd she respond to that?"

"I don't think she really gets it, Momma, because when we ordered the pizza she asked, 'You want a beer?' I told her, no, I can't do anything like that."

"Sounds like she's wrapped up in her world, either ignorant or insensitive."

"Yeah. I've forgotten what it's like to be around people who aren't in recovery. Some don't have a clue. My sponsor's pushing me to meet other sober guys. It's like dating…you have to work up some courage to make the call, find out what you have in common, make plans, and go from there."

"Sounds a little anxiety-provoking."

"Yeah, I'm not all that comfortable doing it, but I'm meeting some good guys."

I can't imagine what each new day is like for Jake. Whenever I'm struggling to change my own negative patterns, I feel like I'm surrounded by treacherous emotions, like I'm behind enemy lines. What must it feel like when every single aspect of your life is a challenge?

31
TOGETHER

Don't turn your head. Keep looking at the bandaged place.
That's where the light enters you.
— JALAL AL-DIN RUMI

ON MOTHER'S DAY, Jake arrives at the train station. He's wearing my favorite shirt. As we drive home, he tells me more about the new house. A couple of weeks ago, New Bridge opened up an old six-bedroom Victorian and he and a number of his buddies got to move into it. There's two guys to a bedroom, two refrigerators, and a big comfy couch in the living room. He tells me since they don't have a dining room table, they all store their bikes in there. "It looks like a bike-rental place," he says.

"It makes me happy when you share little stories with me," I say. "I'm so proud of you."

He smiles.

"I want to get to a point where you can say things like, 'Thanks Mom, that's helpful,' or 'You're beginning to bug me, Mom, so let me handle it.'

He looks over at me slightly surprised, still listening.

"Jake, I'm eager to go forward building an adult-to-adult relationship with you. I want to be able to comfortably say, 'I don't know what you're thinking,' or 'I need you to ask me directly if you need something from me.'"

"Okay, that sounds good," he says, then pauses. "I appreciate you telling me that, Momma."

Two years ago, his reaction would have been different. In fact, the whole conversation would never have happened; I'd have driven in silence next to my sullen son, or he would've made up lies to my probing questions. I shake my head in wonder at how nice this exchange feels.

As my children make pancakes for me—Alea arrived home from college last night—Jake tells us that he and the guys in the sober house just got a new cat.

"Tuxedo is black with a white chest and paws." He puts the spatula down and pulls out his phone to show me a picture. "We got him a quick-release collar with a bell. You can hear the little tinkle of him coming and going."

"Cute."

"We've kept him inside while he gets used to us and the house."

"So you keep all the windows closed?"

"Yeah. He still got out on Wednesday and we were all worried because he didn't come back for like twenty-four hours. We left the door open and put some food out."

"So now do you let him come and go?

"Well...no, we're still kinda worried about him going out into a big scary world. That he'll come back safe."

Bruce and I exchange a glance, and Jake notices. I can see how he recognizes that worry comes with love.

Love is not enough against this disease. Addiction often wrenches people apart, shatters their love. Somehow, love helped pull us through. And now we need that love to help us rebuild broken trust.

At breakfast, I watch as my son passes the syrup to his sister. Who would this young man be without his struggle against addiction? Have his challenges completely shaped him, or are his best traits just now beginning to reemerge? Jake's relationships are dormant, as if he's dropped off the earth for the past two years. Forging back into socializing and making new friends must seem formidable. With this past year of self-examination, he's leaped ahead of many peers psychologically. Still, life must feel tentative.

I'm challenged to stay focused on the present. In an instant, my mind can take off, questioning Jake's future. But I'm learning to recognize how incessant worry can cause my own suffering. As I nurture resiliency, I tell myself, *I don't know, none of us knows,* which helps me shift my focus back to the day that spreads before me, this day right here and now.

My son is wolfing down breakfast in my kitchen, choosing to be with our family. He's embracing recovery. He lives with uncertainty, yet he's living with purpose. As Rumi wrote, "No more than a ball can guess where it's going next."

Bruce gets up to make us all coffee. He and I have begun sharing our Sunday-morning coffee together on our sunny patio. We've situated two padded lounge chairs where we can soak up the warm California sun, gaze at our blooming garden, and talk. I feel my husband's engagement and commitment to our marriage as he strives for better balance. Instead of working late, he's often home to help prepare dinner. He's reclaiming time for himself, for our family, and for me.

Last Mother's Day, I didn't have much hope for my son to live. Now he and Alea are chattering away, clearing the dishes from the table. Jake is taking responsibility for his disease. Alea has gone off to Boulder and proven herself, maneuvering the wild party environment and managing excellent grades. She figured out a way forward through a year packed with relationship challenges. I'm bursting with pride for both of them. I want to climb right up on my kitchen table and sing.

With the dishes done and our cream and sugar just right, the four of us carry our mugs out to the patio. The cloudless sky is cornflower blue and there's not a breath of wind. Jake fetches my sunglasses for me then sits on a patio chair, propping his feet on the end of my chaise lounge. Bella hops up with Bruce and he repositions himself to accommodate her. She licks his calf in devotion then moves to Jake's toes, a stretch but still within her range. Alea rolls up her pant legs to begin working on her summer tan. The simple binding practice of sharing a cup of coffee is delicious.

As grateful as I feel in this moment, I know I must continue to separate my welfare from Jake's. I'll have to learn to make it, whether he does or not. I don't know if there are relapses ahead. Addiction can be battled but it can't always be defeated. People continue to die every day from this disease—a javelin to my heart. Silence is not an option for me. And I wonder if breaking my silence—telling my story—is the start.

In the afternoon, the four of us go off to play tennis, whacking the ball around, laughing. It's as if a tightly wound wire binding my chest is loosening with each and every laugh. Bella is crisscrossing the court, retrieving balls to drop at Jake's feet. Alea and I sit panting on the shady bench while Bruce and Jake play a few more games. Nobody is keeping score.

At home, we once again gather in our backyard, this time in the shade of the magnolia. The blueness of the sky has deepened. I watch a squirrel navigate the tangle of branches overhead then scamper full tilt along our fence top. Alea holds the pitcher of

lemonade she made from fruit picked from our tree. Jake passes
out the glasses. I think of how much we've endured and learned,
lost and gained. And here we are, experiencing joy today.

Alea pours, the ice clinking. I gaze at her face—my son's, my
husband's. Sipping, I taste both the sweetness and the tartness,
savoring both, cherishing them. To be all together for one day,
this Mother's Day, is extraordinary.

EPILOGUE

I have sometimes been wildly, despairingly, acutely miserable, racked
with sorrow, but through it all I still know quite certainly
that just to be alive is a grand thing.
— AGATHA CHRISTIE

ON A SPARKLING BLUE DAY in May 2014, one year after that
extraordinary Mother's Day, Bruce, Alea, and I approached
a church hall in Berkeley a few minutes before the start of New
Bridge's annual graduation ceremony. We spotted Jake, standing handsome and tall on the front steps—two years clean and
sober—chatting with fellow graduates. The three of us stood,
stunned and impressed. He was dressed in fashionable new
linen trousers, the sleeves of his blue dress shirt rolled up to his
bulging biceps. His colorful necktie was tucked into his buttoned
vest—no evidence of that budding pot belly—accentuating his
trim waist. His tobacco-colored leather dress shoes completed
the vision. It was almost as if he and the other beaming graduates were the source of sunshine splashing us all. I had to grab
Bruce's arm for support, stumbling between leaping with joy and

collapsing to the pavement in relief. Jake turned, caught sight of us, and strode over to give us all mighty hugs.

We filed into the church, smiling at all the familiar faces from all those Tuesday nights at New Bridge. We filled every seat, and more people crowded the aisles. The counselors spoke, and then, one by one, the graduates walked to the lectern, faced the crowd, and told their stories with powerful honesty and gratitude.

During the years I was grappling with being the parent of an addicted son, I never pictured reaching this pinnacle. I never dared to imagine, while navigating the lows of those lowest months, the powerful expansion of standing on a summit. I wanted to hug every person there—I mean each and every one—because I knew something of their harrowing journeys. Never did any of us find signposts pointing the way, yet traveling our varied routes, we got here. Celebrating this long-awaited, hard-earned graduation, we all might as well have been singing in unison, belting out the most jubilant tune, as we streamed out of that church hall straight into sunshine.

Back in November, Jake had applied and been accepted as a transfer student to a small prestigious liberal-arts college. His first semester, beginning in January, he took just one class and continued to work full-time at the Fremont startup where he'd started at the bottom rung. That summer, he moved in with us to save on rent and cut his commute in half. Every day Bella would greet him at the front door when he got home from work and entice him into roughhousing. Sometimes he helped me finish cooking, asking if he was slicing the green onions correctly or if he'd set the flame too high under the pot of marinara sauce. When he shared his enthusiasm about his job, told us of promotions and pay-raises, and admitted his nervousness about beginning full-time studies in the fall, Bruce and I felt like recipients of priceless gifts.

I made plenty of mistakes that summer, but I was beginning to recognize them more quickly and apologize more readily. On a fact-finding mission about options for the removal of his wisdom teeth, Jake told the surgeon candidly, "I'm two years in recovery—can I do this without narcotics?" and I sat in silence, worrying about the trigger of sticking an IV needle into his arm. As we were leaving, the nurse—not privy to his search for alternatives—handed Jake a packet containing valium. I reached out, grabbed it before Jake could, and pushed it back at her. Mother bear took over before I could think.

"I won't be needing that," Jake told the nurse calmly. I felt awful for embarrassing him, for conveying mistrust, for seizing control. Outside, I told him how sorry I was. He smiled, letting it roll right off his back, and thanked me for apologizing.

Often I'm stretching, as if my hands are reaching for a challenging chord, playing richer sounds as I practice changing how I do things. It still is not automatic for me to stop and think before leaping into action, or to let go of worry when it's not my problem, or to remain silent and focus on myself when I'm yearning to take control of either of my children's lives. I used to think that once I learned something I would know it forever. But it isn't true. We have to learn basic things over and over again. Each day, there's always something new to ponder and practice. I have to keep reminding myself that letting go of worry fosters a more joyous life, that setting and holding boundaries generates respectfulness and trust, and most important, that my children's lives are not mine to live.

I recall the day our family went to a Giants game at AT&T Park. It was the summer of 2013, back when Jake was still living in the sober house. In the fourth inning, a boisterous guy sitting behind us spilled his cup of beer down Bruce's back. By the fifth inning, the raucous chants of the crowd began to sound slurred.

Despite feeling like we were sitting in a pond of alcohol, it was wonderful to spend the afternoon together.

"So how're things with Sadie?" I asked Jake during a lull.

"I told her," he said.

About six weeks earlier, at Gay Pride in San Francisco, a lovely young woman had approached Jake and asked him if he was gay or straight, single or in a relationship. They went on a few dates—a hike starting at the Cliff house, sushi at the Japanese restaurant we love in Berkeley, a picnic in Tilden Park. Jake had waited to reveal his past because he wanted her to get to know him and like him first.

"What'd she say?

"She seemed pretty open-minded and asked, 'Do you carry it around all the time, the craving?'"

"How did you answer that?"

"I told her no, it's almost like a feeling of revulsion, the idea of using."

This was news to me. Jake was still the same person he was before his disease; he mostly kept things to himself.

"But she's really close with her mother, so she told her, too." He paused a moment while the crowd roared. "Her parents exploded and forbid her to see me. They threatened to cut off paying her rent."

"Oh, Jake."

An opposing batter blasted a ball out to right field. What a slam this must feel like for my son.

"I offered to meet them, but they refused. She called me in tears, not sure what to do."

For the rest of the game, hot, helpless, anger burned; discrimination wasn't something I'd felt before. Those parents should realize their daughter could do a *lot* worse than dating a guy who offered wholesome hikes, home-cooked dinners, honest conversations. Wild parties and getting loaded would not be part of the picture. Jake deserved trust.

And then I thought of Zeke. I had been on the flip side of this quandary. Awful uncertainty comes with a disease that lurks. I hated to admit that I did understand those parents' fear. No assurances come with addiction. No promises will secure the future. Resignation and compassion began to replace my heat.

At that baseball game, it hit me how Jake had changed into a man seemingly overnight. He was fourteen months clean, on a strong forward trajectory, and fully enmeshed in his recovery program and full-time job. He'd been so kind and polite to our waitress when we'd grabbed a bite to eat before the game. He was often quiet, yet when he spoke he was thoughtful, sincere. He had an energy that both encompassed him and radiated out from him, attracting. No wonder a young woman had approached him.

Not long after that, Jake and Sadie parted with great regret. I felt sadness but also trust that Jake would find his way.

By the spring of 2015, Jake was a full-time business major, gaining confidence by the day, making straight A's and working twenty hours a week for a venture capital firm in San Francisco. He, his buddy Joe from New Bridge, and Tuxedo the cat shared an apartment in the East Bay.

On Mother's Day, Jake was swamped with finals, tutoring, and work, so he called instead of visiting. We had an amazing conversation, full of honesty. He told me how challenging work events were when drinking was involved, how his peers questioned his abstinence. He told me that he and Joe had been asked to speak at New Bridge; they were nervous, but found themselves running out of time to say everything they wanted to say. "A couple of the new guys told us how inspiring we were. That was really something." The mighty chain was still in place.

Alea had flown to Boulder the day before, excited about a summer internship, full of new insights after spending the semester studying in Spain. Jake's new stability allowed her to focus on her own self-care. "I still look up to him," she told me, "but in a different way from before. It's not about how cool and popular he is anymore—it's about his resilience and humility." She left me a handmade Mother's Day card, telling me how proud she was of me for writing this book.

I've never been the same since I discovered my son was addicted to drugs. Have I learned more than I suffered? Certainly fear, dread, denial, anger, and guilt turned me into someone I barely recognized. Still, as I discovered words to live by, people to support and guide me, love to fuel me, I evolved into someone new, more even-tempered, more empathetic, clearer about boundaries, certainly less intense, less judgmental. I'm crystal clear about what matters to me now: relationships, intimacy, honesty, love, and family. Growth might have happened another way but this difficulty has enriched me—it's the fight that caused the transformation. Strangely, I wouldn't exchange those dark years for anything. They made our family who we are, more connected, more respectful, more humble, more autonomous, much healthier than we would have been. The surprise is that I've ended up grateful for the experiences I would have done anything to avoid.

There is hope in the lifelong process of recovery. After so much time spiraling down, Bruce and I are grateful for the small pleasures in life—a call from Jake telling us about his week, shared dinners, the four of us piling onto couches to watch a movie, a leisurely walk with the dog. Our family is forging ahead searching less for answers, putting more into practice all that we've learned. Anything can happen with the disease of addiction. For now, love and trust continue to grow.

ACKNOWLEDGMENTS

WITHOUT MY SON there'd be no book. His story is wrapped in mine, and mine in his, and if he'd protested, our family's experience would not have landed on these pages. I'm deeply grateful to him for recognizing the power of stories and for his willingness to let me share his. My profound regard for the battle he has waged hasn't diminished over time—in fact, as he attends to his recovery and pursues his grand dreams, my awe at his fortitude only increases. Jake, you have my love, admiration, and gratitude.

Along the way, so many angels have reached out to Jake, and I thank each and every one of you. Tim and Bev and all the counselors at Cirque and Jaywalker; Doug, Lorri, and David out on the trail; Brian and Frankie in Carbondale; Dave in Boulder—unsung heroes working hard each day to help others live. This story might have ended differently without the unwavering strength of the New Bridge Family—a special heartfelt thanks to Angela and Bill, both wise, skilled, and steadfast in their commitment to helping recovering addicts. And to John R., your friendship and example—to Jake and to all of us—is precious.

Thank you to my fellow travelers at the Wednesday night Al-Anon Parents group. You understand my family's story because you are living it. As I listened to your unique wisdom—your experience, strength, and hope—I learned and felt understood. I still do.

Lydia Bird, my editor, cared deeply about this story from start to finish. Your astute suggestions and insightful comments contributed to a clear framework. At every stage of the book process, you encouraged and guided me with wonderful perception and beautiful editing. I've learned so much and truly could not have come this far without you. Thank you.

Lorri helped shore me up when I was floundering. She, Patty, Katrina, Jon, and Michelle all patiently read drafts, offering corrections and helpful comments. Thank you all.

To Barre, our bond—struggling in sisterhood—helped fill me with understanding and insight. To Sharon, thanks for patiently repeating what I needed to hear. To all my friends, your moral support helped get me through.

I'm grateful to my mother and my sisters and brothers and their families, who worried for me, and with me, and never stopped loving Jake.

And finally, my heartfelt gratitude and infinite love goes to Bruce, Alea, and Jake, who shared every step of the journey then patiently loved and supported me as I worked to tell it.

RESOURCES

THOUSANDS OF BOOKS, articles, films, and websites have been created to address the crisis of addiction. While by no means an exhaustive list, I would like to share the resources I found most helpful in my own search for strength and clarity.

MEMOIR

Cataldi, Libby. *Stay Close: A Mother's Story of Her Son's Addiction.* New York: St. Martin's Press, 2009.

Kucera, Dina. *Everything I Never Wanted to Be: A Memoir of Alcoholism and Addiction, Faith and Family, Hope and Humor.* Downers Grove: Dream of Things, 2010.

Moyers, William Cope, with Katherine Ketcham. *Broken: My Story of Addiction and Redemption.* New York: Viking Penguin, 2006.

Sheff, David. *Beautiful Boy: A Father's Journey Through His Son's Addiction.* New York: Houghton Mifflin, 2008.

Volkmann, Chris, and Toren Volkmann. *From Binge to Blackout: A Mother and Son Struggle with Teen Drinking.* New York: New American Library, 2006.

Wandzilak, Kristina, and Constance Curry. *The Lost Years: Surviving a Mother and Daughter's Worst Nightmare.* Santa Monica: Jeffers Press, 2006.

Articles and Practical Nonfiction

Ball, Carolyn M. *Claiming Your Self-Esteem: A Guide Out of Codependency, Addiction, and Other Useless Habits.* Berkeley: Celestial Arts, 1991.

Beattie, Melody. *Codependent No More: How to Stop Controlling Others and Start Caring for Yourself.* 2nd ed. Center City: Hazelden, 1986.

————. *The New Codependency: Help and Guidance for Today's Generation.* New York: Simon & Schuster, 2009.

Calabresi, Massimo. "The Price of Relief: Why America Can't Kick Its Painkiller Problem." *Time,* June 15, 2015.

Cantan, Thomas, and Evan Perez. "A Pain-Drug Champion Has Second Thoughts." *Wall Street Journal,* December 15-16, 2012.

Conyers, Beverly. *Addict in the Family: Stories of Loss, Hope, and Recovery.* 1st ed. Center City: Hazelden, 2003.

————. *Everything Changes: Help For Families of Newly Recovering Addicts.* Center City: Hazelden, 2009.

Dobbs, David. "Beautiful Brains." *National Geographic,* October, 2011.

Giron, Lisa, Scott Glover, and Doug Smith. "Drug Deaths Now Outnumber Traffic Fatalities in U.S." *Los Angeles Times,* September 17, 2011.

Grieg, Alex. "The New Face of Heroin: Number of affluent teenagers from the suburbs using the drug is shooting up in alarming numbers." DailyMail.com, August 5, 2013.

Hersanek, Joe. *Why Don't They Just Quit? What Families and Friends Need to Know About Addiction and Recovery.* 2nd ed. Loveland: Changing Lives Foundation, 2010.

Jay, Debra. *No More Letting Go: The Spirituality of Taking Action Against Alcoholism and Drug Addiction.* New York: Bantam Dell, 2006.

Jay, Jeff and Debra. *Love First: A Family's Guide to Intervention.* 2nd ed. Center City: Hazelden, 2008.

Jensen, Frances E., M.D., with Amy Ellis Nutt. *The Teenage Brain: A Neuroscientist's Survival Guide to Raising Adolescents and Young Adults.* New York: HarperCollins, 2015.

Ketcham, Katherine, and Nicholas A. Pace, M.D. *Teens Under the Influence: The Truth about Kids, Alcohol, and Other Drugs—How to Recognize the Problem and What to Do About It.* New York: Ballantine Books, 2003.

Miller, Angelyn. *The Enabler: When Helping Hurts the Ones You Love.* 3rd ed. Tucson: Wheatmark, 2001.

Moyers, William Cope. *Now What? An Insider's Guide to Addiction and Recovery.* Center City: Hazelden, 2012.

"Narcotic Pain Relief Drug Overdose Deaths a National Epidemic." University of North Carolina School of Medicine website, April 25, 2011.

Rubin, Charles. *Don't Let Your Kids Kill You: A Guide for Parents of Drug and Alcohol Addicted Children.* Petaluma: New Century Publishers, 2007.

Sheff, David. *Clean: Overcoming Addiction and Ending America's Greatest Tragedy.* New York: Houghton Mifflin Harcourt, 2013.

Sontag, Deborah. "Heroin's Small-Town Toll, and a Mother's Grief." *New York Times,* February 10, 2014.

———. "Addiction Treatment With a Dark Side." *New York Times,* November 16, 2013.

Wainwright, Andrew T., and Robert Poznanovich. *It's Not Okay to be a Cannibal: How to Keep Addiction from Eating Your Family Alive*. Center City: Hazelden, 2007.

Whitcomb, John E. *The Sink or Swim Money Program: The 6-Step Plan for Teaching Your Teens Financial Responsibility*. 5th ed. New York: Viking Adult, 2001.

Williams, Bill. "Ending the Secrecy of a Child's Addiction." *New York Times,* May 19, 2013.

Williams, Greg. "It's Time to Change Everything... But Maybe We Can Just Start By Being a Little Hopeful?" Connecticut Turning to Youth and Families, October, 2009.

SPIRITUALITY AND INSPIRATION

Chödrön, Pema. *Living Beautifully with Uncertainty and Change*. Boston: Shambhala Publications, 2012.

————. *The Fearless Heart: The Practice of Living with Courage and Compassion*. Boston: Shambhala Audio, 2010.

————. *When Things Fall Apart: Heart Advice for Difficult Times*. Boston: Shambhala Publications, 1997.

Griffin, Kevin. *One Breath at a Time: Buddhism and the Twelve Steps*. Emmaus: Rodale, 2004.

Kenison, Katrina. *The Gift of an Ordinary Day: A Mother's Memoir*. New York: Grand Central Publishing, 2009.

Kornfield, Jack. *The Wise Heart: A Guide to the Universal Teachings of Buddhist Psychology*. New York: Bantam Books, 2009.

Lamott, Anne. *Bird by Bird: Some Instructions on Writing and Life*. New York: Anchor, 1995.

————. *Help, Thanks, Wow: Three Essential Prayers*. New York: Riverhead Books, 2012.

————. *Traveling Mercies: Some Thoughts on Faith.* New York: Anchor, 2000.

Lawford, Christopher Kennedy. *Moments of Clarity: Voices from the Front Lines of Addiction and Recovery.* New York: William Morrow, 2009.

Sinor, Barbara, PhD. *Tales of Addiction & Inspiration for Recovery: Twenty True Stories from the Soul (Reflections of America).* Ann Arbor: Modern History Press, 2010.

AL-ANON AND AA LITERATURE

Alcoholics Anonymous (The Big Book). 4th ed. New York: Alcoholics Anonymous World Services, 2001.

Courage to Change: One Day at a Time in Al-Anon II. Virginia Beach: Al-Anon Family Group Headquarters, 1992.

How Al-Anon Works for Families & Friends of Alcoholics. Virginia Beach: Al-Anon Family Group Headquarters, 1995, 2008.

One Day at a Time in Al-Anon. Virginia Beach: Al-Anon Family Group Headquarters, 1968, 1972, 2000.

Paths to Recovery—Al-Anon's Steps, Traditions, and Concepts. Virginia Beach: Al-Anon Family Group Headquarters, 1997.

FILM

The Anonymous People. Directed by Greg Williams. 4th Dimension Productions, 2013.

Moyers on Addiction: Close to Home. Directed by Bill Moyers. VHS. Curriculum Median Group, 1998.

Pleasure Unwoven: A Personal Journey about Addiction. Directed by Kevin McCauley, M.D. DVD. The Institute for Addiction Study, 2009.

CREDITS

THE AUTHOR GRATEFULLY ACKNOWLEDGES permission from these sources to reprint the following:

Excerpts republished with permission of Hazelden from *Love First: A New Approach to Intervention,* by Jeff and Debra Jay. Hazelden, 2nd Edition, 2008. Permission conveyed through Copyright Clearance Center, Inc.

Excerpt taken from *Parenting Teens With Love and Logic,* by Foster Cline and Jim Fay. Copyright © 1992, 2006. Used by permission of Tyndale House Publishers, Inc. All rights reserved.

Excerpt from the Afterword by Patrick MacAfee, Ph.D., of *Stay Close,* by Libby Cataldi. St. Martin's Press, 2009. Used by permission.

Excerpts from "Words of Blame, Words of Shame" by Katherine Ketcham. *Under the Influence* blog, February 2, 2013. Used by permission.

Excerpt from "Help that Hinders" by William C. Moyers. *Beyond Addiction* column (Hazelden Betty Ford Foundation), August 23, 2014. Used by permission.

Excerpts republished with permission of Hazelden from *Addict in the Family: Stories of Loss, Hope, and Recovery,* by Beverly Conyers. Hazelden Foundation, 1st Edition, 2003. Permission conveyed through Copyright Clearance Center, Inc.

Excerpt from *Broken: My Story of Addiction and Redemption,* by William Cope Moyers with Katherine Ketcham. Viking Penguin, 2006. Used by permission.

Excerpt from *Everything I Never Wanted to Be,* by Dina Kucera. Reprinted by permission of Dream of Things. Copyright © 2010 by Dina Kucera.

Excerpt from "It's Time to Change Everything...But Maybe We Can Just Start By Being a Little Hopeful?" by Greg Williams, Connecticut Turning to Youth and Families, October, 2009. Used by permission.

Excerpt from *When Things Fall Apart: Heart Advice for Difficult Times,* by Pema Chödrön, © 1997. Reprinted by arrangement with Shambhala Publications, Inc., Boston, MA.

Excerpt from *Claiming Your Self-Esteem: A Guide Out of Codependency, Addiction, and Other Useless Habits,* by Carolyn M. Ball. Celestial Arts, 1991. Used by permission.

Excerpts from *Living Beautifully with Uncertainty and Change,* by Pema Chödrön, © 2012. Reprinted by arrangement with Shambhala Publications, Inc., Boston, MA.

Excerpt from *The Life Recovery Bible* by David Stoop, Ph.D., and Stephen Arterburn, M.Ed. Copyright © 2006, 2012. Used by permission of Tyndale House Publishers, Inc. All rights reserved.

Made in the USA
San Bernardino, CA
07 May 2016